Dæmonologia Sacra
Or, A Treatise Of Satan's Temptations
Part- III

by

Richard Gilpin

Dæmonologia Sacra
Or, A Treatise Of Satan's Temptations
Part- III
by Richard Gilpin

ISBN: 978-93-60462-85-7

Published by

DOUBLE 9 BOOKS

2/13-B, Ansari Road
Daryaganj, New Delhi – 110002
info@double9books.com
www.double9books.com
Tel. 011-40042856

ABOUT THE AUTHOR

English nonconformist preacher and doctor Richard Gilpin (1625–1700) was well known in the north. Isaac Gilpin of Strickland Ketel in the parish of Kendal, Westmorland, and Ann Tonstall, daughter of Ralph Tonstall of Coatham-Mundeville in County Durham, had their second child. He was born in Strickland and baptized in Kendal on October 23, 1625. He went to school at the University of Edinburgh and graduated with an MA on July 30, 1646. There, he first studied medicine and then religion. There is no record of the date or way of his appointment. He began his preaching in Lambeth and continued it at the Savoy as John Wilkins' assistant. When he came back to the north, he preached at Durham. William Morland was locked up in the house of Greystoke, Cumberland, in 1650. A well-known priest named West had been in charge for about two years before he died of consumption. Gilpin took over after him in 1652 or early 1653. There were four chapels in the parish of Greystoke, and Gilpin sent ministers to all of them. His parish was set up like a congregation, with a small group of communicants and a staff of deacons. Cumberland had not yet accepted the Presbyterian system.

CONTENTS

PART III

Then was Jesus led up of the Spirit into the wilderness, to be tempted of the devil.—Mat. iv. 1.

CHAPTER I

I shall here consider the great temptation which it pleased our Lord Christ to submit unto, as a most famous instance for confirmation and illustration of the doctrine of temptations already handled.

The first verse sets down several remarkable circumstances of this combat, all of them matter of weight and worth: as,

1. First, The time when this fell out; not as a loose and accidental emergency, but as particularly made choice of both by God and Satan, being most fit and proper for the design which each of them were carrying on. This is expressly noted in Mat. iv. 1, 'Then was Jesus led up;' but more full in Mark i. 12, 'Immediately the Spirit driveth him into the wilderness;' manifestly directing us to expect something worthy of our observation in that circumstance. Neither can we miss of it, when the things unto which this directs us are so fully related immediately before. For we find in both these evangelists, which speak so exactly of the time of these temptations, that Christ was baptized of John. This was in order to the fulfilling the righteousness of his office. As the priests under the law, when they came to be thirty years old, entered upon their function by washings, or baptizings and anointings:362 so Christ, that he might answer his type, beginning to be about thirty years of age, was solemnly inaugurated into the great office of the mediatorship by baptism, and the extraordinary descending of the Holy Ghost, by which he was 'anointed with the oil of gladness above his fellows.' To this solemn instalment the Father adds an honourable testimony concerning him, 'This is my beloved Son, in whom I am well pleased,' Luke iii. 23. Immediately after this was he carried to the place of combat. Hence we may infer,

Obs. 1. *That our entering upon a special service for God, or receiving a special favour from God, are two solemn seasons which Satan makes use of for temptation.* Often these two seasons meet together in the same person at the same time. Paul, after his rapture into the third heaven, 2 Cor. xii. 2, 7, which, as some conceive, was also upon his entrance upon the ministry, was buffeted by 'the messenger of Satan.'

Sometime these two seasons are severed; yet still it may be observed that the devil watcheth them. When any servant of God is to engage in any particular employment, he will be upon him. He assaulted Moses by persecution, when he was first called to deliver Israel. As soon as David was anointed, immediately doth he enrage the minds of Saul and his courtiers against him. It was so ordinary with Luther, that he at last came to this, that before any eminent service he constantly expected either a fit of sickness, or the buffetings of Satan. He is no less sedulous in giving his assaults when any child of God hath been under peculiar favours or enjoyments. The church, after a high entertainment with Christ, is presently overcome by a careless, sleepy indisposition, Cant. v. 1, 2.

Though this may seem strange, yet the harshness of such a providence on God's part, and the boldness of the attempt on Satan's part, may be much taken off by the consideration of the reasons hereof.

(1.) First, *On Satan's part*. It is no great wonder to see such an undertaking, when we consider his fury and malice. The more we receive from God, and the more we are to do for him, the more doth he malign us. So much the more as God is good, by so much is his eye evil.

(2.) Secondly, There are in such cases as these several advantages, which, through our weakness and imperfection, we are too apt to give him; and for these he lieth at the catch.

[1.] As first, *Security*. We are apt to grow proud, careless, and confident, after or upon such employments and favours; even as men are apt to sleep or surfeit upon a full meal, or to forget themselves when they are advanced to honour. Job's great peace and plenty made him, as he confesseth, so confident, that he concluded he should 'die in his nest,' chap. xxix. 18. David enjoying the favour of God in a more than ordinary measure, though he was more acquainted with vicissitudes and changes than most of men, grows secure in his apprehension, that he 'should never be moved,' Ps. xxx. 6; but he acknowledgeth his mistake, and leaves it upon record as an experience necessary for others to take warning by, that when he became warm under the beams of God's countenance, then he was apt to fall into security; and — this it seems was usual with him in all such cases — when he was most secure, he was nearest some trouble or disquiet. 'Thou didst hide thy face' — and then to be sure the devil will shew his — 'and I was troubled.' Enjoyments beget confidence; confidence brings forth carelessness; carelessness makes God withdraw, and gives opportunity to Satan to work unseen. And thus, as armies after victory growing secure, are oft surprised; so are we oft after our spiritual advancements thrown down.

[2.] Secondly, *Discouragement and tergiversation* is another thing the devil watcheth for. By his assaults he represents the duty difficult, tedious, dangerous, or impossible, on purpose to discourage us, and to make us fall back. No sooner doth Paul engage in the gospel than the devil is upon him, suggesting such hazards as he knew were most prevalent with our frail natures, if he had not been aware of him, and refused to hearken to what flesh and blood would have said in the case, Gal. i. 16. When God honoured Moses with the high employment of delivering Israel, the hazard and danger of the work was so strongly fixed upon his thoughts, that he makes many excuses: one while pleading his inability and insufficiency, 'Who am I, that I should go to Pharaoh?' Exod. iii. 11. Another while he urgeth Israel's unbelief, and a seeming impossibility to satisfy them of his commission, Exod. iv. 1. After that he deviseth another shift, 'I am not eloquent,' ver. 10. And when all these subterfuges were removed, Satan had so affrighted him with the trouble and difficulty of this undertaking, that he attempts to break away from his duty: ver. 13, 'Send by the hand of him whom thou wilt send;' that is, spare me and send another: and till the anger and displeasure of God was manifested against him, he submitted not. In Jonah the temptation went higher. He, upon the apprehensions mentioned, ran away from his service, and puts God to convince him by an extraordinary punishment. And when Satan prevails not so far as wholly to deter men by such onsets, yet, at least, he doth dishearten and discourage them, so that the work loseth much of that glory, excellency, and exactness, which a ready and cheerful undertaking would put upon it.

[3.] Thirdly, *The fall or miscarriage of the saints at such times is of more than ordinary disadvantage,* not only to others—for if they can be prevailed with to lay aside their work, or to neglect the improvement of their favours, others are deprived of the benefit and help that might be expected from them—but also to themselves. A prevailing temptation doth more than ordinarily prejudice them at such times. The greatness of the disappointment under special service, the unworthy neglect and unanswerableness to special favours, are extraordinary provocations, and produce more than ordinary chastisements, as we see in Jonah's affliction, and the spouse's desertion.

(2.) Secondly, As we have seen the reason of Satan's keenness in taking those opportunities, so may we consider the reasons of *God's permission,* which are these:—

[1.] First, Temptations at such seasons are permitted for more eminent *trial of the upright.* On this account was Job tempted.

[2.] Secondly, *For an increase of diligence, humility, and watchfulness.* If these privileges and mercies will not discourage Satan, what will? And if Satan so openly malign such enjoyments, we may be awakened to hold them faster and set a double guard upon them.

[3.] Thirdly, *For a plentiful furniture of experience.* Temptation is the shop of experience. Luther was so great a gainer by this, that he became able so to speak to the consciences and conditions of his hearers, that the thoughts of their hearts were manifested by his speaking, as if he had had an intelligencer in their own bosoms. Hence did he commend prayer, meditation, and temptation as necessary requisites for the accomplishment of a minister.

Applic. This may administer matter of counsel to us in both cases aforementioned, if we be put upon eminent employments or receive eminent favours.

1. First, *We must not be so secure as to think Satan will be asleep that while, or that we are beyond danger.* While we are receiving kindnesses, he is devising plots and laying snares. With privileges and mercies expect exercises and hazards.

2. Secondly, in particular, *We may receive something of advice from this consideration in reference to both cases.*

(1.) If God is about to employ us in any service,

[1.] We have little need to be *confident of our abilities or performance,* when we know that temptations wait for us.

[2.] We must not only be sensible of our weakness, that we be not confident; but we must be *apprehensive of the strength and power of God to carry us through,* that we be not discouraged.

[3.] We must see our *opposition,* that we may be watchful; and yet must we refuse to give it the least place of consideration in our debates of duty, lest it sway us against duty or dishearten us in it.

(2.) If God be pleased to honour us with peculiar favours, then,

[1.] Though we must improve them to the full, yet must we not feed on them without fear.

[2.] We must not stay in the enjoyment or play with the token, but look to the tendency of such favours and improve them to duty, as to their proper end.

CHAPTER II

2. The second circumstance acquaints *how Christ was carried to the combat*. In solemn combats and duels, the persons undertaking the fight were usually carried to the place with great solemnity and ceremony. Christ in this spiritual battle is described as having the conduct of the Spirit, 'He was led up of the Spirit,' &c. What this Spirit was is, though by a needless and over-officious diligence, questioned by some; but we need not stay much upon it, if we consider the phrase of the evangelists, who mention *Spirit* without any note of distinction—which of necessity must have been added if it had intended either his proper spirit as man, or the wicked spirit Satan—directing thereby to understand it of him to whom the word Spirit is more peculiarly attributed, viz., the Holy Ghost. Or if we observe the close connexion in Luke betwixt that expression of Christ's being 'full of the Holy Ghost,' and his being 'led by the Spirit,' it will be out of controversy that the Holy Spirit is here intended. Hence was it that Beza translates it more fully, 'Jesus being full of the Holy Ghost, was led, *eodem Spiritu*, of the same Spirit;' and the Syriac, in Matthew, doubts not to express it by the Holy Spirit. And what else can be imagined, when in this text the Spirit that led him up, and the devil that tempted, are mentioned in so direct an opposition? 'He was led of the Spirit into the wilderness to be tempted of the devil.' The manner of his being carried thither is expressed by such words as signify, though not an external rapture like that of Philip, a strong inward motion and impulse upon him. The Spirit driveth—ἐκβάλλεν—him, saith Mark. The Spirit 'led him'—ἤγετο—saith Luke, using the same word by which the Scripture elsewhere expresseth the power of the Spirit upon the children of God, who are said to be 'led' by him.

Obs. 2. Hence note *that the Spirit of God hath a hand in temptations*. Christ was led by the Spirit to be tempted. This must not be understood as if God did properly tempt any to sin, either by enticing their hearts to evil, or by moving and suggesting wicked things to their minds, or by infusing evil inclinations, or by any proper compliance with Satan to undermine and delude us by any treachery or deceit. None of these can be imagined without apparent derogation to the holiness of God, 'who tempteth no man, neither can he be tempted with evil,' [James i. 13.] But what we are to understand by the Holy Spirit's concerning himself in temptations, is included in these particulars:—

1. First, God gives *commission to Satan*, without which his hand would be sealed up under an impossibility of reaching it out against any.

2. Secondly, *Opportunities and occasions do depend upon his providence*, without which nothing comes to pass. Neither we nor anything else do or can move without him.

3. Thirdly, The Spirit *oversees the temptation as to measure and continuance.* The length and breadth of it is ordered by him.

4. Fourthly, *The issue and consequences of every temptation are at his appointment.* The ways of its working for our exercise, humiliation, or conviction, or for any other good and advantage whatsoever, they all belong to his determination.

So that it is not improper to assert that God and Satan do concur in the same temptation, though the ways of proceeding, with the aims and intentions of both, be directly different and contrary. Hence is it that the temptation of David, 1 Sam. xxiv. 1, and 1 Chron. xxi. 1, are upon several regards attributed both to God and Satan.

Appl. 1. This note is of use to remove those harsh interpretations which poor tempted Christians meet withal, commonly from such as have not touched their burdens with the least of their fingers. Men are apt in these cases to judge,

(1.) First, *The ways of religion, as being ways, at least in the more serious and rigid practice of them, of intolerable hazard and perplexity,* and only upon an observation that those who most addict themselves to a true and strict observance of duty and command usually complain of temptations, and express sometimes their fears and distress of heart about them. This is your reading, your praying, and hearing. Such preaching, say they, leads men to despair and perpetual disquiet; and upon the whole they conclude it dangerous to be religious above the common rate of those that prosecute it in a slow and careless indifferency.

(2.) Secondly, The like severity of censure do they use in reference to *the spiritual state of the tempted,* as if they were vessels of his hatred, and such as were by him given up to the power of this 'wild boar of the forest' to devour and tear. All kind of distresses are obnoxious to the worst of misjudgings from malevolent minds. The sufferings of Christ produced this censorious scoff, 'Let God deliver him, if he will have him,' [Mat. xxvii. 43.] David's troubles easily induced his adversaries to conclude that 'God had forsaken him, and that there was none to deliver him,' Ps. lxxi. 11. But in troubles of this nature, where especially there are frightful complainings against themselves, men are more easily drawn out to be peremptory in their uncharitable determinations concerning them, because the trouble itself is somewhat rare, and apt to beget hideous impressions; and withal the vent which the afflicted parties give by their bemoaning of their estate, in hope to ease themselves thereby, is but taken as a testimony against themselves, and the undoubted echoes of their real feelings.

(3.) Thirdly, *Their sins are upon this ground misjudged and heightened.* Unusual troubles with common apprehension argue unusual sins. The viper upon Paul's hand made the barbarians confident he was a man of more than ordinary guilt and wickedness, Acts xxviii. 4. David's sickness was enough to give his enemies occasion to surmise that it was the punishment of some great transgression. 'An evil disease,' say they, 'cleaveth to him,' Ps. xli. 8. Those that were overwhelmed by the fall of the tower of Siloam, and those whose blood Pilate mixed with their sacrifices, were judged greatest sinners, Luke xiii. 4. But in inward temptations, this misjudging confidence is every way more heightened; and those that are most molested are supposed to have given more away to Satan.

(4.) Fourthly, Temptations are also misjudged *to be worse than they are.* They are indeed things to be trembled at; but they are not properly of an astonishing, amazing, or despairing consideration, as men are apt to think that view the workings of them at a distance.

Against all those unrighteous surmises, the poor afflicted servants of Christ may have relief from this truth in hand, that the Holy Spirit of God hath a hand in temptations: and therefore it is impossible that everywhere they should be of such a signification. Were they in themselves no way serviceable to God's glory in the gracious exercise of his children, the Spirit of wisdom and holiness would not at all have a hand in them. If under Satan's assaults you meet with those that by such a harshness of censure would aggravate your troubles, and so grieve those whom God hath saddened, you may boldly appeal from them to him that judgeth righteously. And indeed, if men would but consider, in the saddest case of this nature, either,

[1.] *The end of the Lord in permitting temptations,* which, if seen, would give a high justification of his dealing, and force men to applaud and magnify his wisdom, rather than to censure it. Or,

[2.] If they could but see the *secret ways of God's support,* how he acts his part in holding them by the hand, in counterworking of Satan, and confounding him under the exercise of his highest malice, and also in the ways of his preservation and deliverance. Or,

[3.] *If the harmlessness of temptations, when their sting is taken out, were but weighed,* men would change their minds as readily as the barbarians did, when they saw the viper not effect that mischief they supposed upon Paul;

and would see cause to stand amazed at the contrivances of so much power and wisdom, as can turn these to quite other ends and uses, than what they of themselves seem to threaten.

Applic. 2. This consideration will further express its usefulness *in comforting us under temptations.* It might have been Paul's great discouragement, that in his answer before Nero no man stood with him, 2 Tim. iv. 16; but this was his support, that God was with him. The like encouragement we have under all assaults of Satan, that we are not left to ourselves, but the Spirit of God is with us, and that he concerns himself on a design to oversee and overrule his work, and to put a check upon him when there is need. So that he cannot tempt as he will, nor when he will, nor in what he would, nor as long as he would; but that in all cases, we may rely upon the great master-contriver, for relief, help, mitigation, or deliverance, as there is need.

Obs. 3. In that the evangelists do not say that Christ cast himself upon a temptation, neither did go to undertake it till he was led to it, we note, *that whatever may be the advantage of a temptation by the Spirit's ordering of it, or what security from danger we may promise to ourselves upon that account, yet must we not run upon temptations; though we must submit when we are fairly led into them.* The reasons of this truth are these:—

(1.) First, There is so much of *the nature of evil in temptations that they are to be avoided if possible.* Good they may accidentally be, that is, beyond their proper nature and tendency, by the overruling hand of God; but being in their own natural constitution evil, it is inconsistent with human nature to desire them as such.

(2.) Secondly, *To run upon them would be a dangerous tempting of God;* that is, making a bold and presumptuous trial, without call, whether he will put forth his power to rescue us or not. Now he that runs upon a temptation hath no promise to be delivered out of it. And besides, runs upon so desperate a provocation, that in all probability he shall miscarry in it, as a just punishment of his rashness.

Quest. But inquiry may be made, When do men run uncalled and unwarrantably upon temptation? I answer, many ways. As,

Ans. [1.] First, When men engage themselves *in sin and apparent wickedness, in the works of the flesh.* For it can never be imagined that the holy God should ever by his Spirit call any to such things as his soul abhors.

[2.] Secondly, When men run upon *the visible and apparent occasions and causes of sin.* This is like a man's going to the pest-house. Thus do they, that though they design not to be actors in evil, yet will give their company and countenance to persons actually engaged in evil.

[3.] Thirdly, When men *unnecessarily, without the conduct either of command or urging an unavoidable providence, do put themselves, though not upon visible and certain opportunities, yet, upon dangerous and hazardous occasions and snares.* Peter had no errand in the high-priest's hall; his curiosity led him thither; he might easily have foreseen a probable snare; but confidently putting himself forward, where his danger was more than his business, he ran upon the temptation, and accordingly fell. The like did Dinah, when she made a needless vagary to see the daughters of the land; where she met with her sin and shame, Gen. xxxiv. 1. Neither do they otherwise, who dare adventure themselves in families—whilst yet they are free and may otherwise dispose of themselves—where they see snares and temptations will be laid before them. The case indeed is otherwise to those that are under the necessary engagement of relation, natural or voluntary, if it be antecedent to the hazard, to live in such places or callings; they have a greater promise of preservation than others can lay claim to, Ps. xci. 11; Prov. x. 29.

[4.] Fourthly, Those run upon temptation, that adventure *apparently beyond their strength, and put themselves upon actions good or harmless, disproportionably to their abilities.* The apostle gives the instance in marriage abstinence, 1 Cor. vii. 5, which he cautions may not be undertaken at a careless adventure for fear of a temptation: and by this may we judge other things of like nature.

[5.] Fifthly, They are also guilty that design an *adventure unto the utmost bounds of lawful liberty.* Those that have a mind to try conclusions, how near they may make their approaches to sin, and yet keep off from the defilement, such as would divide a hair betwixt good and evil, have at best but a hair's breadth betwixt them and sin; but how easily are they brought over that. Like a man that walks upon the utmost verge of a river's brink, ofttimes meets with hollow ground and a dangerous slip before he is aware.

[6.] Sixthly, Those also may be reckoned in the number of such as rush upon their danger, *who go abroad without their weapons, and forget in the midst of daily dangers the means of preservation.* Thomas, by his neglect, slid into a greater unbelief than the rest of the apostles. David's unwatchful heart was easily smitten by the intelligence which his eyes brought him. They that would plead their innocency against temptation had need to carry their arms and preservatives still with them.

Applic. This truth is a sufficient caution against the *rash adventurousness of those who forwardly engage themselves in matters of temptation.* As the former observation told us, temptations are not to be feared, so this also tells they are not to be slighted. The carriage of the Philistines when the ark came among them is matter of imitation to us. We may tremble justly when we hear of their approach, but our hazard should be the whetstone of our courage, and our danger should bring us to resolves of a more stout resistance, that we may 'quit ourselves like men.'

The apostle, Gal. vi. 1, seems to imply, when he tells those that were more severe and careless of others, that 'they may also be tempted,' that the best of men do little know what a change a temptation may make upon them; a small temptation may be too strong for them, and may carry them to what they never thought of; nay, may break down the strongest of their resolves, and snap their purposes as a thread in a flame. It did so with Peter, who was quickly overcome by that which he had with so much confidence undervalued.

CHAPTER III

3. The third circumstance next to be considered is *the place of this combat*, *'the wilderness.'* To inquire what or where this wilderness was, is not only impertinent and useless, as to anything we can observe from it in reference to temptation, but also a matter of mere uncertain conjecture; only they that would understand it of a place more thinly peopled are expressly contradicted by Mark i. 13, where it is said, 'he was with the wild beasts;' noting thereby a desolate and dangerous solitude, far remote from human society and comfort.

It is much more our concern to seek after the reasons of his choice of that place, or rather among those many that are given, to satisfy ourselves with what may have the greatest appearance of truth. They that think Christ hereby designed to shew the uncertain changes and vicissitudes of outward things in this life, or to point at the future low estate of his church in the world, that it should sojourn in a wilderness; or to direct those that have dedicated themselves to God to withdraw from the blandishments and allurements of the earth, with a great many more hints of instruction and document of that kind; they, I say, that offer no other, seem not to attend to the true design of the choice of this place, which notwithstanding is evidently discovered to have been done in order to the temptation.363 'He was led into the wilderness to be tempted.' The place then was subservient to the conflict, as the proper theatre on which so great a contest was to be acted. And if we shall but mind what special consideration was to be had of such a place, — a howling desolate wilderness, — we may with ease pitch upon these following reasons: —

(1.) First, It pleased God to have an eye to *the glory of Christ's conquests*, when in a single combat he should so remarkably foil the devil, without any the least advantage on his part, there being none that might be the least support or encouragement to him.

(2.) Secondly, The condition of the place *gave rise to the first temptation*. For in that he 'hungered' in a barren wilderness, it gave occasion to Satan to tempt him more strongly to 'turn stones into bread.'

(3.) Thirdly, In the choice of such a place God seems to offer Satan a special *advantage in tempting*, which was the solitude and danger of his present condition.

To omit the two former considerations, as not altogether so useful, further than what I shall be engaged to speak to afterwards, this last affords this observation:

Obs. 4. *That solitude affords a great advantage to Satan in the matter of temptation.* This advantage ariseth from solitude two ways:

(1.) First, *As it doth deprive us of help.* So great and many are the blessed helps arising from the society and communion of such as fear the Lord, as counsel, comfort, encouragement from their graces, experiences, and prayers, &c., that the woe pronounced to him 'that is alone' is not groundless, Eccles. iv. 10. Christians in a holy combination can do more work, and so have a good reward for their labour. They can mutually help one another when they fall; they can mutually heat and warm one another; they can also strengthen one another's hands to prevail against an adversary. He then that is alone, being deprived of these advantages, lieth more open to the stroke of temptation.

(2.) Secondly, *Solitude increaseth melancholy,* fills the soul with dismal apprehensions; and withal doth so spoil and alter the temper of it that it is not only ready to take any disadvantageous impression, but it doth also dispose it to leaven and sour those very considerations that should support, and to put a bad construction on things that never were intended for its hurt.

Applic. This may warn us to take heed of giving Satan so great an advantage against us, *as an unnecessary solitude may do.* I know there are times and occasions that do justly require us to seek a solitary place for the privacy of duty, or for secret lamentations, as Jeremiah desired, chap. ix. 1, 2, or to avoid the trouble and snare arising from our mixing with an assembly of treacherous and wicked men. This is no more than care and watchfulness. But when these reasons urge not, or some of like nature, but either out of pettish discontent or a mopish reservedness, we withdraw from those aids and comforts which are necessary for our support, we do strengthen Satan's hands against us and weaken our own.

CHAPTER IV

4. The fourth circumstance was *the end*. There was no other design in the main of Christ's being led up and into the wilderness, but that he might be 'tempted.' In this two things seem to be matter of equal wonder:—

(1.) First, *Why Christ would submit to be tempted*. For this many great and weighty reasons may be given. As,

[1.] First, Thus was Christ *evidenced to be the second Adam, and the seed of the woman*. His being tempted, and in such a manner, doth clearly satisfy us that he was true man; and that in that nature he it was that was promised 'to break the serpent's head.'

[2.] Secondly, This was a fair *preludium and earnest of that final conquest over Satan, and the breaking down of his power*.

[3.] Thirdly, There was a more peculiar aim in God by these means of temptation to qualify him with *pity and power to help*, 'For in that he suffered being tempted, he is able to succour them that are tempted,' Heb. ii. 18. And having experience of temptation himself, he became a merciful high-priest, apt to be 'touched with the feeling of our infirmities,' Heb. iv. 15.

[4.] Fourthly, *The consequence of this experimental compassion in Christ*, was a further reason why he submitted to be tempted, to wit, that we might have the greater comfort and encouragement in the expectancy of tender dealing from him. Hence the apostle, Heb. iv. 16, invites to 'come boldly to the throne of grace at any time of need.'

[5.] Fifthly, A further end God seemed to have in this, viz., *to give a signal and remarkable instance to us of the nature of temptations*; of Satan's subtlety, his impudency, of the usual temptations which we may expect; as also to teach us what weapons are necessary for resistance, and in what manner we must manage them.

(2.) Secondly, It seems as strange that Satan would *undertake a thing so unfeasible and hopeless as the tempting of Christ*. What expectation could he have to prevail against him, who was 'anointed with the oil of gladness above his fellows'? [Ps. xlv. 7.] Some answer,

[1.] First, That Satan might possibly *doubt whether Christ were the Son of God or no*. But the improbability of this I shall speak of afterwards.

[2.] Secondly, Others attribute it to his *malice*, which indeed is great, and might possibly blind him to a desperate undertaking. But,

[3.] Thirdly, We may justly apprehend *the power of sin over Satan to be so great that it might enforce him to the bold attempt of such a wickedness*. We see daily that wicked men, by the force of their own wicked principles, are restlessly hurried upon acts of sin, though they know the prohibition, and are not ignorant of the threatened danger. Satan is as great a slave to his own internal corrupt principles as any. And whatsoever blind fury is stirred up in man by the power of his lust, we may very well suppose the like in Satan.

[4.] Fourthly, *There is a superior hand upon the devil, that sways, limits, and orders him in his temptations*. He cannot tempt when he would, neither always what he would, but in his own cursed inclinations and the acting of them, he is forced to be subservient to God's designs. And in this particular, whatever might be Satan's proper end or principle, it is evident that God carried on a gracious design for the instruction and comfort of his children.

The end of Christ's going to the wilderness being that he might be tempted, if together with this the holiness and dignity of Christ in respect of his person and office be considered, we may note from it,

Obs. 5. *That neither height of privilege, nor eminency of employment, nor holiness of person, will discourage Satan from tempting, or secure any from his assaults*. The best of men in the highest attainments may expect temptations. Grace itself doth not exempt them.

(1.) For first, None of these privileges *in us, nor eminencies of grace, want matter to fix a temptation upon*. The weaknesses of the best of men are such that a temptation is not rendered improbable, as to the success, by their graces. Nay, there are special occasions and inclinations in them, to encourage temptations of pride and neglect. He found indeed nothing in Christ that might offer the least probability of prevalency; but in the best of men, in their best estate, he can find some encouragement for his attempts.

(2.) Secondly, None of us are beyond the necessity of such exercises. It cannot be said that we need them not, or that there may not be holy ends wherefore God should not permit and order them for our good. Temptations, as they are in God's disposal, are a necessary spiritual physic. The design of them is to humble us, to prove us, and to do us good in the latter end, Deut. viii. 16. Nothing will work more of care, watchfulness, diligence, and fear in a gracious heart, than a sense of Satan's designment against it. Nothing puts a man more to prayer, breathing after God, desiring to be dissolved, and running to Christ, than the troublesome and afflictive pursuits of Satan. Nothing brings men more from the love of the world, and to a delight in the ordinances of God, than the trouble which here abides them unavoidably from Satan. This discipline the best have need of. There are such remainders of pride and other evils in them, that if God should not permit these pricks and thorns to humble them, and thereby also awaken them to laborious watchfulness, they would be careless, secure, and sadly declining. This made Augustine conclude that it was no way expedient that we should want temptations,364 and that Christ taught us as much when he directed us not to pray that we should 'not be tempted,' but that we might not be 'led into the power and prevalency of temptation.'

(3.) Thirdly, *The privileges and graces of the children of God do stir up Satan's pride, revenge, and rage against them.* And though he hath no encouragement to expect so easy a conquest over these as he hath over others, who are captivated by him at pleasure; yet hath he encouragements to attempt them, for the singular use and advantage he makes of any success against them, the difficulty of the work being recompensed by the greatness of the booty. For the fall of a child of God, especially of such as are noted above others, is as when 'a standard-bearer fainteth,' [Isa. x. 18;] or as the fall of an oak, that bears down with it the lower shrubs that stand near it. How the hearts of others fail for fear, lest they should also be overcome; how the hearts of some grow thereby bold and venturesome; how a general disgrace and discredit thereby doth accrue to religion, and the sincere profession of it, are things of usual observation. If such men had not in them something of special prey in case of conquest, his pride would not so readily carry him against the heads and chief of the people, while he seems to overlook the meaner and weaker. Out-houses, though more accessible, are not the objects of the thief's design, but the dwellinghouse, though stronger built and better guarded, because it affords hopes of richer spoil, is usually assaulted. Neither do pirates so much set themselves to take empty vessels, though weakly manned, but richly laden ships, though better able to make resistance, are the ships of their desire.

Applic. 1. This may be applied for *the encouraging of those that think it strange that temptations do so haunt them,* especially that they should, in their apprehension, be more troubled by him when they fly furthest from him. The consideration of this will much allay these thoughts, by these inferences which it affords:—

(1.) First, *There is nothing unusual befalls these complainants.* Satan frequently doth so to others; they cannot justly say their case is singular, or that they are alone in such disturbances; it is but what is common to man. If they urge the uncessantness of the devil's attempts, Christ and others have felt the like. If they object the peculiar strangeness and horridness of the temptation, as most unsuitable to the state of an upright soul, Christ met with the like. He was tempted to self-destruction, to distrust, to blasphemy itself in the highest degree.

(2.) Secondly, *There is a good advantage to be made of them*: they are preservations from other sins that would otherwise grow upon us.

(3.) Thirdly, These temptations to the upright do but argue Satan's loss of interest in them, and their greater sensibility of the danger. The captivated sinners complain not so much, because they are so inured to temptation that they mind not Satan's frequent accesses. He that studies humility is more sensible of a temptation to pride than he that is proud.365

2. Secondly, This is also of use to those that are apt to be *confident upon their successes against sin through grace*. Satan, they may see, will be upon them again; so that they must behave themselves as mariners, who, when they have got the harbour, and are out of the storm, mend their ship and tackling, and prepare again for the sea.

Lastly, If we consider the unspotted holiness of Christ, and his constant integrity under these temptations, that they left not the least of taint or sinful impression upon him, we may observe,

Obs. 6. *That there may be temptations, without leaving a touch of guilt or impurity behind them upon the tempted.*

It is true this is rare with men. The best do seldom go down to the battle, but in their very conquests they receive some wound; and in those temptations that arise from our own hearts, we are never without fault; but in such as do solely arise from Satan, there is a possibility that the upright may so keep himself, that the wicked one may not so touch him as to leave the print of his fingers behind him.

Quest. But the great difficulty is, How it may be known when temptations are from Satan, and when from ourselves?

Ans. To answer this I shall lay down these conclusions:—

(1.) First, The same sins which *our own natures would suggest to us, may also be injected by Satan*. Sometimes we begin by the forward working of our own thoughts upon occasions and objects presented to us from without, or from the power of our own inclination, without the offer of external objects, and then Satan strikes in with it. Sometimes Satan begins with us, and by his injected motions endeavours to excite our inclinations; so that the same thing may be sometime from ourselves, and sometimes from Satan.

(2.) Secondly, *There is no sin so vile, but our own heart might possibly produce it without Satan*. Evil thoughts of the very worst kind, as of murders, adulteries, thefts, false witness, and blasphemies may, as Christ speaks,

Mat. xv. 19, be produced naturally from our own hearts; for seminally all sins, the very greatest of all impieties, are there. So that from the greatness and vileness of the temptation we cannot absolutely conclude that it is from Satan, no more than from the commonness of the temptation, or its suitableness to our inclination, we can conclude infallibly that its first rise is from ourselves.

(3.) Thirdly, There are many cases wherein it *is very difficult, if not altogether impossible, to determine whether our own heart or Satan gives the first life or breathing to a temptation.* Who can determine, in most ordinary cases, when our thoughts are working upon objects presented to our senses, whether Satan or our own thoughts do run faster? Yea, when such thoughts are not the consequent of any former occasion, it is a work too hard for most men to determine which of the parents, father or mother, our own heart or Satan, is first in the fault. They are both forward enough, and usually join hand in hand with such readiness, that he must have a curious eye that can discover certainly to whom the first beginning is to be ascribed.

The difficulty is so great, that some have judged it altogether impossible to give any certain marks by which it may be determined when they are ours and when Satan's.366 And indeed the discoveries laid down by some are not sufficient for a certain determination; and so far I assent, that neither the suddenness of such thoughts—for the motions of our own lusts may be sudden—nor the horridness of the matter of them, are sufficient notes of distinction. That our own corrupt hearts may bring forth that which is unnatural and terrible, cannot be denied. Many of the sins of the heathens mentioned in Rom. i. were the violent productions of lust against natural principles; and to ascribe these to the devil, as to the first instigator, is more than any man hath warrant to do. Yet though it be confessed that in some cases it is impossible to distinguish, and that where a distinction may be made, these notes mentioned are not fully satisfactory, there may, I believe, be some cases wherein there is a possibility to discover when the motions are from Satan, and that by the addition of some remarkable circumstances to the fore-named marks of difference.

(4.) Fourthly, Though it be true, which some say,367 that in most cases it is needless altogether to spend our time in disputing whether the motions of sin in our minds are firstly from ourselves or from Satan, our greatest business being rather to resist them than to difference them; yet there are special cases wherein it is very necessary to find out the true parent of a sinful motion, and these are when tender consciences are wounded and oppressed with violent and great temptations, as blasphemous thoughts, atheistical objections, &c. For here Satan in his furious molestations aims mainly at this, that such afflicted and tossed souls should take all these thoughts which are obtruded upon their imaginations, to be the issue of their own heart. As Joseph's steward hid the cup in Benjamin's sack, that it might be a ground of accusation against him, so doth the devil first oppress them with such thoughts, and then accuseth them of all that villainy and wickedness, the motions whereof he had with such importunity forced upon them; and so apt are the afflicted to comply with accusations against themselves, that they believe it is so, and from thence conclude that they are given up of God, hardened as Pharaoh, that they have sinned against the Holy Ghost, and finally that there is no hope of mercy for them. All this befalls them from their ignorance of Satan's dealings, and here is their great need to distinguish Satan's malice from their guilt.

(5.) Fifthly, Setting aside ordinary temptations, wherein it is neither so possible nor so material to busy ourselves to find out whether they are Satan's or ours;—in extraordinary temptations, such as have been now instanced, we may discover if they proceed from Satan, though not simply from the matter of them, not from the suddenness and independency of them, yet from *a due consideration of their nature and manner of proceeding, compared with the present temper and disposition of our heart.* As,

[1.] First, When unusual temptations intrude upon us with a high impetuosity and violence, while our thoughts are otherwise concerned and taken up.368 Temptations more agreeable to our inclination, though suddenly arising from objects and occasions presented, and gradually proceeding, after the manner of the working of natural passions, may throng in amidst our thoughts or actions that have no tendency that way, and yet we cannot so clearly accuse Satan for them; but when things that have not the encouragement of our affections are by a sudden violence enforced upon us, while we are otherwise concerned, we may justly suspect Satan's hand to be in them.

[2.] Secondly, While such things are borne in upon us, against the actual loathing, strenuous reluctancy, and high complainings of the soul, when the mind is filled with horror and the body with trembling at the presence of such thoughts.369 Sins that owe their first original to ourselves, may indeed be resisted upon their first rising up in our mind; and though a sanctified heart doth truly loathe them, yet they are not without some lower degree of tickling delight upon the affections; for the flesh in those cases presently riseth up with its lustings for the sinful motion; but when such unnatural temptations are from Satan, their first appearance to the mind is a horror without any sensible working of inclination towards them; and the greatness of the soul's disquiet doth shew that it hath met with that which the affections look not on with any amicable compliance.

[3.] Thirdly, Our hearts may bring forth that which is *unnatural in itself, and may give rise to a temptation that would be horrid to the thoughts of other men,* but that it should of its own accord, without a tempter, on a sudden bring forth that which is directly contrary to its present light, reason, or inclination; as for a man to be haunted with thoughts of atheism, while he is under firm persuasions that there is a God; or of blasphemy, while he is under designs of honouring him, is as unimaginable as that our thoughts should of themselves contrive our death, while we are most solicitous for our life; or that our thoughts should soberly tell us it is night when we see the sun shine. Temptations that are contrary to the present state, posture, light, and disposition of the soul are Satan's. They are so unnatural as to its present frame, that the production of them must be from some other agent.

[4.] Fourthly, Much more evident is it that such proceed from Satan, when they are of *long continuance and constant trouble,* when they so incessantly beat upon the mind, that it hath no rest from them, and yet is under grievous perplexities and anxieties of mind about them.

Applic. The consideration of this is of great use to those that suffer under the violent hurries of strange temptations.

(1.) First, In that sometime they can justly complain of the affliction of such temptation, when they have no reason to charge it upon themselves as their sin. It is one thing to be tempted, and another to consent or comply. To be tempted, and not to be brought into temptation, is not evil. Satan only barks when he suggests, but he then bites and wounds when he draws us to consent.370

(2.) Secondly, That not only the *sin but the degree also,* by just consequence, is to be measured by the consent of the heart. If we consent not, the sin is not ours, and the less degree of consent we give, the less is in the sin.

CHAPTER V

Of Christ's fast, with the design thereof.—Of Satan's tempting in an invisible way.—Of his incessant importunities, and how he flies when resisted.—Of inward temptations, with outward afflictions.—Several advantages Satan hath by tempting in affliction.

I am next to explain the fast of Christ, the end and design whereof, because it is not expressly mentioned, is variously conjectured. Not to insist in this discourse, which is designed for practice, on the controversy about the Quadragesimal fast, that which I shall first consider is the opinion of Musculus,371 who, upon this ground that his fast was not the principal thing for which the Spirit led him into the wilderness; for he was not led to fast, but to be tempted—thereupon concludes, that this was only a consequent of his solitary condition in the wilderness, and no other thing than what befell Moses and Elias, who being engaged by God to attend him in such a service, where the ordinary means of the support of life were wanting, were therefore kept alive by him in an extraordinary way without them. Thus he thinks the fasting was not, at least principally, designed, but that he being to undergo a temptation in a desolate wilderness where he had no meat to eat, there God restrained his hunger, so that he neither desired nor needed any. If we acquiesce in this, it will afford this doctrine:—

Doct. 1. *That when God leads forth his children to such services as shall unavoidably deprive them of the ordinary means of help or supply, there God is engaged to give extraordinary support, and his people may expect it accordingly.*

This is a great truth in itself, and a great and necessary encouragement to all the children of God that are called out to straits; but I shall not insist on this as the genuine product of this fast.

If we look further amongst protestant divines, we shall observe it taken for granted, that Christ fasted upon design, and this is generally reduced to those two heads:—

(1.) First, Either for *instruction*: as to shew that he was *God, by fasting so long*, and that under the trouble of molesting and disquieting temptations; whereas the fasts of like date in Moses or Elias were accompanied with the quiet repose of their thoughts; or to shew that he was *man, in that he really felt the natural infirmities of the human nature, in being hungry;* or to teach us *the usefulness of fasting in the general,* when fit occasions invite us thereto; or,

(2.) Secondly, For confirmation of his doctrine, to put an honour and dignity upon his employment;372 as Elias fasted at the restoring of prophecy, and at the Reformation. As Moses fasted at the writing of the law, so Christ began the gospel of the kingdom with fasting. However, that these things cannot be spoken against, being conclusions warrantably deducible from this act of Christ's; yet these seem not, in my apprehension, to come fully up to the proper end of this undertaking of his; which seems not obscurely to be laid before us in that passage of Luke iv. 2, 'being forty days tempted of the devil; and in those days he did eat nothing;' where we see that his being 'tempted forty days' was the principal thing, and that his fasting had a plain reference and respect to his temptation. Thus far, I suppose, we may be secure, that we have the design in the general, that his fasting was in order to his temptation. But then whether this was designed as an occasion of the temptations, or as a remedy against them, it is not so easy to determine. That one of those, at least, was intended, cannot be denied by those that will grant that his fast related to the combat; and it seems not to labour of any repugnancy or absurdity, if we say that it is possible that both these ends might be aimed at, and accordingly I shall proceed to observe upon them. There are only some other things to be first despatched out of the way: as

The continuance of the fast, why it was forty days, neither more nor less. Though some adventure to give reasons for it,373 not only papists, who, according to their wont, are ridiculous and trifling in this matter; but also protestants, supposing that some regard was, or ought to be, had to his fulfilling the times of the fasts of Moses and Elias; yet I think it is neither pertinent nor safe to determine anything about it, only it observes to us that the continuance of this was a considerable time.

We are more concerned to inquire whether Christ was under any conflict of temptation all that time;374 which although some deny, lest they should favour a seeming contradiction among the evangelists, yet the words of Luke are so express, 'being forty days tempted of the devil,' Luke iv. 2, that no tolerable evasion can be found to cast these temptations to the end of the forty days; for he tells us, he was not only tempted after the expiration of the forty days, but that he was tempted during the continuance of the forty days beside; only there was a difference in the kinds of these temptations, in regard of the way wherein Satan managed them, and this also is fully set down by Matthew, 'And when the tempter came to him,' which with the other expression of Luke compared, shews us, that during the space of the forty days Satan tempted Christ, and yet came not to him till afterward — that is, he managed those temptations in an invisible way. Hence we may note,

Doct. 2. That Satan doth usually tempt in an invisible way and manner. To explain this a little, I shall evidence it by a few considerations. As,

(1.) First, *That he hath a hand in all sins first or last, and then it must needs be in an invisible way.* His work is to tempt, to go about laying snares to draw men to sin. Wicked men are 'of their father the devil,' John viii. 44, and do his works. Carnal desires are 'his lusts;' giving way to anger is 'giving place to the devil,' Eph. iv. 26, 27, and resisting of sin is called in the general, 'a resisting of the devil,' &c., James iv. 7. In all this work of Satan, men do not see him. When he puts evil motions into their hearts they do not perceive him, and therefore doth he his work in an invisible way.

(2.) Secondly, We have sufficient discoveries of these private paths of his: for, [1.] Sometime he tempts by *friends*: he tempted Job by his wife, Christ by Peter. [2.] Sometime by *external objects*, as he drew out Achan's covetousness, and David's uncleanness, by the eye. [3.] Sometime by *injecting thoughts and motions* to our mind. [4.] Sometime by exercising an *invisible power upon our bodies*, in stirring up the humours thereof, to provoke to passion or excessive mirth. All these ways, of which I have discoursed before more largely, are secret and invisible, and by such as these he most usually tempts.

(3.) Thirdly, *The wiles, depths, secrets, and devices of Satan,* which the Scripture tells us are his most familiar ways and courses, they in their own nature imply a studied or designed secrecy and imperceptibility.

(4.) Fourthly, He hath peculiar *reasons of policy* for his invisible way of dealing; for the less visible he is, the less suspicious are his designs, and consequently the less frightful and more taking. By this way he insinuates himself so into our bosoms, that he gets a party in us against ourselves before we are aware; whereas in vain he knows he should spread his net if his designs and enmity were discovered to us.

Applic. This must teach us to suspect Satan where we see him not, and so to converse with objects and occasions as still fearing that there may be *anguis in herba*, a secret snare laid for us to entrap us at unawares.

If we again cast our eyes upon what hath been said, that Christ was tempted 'all the forty days,' it will then give us this observation:—

Doct. 3. *That Satan is sometime incessant in temptations, and sets upon us with continued importunities.*

Here we may note a distinction of temptations, besides that of invisible and visible, of which I have spoken, that some are moveable and short fits, and as it were skirmishes, in which he stays not long, and others are more fixed and durable. We may call them solemn temptations, in which Satan doth, as it were, pitch down his tents, and doth manage a long siege against us. Of these last sort is this observation.

Thus he tempted Paul, continuing his assault for some time before he departed, 2 Cor. xii. 8. Thus also he dealt with Joseph, who was solicited day by day for a long time together, Gen. xxxix. 10. Of these I shall note a few things. As,

(1.) First, Such temptations are not without a *special commission*. He cannot indeed tempt at all without leave, but in the ordinary course of his temptations he hath a general commission under such restraints and limitations as pleaseth the Most High to put upon him; but in these he must have a special order, as we see in Job's case.

(2.) Secondly, Such temptations have also *a special ground*. Either the present state and posture of our condition is such as Satan apprehends highly advantageous for his design, and therefore he desires to have the winnowing of us at such a season; or there are more than ordinary dispositions and inclinations in our heart to what we are directly tempted to, or to some other consequent design. These animate and encourage him to high resolves of prosecuting us more closely, upon an expectation that a continued solicitation is most likely to prevail at the long run.

(3.) Thirdly, It is possible that such temptations *may stand out against the endeavours of many prayers*, and that we shall find they are not so easily shaken off as the viper that was upon Paul's hand. Paul, 2 Cor. xii. 8, prayed thrice against the messenger of Satan, that is, as Estius and others interpret, he prayed often and fervently, and yet it departed not.

(4.) Fourthly, Such temptations give *no rest nor intermission*; men are haunted and dogged by them; what way soever they go, they still hear the same things, and cannot command their thoughts to give an exclusion to his motions, but still by renewed disputes and arguings, or by clamorous importunities, they are vexed and tormented: which surely shews a high degree of earnestness and impudency in Satan.

(5.) Fifthly, These are consequently *very burdensome, exceeding irksome and tiresome to us*. Paul calls them 'buffetings,' for their trouble and molestation. Satan so molested Job in his affliction by inward accusations and troubles of terror, that, as an overwearied man, he cries out he had no quiet, and that he was disappointed of his hope of ease in sleep, because he was then 'scared with dreams and terrified with visions,' [Job vii. 14.]

(6.) Sixthly, These are also upon a special design *on God's part, either to find us work and to keep us doing, or to prevent sin and miscarriage*; to keep down our pride, lest we should be 'exalted above measure,' [2 Cor. xii. 7;] to awaken us from slothfulness and security, lest we should 'settle upon our lees,' [Jer. xlviii. 11;] or to be an occasion of his grace, and an evidence of his power in our preservation, satisfying us and others, that in the greatest shocks of our spiritual battle his 'grace is sufficient for us,' [2 Cor. xii. 9.] Upon these, and such like designs as these, doth the most wise God permit it.

(7.) Seventhly, Satan doth not attempt temptations of this kind but upon *a special design*, and that either because he hopes by a violent and pertinacious impetuosity at length to prevail, or that he would please himself to molest us; for surely the cries and complainings of God's children are music in his ears; or at least upon a design to discourage us in our services, and to make way for other temptations of murmuring, blasphemy, despair, &c., which are as a reserve or ambushment laid in wait for us. The inferences from hence are these two:—

Applic. 1. That the children of God under such temptations may be encouraged under a patient expectation, by considering that Christ did undergo the like assaults from Satan. It is in itself tedious and disheartening, but they may see,

(1.) First, That this way of trouble *is usual, and that to the best*; and therefore they should not faint under it.

(2.) Secondly, That grace *is sufficient to preserve from the prevalency of the most earnest temptations* even there, where our heavenly Father thinks it not fit to preserve us from the trouble of them. When Paul gives the highest security that the faithfulness of God can afford, that temptations shall not be above strength, 1 Cor. x. 13, or the ability that shall be given them, he tells them they are not to expect always such aids as shall presently drive away the temptation, that it must immediately vanish, or that their temptations shall become light and contemptible, but that God's faithfulness will be no further engaged in the general, than [1.] to make their temptations tolerable, that they 'may be able to bear them,' though not without much to do. [2.] That the 'way of escape' shall be concurrent with the continuance of the temptation, that though the temptation abide, yet we shall be aided under it. [3.] That yet he is as careful of our help in temptations as he is ready to commissionate them, when need requires. His resolves that we should be tempted, and his resolves that we should be succoured, they bear the same date. 'With the temptation he will make a way to escape.' ¯

(3.) Thirdly, That such temptations do not argue [1.] either a likelihood, much less a necessity, that they should prevail; nor [2.] any want of care and love in God; nor [3.] do they always evidence a more than ordinary proneness and inclination in us; for Christ, who was most averse to the least of sin, who was highest in God's love, against whom there was no possibility he should prevail, yet was thus tempted.

Applic. 2. Secondly, In such continued violences it will concern us to *make stout resistances*; according to the counsel of James, chap. iv. 7, 'Resist the devil, and he will fly.'

Obj. But I have done so, and yet the temptation is the same, and still continues.

Ans. (1.) First, It is not enough *to resist, but we must continue to do so.* Some make limited resistances, as besieged persons that set a time for their holding out, and then if they be not relieved at that time, they yield; but we must resolve a perpetual resistance, as long as the temptation lasts. When one hand is beaten off, we must hold by another; when both are beaten off, we must, as it were, hold by our teeth.

(2.) Secondly, In a faithful resistance, we may *cast the whole matter upon God*, and engage him in the quarrel; as David: 'I will say unto God, Why hast thou forsaken me?' &c.

Obj. But how is it consistent with truth that the temptation should continue, when James tells us that Satan will fly upon resistance?

Ans. (1.) It may be *the resistance is not as it ought, and so the blame is ours.* If we be not serious, as some who defy the devil in words, and resist him by crossing themselves, things which doubtless the devil laughs at; or if in the confidence of a presumptuous bravado, or if not with that humility and care that is requisite, it will be no wonder if he depart not.

(2.) Secondly, *He doth fly at every resistance more or less;* he doth give back, and is discouraged, and is a loser by every opposition.

(3.) Thirdly, Though the scripture say that he shall fly,—that is, sooner or later,—yet it doth not say *that he shall do so immediately,* though most usually he doth so where he is peremptorily rejected. But in some cases time must be allowed; for the devil, as it is in Chrysostom's comparison, stands like a fawning dog scratching and waving his tail, and if anything be given him, it makes him importunate for more; yet though we give him nothing, we cannot expect that the first or second denial should make him cease his trouble: as he hath been encouraged by former compliances, so will he not be discouraged but with many and continued denials.

If we consider the fast of Christ as an occasion designed by God for an advantage to the temptation, and then look upon his condition in the wilderness, being under hazards from wild beasts, in want of necessaries, and without a possibility of supplies in a usual way, and also under the discomforts of cold and long nights,—for according to the conjectures of some this was about our October and November375—then we may observe,

Doct. 4. That it is Satan's way to second outward distresses and afflictions with inward temptations. We see the like carriage of Satan toward Job. His affliction was followed with many temptations. All his friends, in urging him with hypocrisy, were no other than parties to Satan's design, though they knew it not apparently. His wife is set on by the tempter, as the serpent against Eve, to provoke him to 'curse God and die.' Besides all this, whosoever shall consider what inward workings of heart, spiritual trouble and conflict, his words frequently express, they will quickly find that when God put Job into Satan's hand, under that only limitation of not touching his life, he gave Satan a liberty to pursue him with inward temptations as well as outward vexations. When Israel was pinched with the straits of the wilderness, Satan was most busy with them to put them upon distrust, murmuring, revolt, disobedient oppositions, idolatry, and what not. David gives in his experience to confirm this truth. He never met with outward troubles but he had also inward temptations with them, as fretting, disquiet, sad apprehensions of God's wrath, haste, distrust, fear, &c., as the relation of his several straits do testify. And besides these, the generality of God's children find it so. Outward afflictions seldom pass alone. When they have 'fightings without,' they have 'fears within' usually. Seldom have they a sickness, or meet with a sad providence, but they have Satan busy with their souls, molesting their peace, or endeavouring to ensnare them. Thus their feet are never in the stocks but the iron enters into their soul. And for this reason is it that outward afflictions and troubles are called temptations in Scripture, because temptations usually accompany them, and they are indeed the solemn seasons that Satan desires to improve for that end; and for that is it that Luke expresseth that which we translate a time of temptation by καιρὸς πειρασμοῦ, which signifies an occasion or opportunity of temptation, Luke viii. 13; 1 Peter i. 6; 2 Peter ii. 9.

The temptations that Satan drives on, upon the advantage of an afflicted estate, are these: —

(1.) First, To drive men upon *impatient outbreakings against God*, as the Israelites in the wilderness turn upon Moses with this, 'Hast thou brought us into the wilderness to slay us?' [Exod. xiv. 11.] To this tended Job's temptation by his wife, 'Curse God, and die,' as it is in our translation, which cannot in anywise admit of the excuse that Beza makes for her, as if she gave wholesome advice, 'to die blessing of God,' because he reproves her sharply as having spoken foolishly and wickedly; but at best it is an ironical scoff at Job's integrity, 'Dost thou bless God while thou art killed by his displeasure?' if it be not a direct suggestion of revengeful despite. At such times men are too apt to entertain cruel thoughts of God, and sadly reflective upon his mercy or justice.

(2.) Secondly, In this posture of affliction he strives to put them *upon direful conclusions against themselves*, as if God called solemnly their sin to remembrance, and that they are forsaken of God, and marked out for destruction, the pledge and earnest whereof they take these troubles to be. We may observe that David's afflictions awakened his conscience to object guilt and miscarriage, so that he is as earnest to deprecate the marking and remembrance of his sin as he is to pray against his troubles. For this see Ps. xxv. 6, 7, xxxviii. 1, 4.

(3.) Thirdly, He pusheth them usually upon *contempt of religion, and abandoning the ways of God*. We are too apt to blame religion for all our troubles; and as we expect that our owning the ways of God should secure us from outward affliction, so when we find it otherwise we are too forward to say, 'We have washed our hands in vain,' &c., [Ps. lxxiii. 13.]

(4.) Fourthly, *The sin of distrust is another evil that he drives at*; he would have men conclude that God cannot or will not deliver. 'Can God prepare a table in the wilderness?' said the Israelites, by the power of temptation, when they were distressed, [Ps. lxxviii. 19.]

(5.) Fifthly, Another evil aimed at in such a case, is to put us upon *indirect courses and ways to escape from our troubles. Flectere si nequeo superos,* &c. Saul went to the witch of Endor when God answered him not. Distresses naturally prompt such things, and a little temptation makes us comply, as is noted by the wise man's desire, 'Give me not poverty, lest I put out my hand and steal,' [Prov. xxx. 9.] Distresses of poverty put men upon theft and unlawful ways.

The reasons of Satan's tempting the afflicted are these:—

(1.) First, That outward afflictions are *a load and burden*. This gives a probability that his designs may the better take place. It is easy to overthrow those that are bowed down, to break those that are bruised, to master those that are weary and weak-handed.

(2.) Secondly, An afflicted estate is *a temptation of itself, and naturally dictates evil things*. It is half of his design brought to his hand, it affords variety of matter for a temptation to work on.

(3.) Thirdly, Such a condition *strongly backs a temptation, and furnisheth many arguments for a prevalency*; for troubles are serious things; they speak to the heart, and what they speak, they speak fiercely; they represent things otherwise than common discovery can do, and for the most part they shew an ingenuity in multiplying fears, and aggravating hazard, and ascertaining suspected events, so that Satan can scarce desire a fairer hit than what these offer him.

(4.) Fourthly, They also give him the advantage *of darkness*; for to such their 'way is hid,' Job iii. 23, and God hath hedged them in; they neither know where they are, whether their trouble be a chastisement of sin, or for trial, or for prevention of miscarriage, or to make way for more comfortable manifestations; and as little know they how to behave themselves in their trouble, or how and when to get out of it. In such groping uncertainties, it is scarce possible but they should be put wrong.

(5.) Fifthly, An afflicted condition brings *on weakness and indisposition to duty*; it makes the hands weak, and the knees feeble. This made Job to faint, chap. iv. 5; this dried up David's strength. The first assault of an affliction doth stound, and put it into such a confusion, that hope turns back, and faith is to seek, and every grace so out of order, that a man shall be unable to do anything of duty in a comfortable manner.

(6.) Sixthly, In this case men are apt to conclude *their prayers are not heard*: 'I cry in the day-time, and thou hearest not,' [Ps. xxii. 2,] says David; 'Hath the Lord forgotten to be gracious?' [Ps. lxxvii. 9.] And with such seeming probability is this urged upon us by affliction, that Job professeth he could not believe his own sense and knowledge in such a case. 'If I had called, and he had answered me; yet would I not believe that he had hearkened unto my voice,' Job ix. 16.

(7.) Seventhly, Afflictions strongly *fix guilt upon us*, and represent God 'searching out our iniquities, and inquiring after our sin,' Job x. 6.

(8.) Eighthly, They *imbitter the spirit*, and beget impressions upon the mind, of very hard thoughts of God.

(9.) Ninthly, They violently push men on *to speak unadvisedly*. There is such a swelling ferment of the old leaven of impatience and distrust in the mind, that it is matter of pain and difficulty to be silent: 'Their belly is as wine that hath no vent; it is ready to burst like new bottles,' and they are 'weary with forbearing and cannot stay, and must speak let come on them what will,' Job xxxii. 19.

All these advantages doth an afflicted condition bring to Satan; and who can think that he who is so studious of our ruin will be willing to miss so fair an opportunity?

Applic. (1.) First, This must teach us to have *a watchful eye over affliction*. Though at all times we must expect Satan's stratagems, yet in troubles especially prepare for them; according to the wise man's advice, 'In a day of adversity, consider,' [Eccles. vii. 14.]

(2.) Secondly, Seeing Satan takes advantage of the sharp humours of impatience and distrust, we must be particularly careful not *to touch too much upon the harshness of our troubles*, because this is that that sets fretting and distracting thoughts on work. Afflictions, like the pillar of the cloud and fire in the wilderness, have a light and darkness; and accordingly, those that converse with the dark side of troubles envenom their imaginations, and poison their thoughts with dark and hideous conclusions, and, in a word, draw forth nothing but the wormwood and the gall; whereas those that study and view the light side of them are full of praise and admiration for the gracious mixtures, comfortable mitigations, encouraging supports, &c., which they observe. It is wisdom then to keep upon the right side of them.

Though it be the design of God to turn the dark side of the cloud to us, yet may we have a competent light to guide us if we would improve it. When the sun is set, the moon may be up. Nay, it is our duty to strive to recover the right side of the cloud. He hides that we may seek.

If this fast of Christ's be considered as a remedy against temptations, then may we observe *that solemn temptations are to be resisted with fastings and prayers*. Of this I shall forbear to speak, till I come to speak of Christ's answer, and the repulse of Satan.

CHAPTER VI

That Christ's temptations were real and not in vision.—That temptation is Satan's employment, with the evidences and instances thereof.—Of Satan's tempting visibly, with the reasons thereof.

Next follows a particular account of those more eminent temptations wherewith Christ was assaulted by Satan. Before I speak of these, I must necessarily remove this stumbling-block out of the way, viz., whether Christ was really tempted, or only in a vision. That this was but visionary hath been supposed; not only by some, whose conceits in other things might justly render their supposals in this matter less worthy of a serious consideration,376 but also by very grave and serious men,377 whose reasons, notwithstanding, are not of that weight as to sway us against the letter and history of these temptations, which give us a full account of these things as really transacted, without the least hint of understanding them as done only in a vision. For,

(1.) First, It is a dangerous thing to depart from the literal sense of what is historically related. If we take such a liberty, we may as well understand other historical passages after the same rate, and so bring the history, not only of Christ's suffering to a visionary and fantastical cross, but also of all the New Testament to a very nothing.378

(2.) Secondly, The circumstances of the temptation are so particularly set down—as the devil's coming to him, leaving him, taking him to the temple. &c.—that if we may expect in anything to secure ourselves from a visionary supposition, we may do it in this history.379

(3.) Thirdly, This imagination doth wholly *enervate and make void the very end and design of Christ's being tempted*; for where were the glory of this victory over Satan, if it were only a visionary temptation, and a visionary conquest? or where were the comfort and encouragement which believers— from the apostle's authority, Heb. ii. 18, and iv. 16—might reap from this, that Christ imagined himself to be tempted, when really he was not so? Nay, how impossible is it to make that expression of the apostle, 'He was tempted in all points like as we are,' to agree to an imaginary temptation? except we also say that we are only tempted visionarily and not really?

(4.) Fourthly, Neither is it a plea of any value against this truth, that it seems to derogate too much from the honour and authority of our Saviour, that Satan should so impudently assault him with temptations to worship him, and should carry him at pleasure from place to place, when we find that he voluntarily submitted to higher indignities from Satan's instruments, and 'turned not away his cheek' from those that 'smote' him, spit upon him, and contumeliously mocked him, and at last submitted to death, even the death of the cross.380

As for those objections from πτερύγιον ἱεροῦ, the pinnacle of the temple, upon which Scultetus thinks it was impossible for Christ to stand; as also the objection of the impossibility to shew the kingdoms of the world from any mountain, I shall answer them in their proper place. In the meantime I shall return to the verse in hand, in which I shall first pitch upon the general *proœmium*, or introduction to these special temptations, which is this, 'The tempter came to him.'

In this we are to take notice of the name given to Satan, and also the way and manner of the assault, in that expression, 'he came to him.'

There are three distinct names given to him in these temptations. [1.] His name 'Satan' shews his malice and fury, which is the ground and fountain whence all that trouble proceeds which we meet with from him. [2.] He is styled 'the tempter,' and that signifies to us how he puts forth this malice, his way and exercise in the exerting of it. [3.] He is called 'the devil' or accuser, expressing thereby the end and issue of all. From this name, then, here given, we may observe: —

Obs. 1. First, That it is Satan's work and employment to tempt men. We need not here dispute whether it be proper to Satan to tempt—that is, an soli, et semper competat, whether it agree to him only and always, which some indeed affirm in such a sense as this, that men do tempt men as Satan's instruments, the world tempts as it is the object and matter of temptations, but Satan tempts as the proper author and engineer of temptations. Others there are that think that men can and do properly tempt themselves, according to James i. 'Every man is tempted, when he is drawn away of his own lust.'381 But the question is altogether needless as to us; though we and others may be true and proper tempters, yet this hindereth not but that it is most true, that Satan makes temptation his very work and business. And therefore not only here, but in 1 Thes. iii. 5, the devil is described by his employment, 'Lest by any means the tempter,' or he that tempteth, 'hath tempted you:' which the ordinary gloss doth thus explain, Diabolus, cujus est officium tentare. This name, then, is put upon Satan, κατ' ἐξοχὴν, by way of eminency. Implying, [1.] That though there be never so many tempters, yet Satan is the chief. [2.] That he makes temptation his proper employment.

That Satan doth so, I shall evidence by these few notes:—

[1.] First, Temptation is in itself *a business and work*. For if we consider either the work of any one temptation, where Satan is oft put to it, after suggestion to persuade, and after persuasion to instigate and provoke; or if we consider what furniture, tools, means, and instruments are requisite, and what it may cost to bring all things together into fit order and method; or if we think of the various ways and manners of temptation, that some are mediate, some immediate; some inward, some outward; some moveable, some fixed and solemn; some enticements to evil, some affrightments from duty, others invasions of our peace and joy; or lastly, if we call to mind what study, what art, what fetches and contrivances the devil is sometimes put upon, we shall easily see that it keeps him doing, and that he eats not the bread of idleness that hath that employment to follow.

[2.] Secondly, Satan *gives up himself unto it, is wholly in it*. He 'walks to and fro,' 'goes about' seeking advantages of this nature, 'compasseth sea and land' to proselyte men to his slavery, useth all means, upon all men, at all times, with all diligence. Hence was it that Latimer, in his homely way of speaking, called him 'a busy bishop in his diocese,' and excited the sluggish to learn laboriousness of the devil.

[3.] Thirdly, *He takes a delight in it, not only from a natural propensity, which his fall put upon him, whereby he cannot but tempt*—as an evil tree cannot but bring forth evil fruits—but also from the power of a habit acquired by long exercise, which is accompanied with some kind of pleasure; and further, whatever pleasure may be supposed to arise from revengeful pride or companionship in evil, he hath of that in full measure, pressed down, and running over. *Solamen miseris*, &c.

[4.] Fourthly, All other things in Satan, or in his endeavours, have either a *subserviency, or some way or other a reference and respect to temptation*. His power, wisdom, malice, and other infernal qualifications, render him able to tempt; his labour and diligence in other things are but the work of one that prepares materials and occasions; his other business of accusing, affrighting, destroying, tormenting, are but the ends and improvements of tempting.

[5.] Fifthly, *He cares not how it goes on, so that it go on*; as a man that designs to be rich, cares not how he gets it; which shews that tempting in general is his design. Of this we have many instances, as [1.] He sticks not to lie and dissemble; he will tell them of the 'kingdoms of the world, and the glory of them,' and a thousand fair promises which he never intends. [2.] He will tempt for a small matter; if he can but gain a little, or but molest us, yet he will be doing. [3.] He will not give over for a foil or disappointment. [4.] He is not ashamed to tempt contradictory things: he tempted Christ against the work of redemption, 'Master, spare thyself,' [Mat. xvi. 22.] He tempted Judas to further it in betraying him. [5.] Any temptation that he sees will hold, he takes up. Hence is it that he tempts not the Jews now to idolatry, because he hath them fast in another snare, being strongly led to an opposition and contempt of Christ. [6.] He will sometime tempt where he hath not probability to prevail, even against hope. Thus he tempted Christ and Paul.

Applic. (1.) The use of the observation is this, *If it be his business to tempt, it must be our work to resist.*

[1.] First, To resist *is a labour*. It is not an idle formality, consisting in words of defiance, or a few ridiculous crossings and sprinklings of holy water, or spitting at the name of him, as ignorant people are wont to do.

[2.] Secondly, *We must give up ourselves to this work*, always fighting and opposing.

[3.] Thirdly, It will be necessary to *make use of all helps*, as prayer, fasting, the counsel and support of holy and experienced men.

[4.] Fourthly, *We must also cast off all hindrances*. Whatsoever in us is apt to take fire or give advantage must be laid off, as pride, which doth prognosticate a fall, and security, which betrays the best, or presumption, which provokes God to leave those of highest attainments, Neh. xiii. 16.

2. Secondly, In this general introduction, we may cast our eye upon *the way and manner of the assault*. When it is said, 'the tempter came unto him,' we are unavoidably forced to suppose another manner of coming than that whereby he tempted him for forty days together. And when we call to mind that at his coming here mentioned, he carried Christ to the temple, and from thence to a high mountain, and there propounded himself an object of worship; we can imagine no less than that Satan here came visibly to him. But in what shape or manner of appearance it is altogether uncertain, though it is most probable it was not in the form of a brute, but in some lustre of majesty or glory, as an angel, because a deformed or base appearance had been unsuitable to the boast of giving 'the kingdoms of the world,' or to his desire that Christ should 'fall down and worship him.' Hence we may observe: —

Obs. 2. *That Satan sometimes tempts in a visible appearance, and by voice.*

[1.] First, The possibility of this is evident from the apparitions of angels. Satan is still an angel, and there is nothing of a natural incapacity in him as to an outward appearance to our eyes and senses, more than in glorified spirits.382

[2.] Secondly, *In the first temptation he did no less, when he used the serpent as a trunk to speak through, and an instrument to act by.* In possessions he speaks audibly, and evidenceth a real presence.

[3.] Thirdly, *Undoubted instances may be given of Satan's tempting and molesting visibly.* I deny not but there are a great many idle stories of this kind, and a number of ridiculous figments; but it would be unreasonable and highly prejudicial to the truth of history, and the common faith of mankind, to refuse credit to the serious accounts of sober men, because of some foolish and unwarrantable fables.

What is related of Luther and his several troubles from Satan this way, is evident in the story of his life. Cyrillus tells us of one Eusebius, disciple of Jerome, who when he was dying, cried out of the devil's appearing to him. The like is storied of St Martin and others, and of these, you may read more collected by Mr Clark.383

If we would inquire into the reasons of Satan's appearing thus, we cannot more fitly pitch upon any other than these:—

[1.] First, Either he thinks a great affrightment necessary in some cases, and for that end appears. Or,

[2.] Secondly, He sees his appearance needful, to give a greater evidence and certainty to the reality of the pleasures of sin which he promiseth. That is the common ground of his appearing in the ways and designs of witchcraft.

[3.] Or thirdly, In the height of rage, when he perceives other ways not available, and when he hath to do with persons not ignorant of his devices, where he sees he hath no need of a visor, or covert ways of dealing, then he sticks not, if permitted, to tempt or molest openly.

This must teach us not to wonder at such temptations, much less to judge those that may be so molested, as if Satan had a greater share in them, seeing Christ was thus tempted.

CHAPTER VII

I have done with the *proœmium* to the temptations. Yet before I open them particularly, I shall take a general view of them. First, By comparing these with the other temptations of Christ during the forty days. Secondly, By comparing these with the temptations of men.

1. First then, If we compare these with the former temptations, and observe that we have no account given us of those temptations, but only in the general, 'that he was tempted,' whereas these are particularly set down and recorded, we cannot apprehend less than this, *that these last temptations were certainly greater and more remarkable temptations.* Hence note,

Obs. 3. That it is Satan's method to be gradual in his temptations, and that he keeps his greatest temptations to the latter end.

That Satan is gradual in his temptations; this is true of him, if we regard,

(1.) First, *The manner of his proceeding,* that he drives slowly, entreats gently, and is very careful that he do not over-drive men, but after they are accustomed to his way, he puts on imperiousness and commands them.

(2.) Secondly, *If the matter of temptation be regarded,* he is gradual there also. He tempts to little sins first, then to greater.

I shall illustrate both these particulars by the example of Thomas Savage, apprentice to Mr Collins, vintner at the Ship Tavern, in Ratcliffe, who suffered in *anno* 1660, for murdering his fellow-servant. He confesseth that the devil took this course with him: he first tempted him to neglect of duty, then to contempt of ordinances and profanation of the Sabbath, then to drinking, then to fornication, then to rob and steal from his master, and last of all to murder; and takes particular notice that in this last temptation, to kill his fellow-servant, there was a violent and more than ordinary power of Satan upon him, to instigate him to that wickedness. All this you may read at large in the printed narration of his life.

(1.) The reasons of his gradual proceedings are,

[1.] First, *He would discover no more of himself in any temptation than he is necessitated unto for the gaining his end,* lest he cross his own design, and instead of drawing men to wickedness, scare or affright them from it.

[2.] Secondly, *Sins are mutually preparatory to each other.* Smaller proffers and temptations do insensibly prepare and incline the heart to greater.

(2.) Secondly, That he keeps his greatest temptations last, is a consequence of the former; for which, besides what is now spoken, these reasons may be given:—

[1.] First, *There is provocation given him in refusing his lesser assaults.* His 'head is bruised' by every refusal, he is set at defiance, which calls him out to stronger opposition. He perceives by often repulses that those with whom he hath to do are not subjects of his kingdom, and that his 'time is short,' and therefore no wonder is it, if he assault most furiously and with all his strength.

[2.] Secondly, *There is also policy in it.* When he hath brought down our strength and weakened our courage, then a violent onset is fair to procure him a victory.

But because I mention a great temptation, it may not be amiss both for the further explaining of the text, and illustration of the matter, to shew what is a great temptation. These were great temptations to Christ, and there are several things remarkable in them, which, wherever they appear, they will denominate the temptation great, and the more of them are conjoined together, and in higher degree, it may justly be called still the greater. As,

(1.) First, In these temptations, we may note there were *external objects as well as insinuated suggestions.* Inward motions are real temptations, but when they have the objects and things presented to the eye or the senses, then do they strongly urge. At this advantage the devil tempted Eve. He urged her when the fruit was within the view. Thus he tempted Achan, when the gold and garment were in his eye.

(2.) Secondly, *These temptations were complex*, consisting of many various designs, like a snare of many cords or nooses. When he tempted to turn stones to bread, it was not one single design, but many, that Satan had in prosecution. As distrust on one hand, pride on another, and so in the rest. The more complicated a temptation is, it is the greater.

(3.) Thirdly, These were also perplexing, entangling temptations. They were dilemmatical,384 such as might ensnare, either in the doing or refusal. If he had turned stones into bread, he had too much honoured Satan by doing it at his motion. If he did not, he seemed to neglect his own body, in not making necessary provisions for himself, being now hungry.

(4.) Fourthly, *These temptations proceeded upon considerable advantages.* His hunger urged a necessity of turning stones into bread. His present straits, and the lowness of his condition, seemed to speak much for the reasonableness of giving proof of his divine nature, by casting himself down from the temple, and of doing anything that might tend to a more plentiful being and support in the world. Advantages strengthen temptations.

(5.) Fifthly, *These temptations were accompanied with a greater presence and power of Satan.* He appeared visibly in them, and was permitted to touch and hurry the body of Christ, and to depaint and set forth the glory of the world, doubtless in the most taking way, to the eye of Christ.

(6.) Sixthly, *The matter of these temptations,* or the things he tempted Christ to, *were great and heinous abominations*: a distrust of providence, a presumption of protection, and a final renunciation of the worship due to him, and transferring it to the most unworthy object, God's professed enemy; and yet were they seconded by the strongest, most powerful, and most prevailing means, as his present straits, his infallible assurance of sonship, pleasure, and glory. Where the matter is weighty, and the medium strong and pressing, there is the temptation great.

(7.) Seventhly, *All these temptations pretended strongly to the advantage and benefit of Christ,* and some of them might seem to be done without any blame, as to turn stones to bread, to fly in the air. The more kindness a temptation pretends to us, it is the stronger.

(8.) Eighthly, *Satan urged some of them in a daring, provoking way;* 'If thou be the Son of God?' as if he had said, I dare thee to shew thyself what thou pretendest to be. These kind of provocations are very troublesome to the most modest and self-denying, who can scarce forbear to do what they are urged unto at such times.

(9.) Ninthly, *These temptations seem to be designed for the engagement of all the natural powers of Christ*; his natural appetite in a design of food; his senses in the most beautiful object, the world in its glory; the affections, in that which is most swaying, pride, and delight in extraordinary testimonies of divine power and love, in supporting him in the air, &c.

(10.) Tenthly, *Some of these warranted as duty, and to supply necessary hunger, others depending upon the security of a promise,* 'He shall give his angels charge,' &c. The greater appearance of duty, or warrantableness, is put upon sin, the greater is the temptation.

By these ten particulars may we, as by a standard, judge when any temptation is great or less.

Applic. 1. *Let us then take heed of small temptations, or the smoother proceedings of Satan, as we would avoid the greater attempts that are to follow.* Where he is admitted to beat out our lusts with a rod or a staff, he may be suspected to bring the wheel over them at last, [Isa. xxviii. 27, *seq.*]

Let us also after our assaults expect more and greater, because the greatest are last to be looked for. This holds true in three cases. [1.] In solemn temptations, where Satan fixeth his assaults, there the utmost rage is drawn out last. [2.] In the continuance and progress of profession, the further we go from him and the nearer to God, be sure of the highest measure of his spite. [3.] At the end of our race: for if he miss his prey then, it is escaped for ever, as a bird unto its hill.

Obj. But some may say, I am but a messenger of sad tidings; and that by bringing such a report of giants and walled cities, I may make the hearts of the people to faint.

Ans. I answer; This is bad news only to the sluggish, such as would go to heaven with ease, and in a fair and easy way; but to the laborious resolute soldiers of Christ this is no great discouragement: for, [1.] It doth but tell them of their work, which as they are persuaded of, so it is in some measure their delight, as well as their expectation. [2.] It doth but tell them, Satan's malice and fury, which they are assured of, and are most afraid of it sometimes, when it seems to lie idle and as asleep. [3.] It doth tell them that Satan's thoughts concerning them are despairing, he fears they are going, or gone from him. If they were his willing servants, there would be no hostility of this nature against them.

I have thus compared these special temptations with those wherewith our Lord Christ was exercised during the forty days. I shall,

Secondly, Compare these temptations of Christ with those that usually befall his members, in which there is so much suitableness and agreement both in matter and manner, that it cannot be unuseful to take notice of it, which will the better appear in instances. First, then, let us consider the first temptation of Eve: Gen. iii. 6, 'And when the woman saw that the tree was good for food, and that it was pleasant to the eyes, and a tree to be desired to make one wise,' &c. Here are all the arguments and ways summed up by which Satan prevailed upon her. It was 'good for food;' here he wrought upon the desire of the natural appetite. It was 'pleasant to the eyes;' here he took the advantage of the external senses. It was 'to be desired to make one wise;' here he inflamed the affections. Let us again call to mind the general account of temptations in 1 John ii. 16, 'All that is in the world, the lust of the flesh, the lust of the eyes, and the pride of life;' where the apostle designedly calls all off from a love of the world, because of the hazard and danger that we lie open unto, from the things of the world, striking upon and stirring up our lusts; which he ranks into three general heads, according to the various ways whereby these outward things do work upon us, in exciting our natural powers and apprehensions to sinful lustings; and these are so fully agreeing with those three in Eve's temptation, that I need not note the parallel. Let us now cast our eyes upon these temptations, and the suitableness of Satan's ways and dealings will immediately appear. When he tempted Christ to turn stones into bread, there he endeavoured to take advantage of the 'lust of the flesh,' which in 1 John ii., I understand in a more restrained sense, not for the lustings of corrupt nature, but for the lustings of the body in its natural appetite, according to that expression of Christ, 'The spirit is willing, but the flesh'—or body—'is weak.' And if we should not so restrain it in this place, the lust of the flesh would include the lust of the eyes and the pride of life, contrary to the clear scope of the text, for these are also the lustings of corrupt nature. When he further tempted him 'to cast himself down,' he pushed him upon 'the pride of life;' when he shewed him 'the kingdoms of the world, and the glory of them,' he attempted to gain upon him by the 'lust of the eyes.' From this proportion and suitableness of temptation to Christ and his members, observe,

Obs. 4. That Satan usually treads in a beaten path, using known and experienced methods of temptation. It is true, in regard of circumstances, he useth unspeakable varieties in tempting, and hath many more devices and juggles than can be reckoned up; yet in the general he hath digested them into method and order, and the things upon which he works in us are the same. Thus he walks his round, and keeps much-what the same track, not only in different persons, but also in the same men, using the same temptations over and over; and yet this argues no barrenness of invention or sluggishness in Satan; but he hath these reasons for it:—

[1.] First, Because the same temptations being suited to human nature in general, will, with a small variation of circumstance, suit all men: their inclinations generally answering to one another, as face answers to face in water.

[2.] Secondly, These standing methods are famous with him, as generally powerful and taking; and it can be no wonder if Satan practise most with these things that have the largest *probatum est* of experience to follow them.

[3.] Thirdly, The more experienced he is in any temptation, the more dexterously and successfully still he can manage it; so that we may expect him more cunning and able in what he most practiseth.

Applic. This may be some satisfaction to those that are apt to think of themselves and their temptations as Elias did in his persuasion, 'I alone am left,' [1 Kings xix. 14.] Where Satan useth anything of vigour and fierceness, we are apt to say, 'None are tempted as we,' none in like case, we are singular, they are peculiar and extraordinary temptations, &c.; but it is a mistake. Even that of Solomon may be applied to these, 'There is nothing new,' [Eccles. i. 9,] nor anything befallen us which others have not undergone before us; and would but Christians be so careful to observe the way of the serpent upon their hearts as they might, and so communicative of their experiences as they ought, the weak and heavy laden would not go so mourning under such apprehensions as commonly affright them, that none were ever so tempted as they are. It would be some support at worst, when the most hellish furies do oppress them, to know that others before them were in these deeps, and as fearful of being overwhelmed as themselves, and yet were delivered. The deliverances of those that have escaped the danger, is ground of hope to those that are at present under it.

Obs. 5. *The usual advantages that Satan takes against us is from our natural appetite, our external senses, or our passions and affections.* All these are usual ways by which Satan works against us, as appears from what hath been said; neither are any of them so mean and contemptible, but that we have cause to fear the power and influence of them. Hence the Scripture cautions descend to the eyes: 'Look not upon the wine when it is red in the cup,' [Prov. xxiii. 31;] 'Be sober, be vigilant,' &c., [1 Peter v. 8.] The appetite is not so easily kept in, but that it may prevail to gluttony and drunkenness; and some are so powerfully carried by this, that they are said 'to make their bellies their god,' [Phil. iii. 19.] Of the power of sense and affection, elsewhere hath been spoken.

CHAPTER VIII

Having thus considered these temptations as they lie before us in their general prospect, I shall now speak of this first special temptation in particular, in which—(1.) The rise, or occasion; (2.) The temptation itself; (3.) The argument by which Satan would enforce it, are to be distinctly noted.

1. First, *As to the rise of it*, it is questioned by some why Satan begins with this first. The cause they assign, in part at least, is from his first success against Eve, in a temptation about eating, as if this were the chief and most hopeful arrow in his quiver. But we need not go so far, when the evangelist is so punctual in setting it down, in the latter end of the former verse, 'he was an hungered.' This the devil took notice of, and from hence took the rise of his temptation, that by 'turning stones to bread,' for the satisfaction of his present hunger, he might be induced to make way for the secret stratagems which he had prepared against him on this occasion. Here I note,

Obs. 6. That where Satan hath a design against any, he doth take the advantage of their condition, and suits his temptation accordingly. Thus, if men be in poverty, or in the enjoyments of plenty, in sickness or health, if in afflictions, under wrongs, in discontents, or carried to advancements and honours, or whatever else may be considerable relating to them, he observes it, and orders his designs so as to take in all the advantages that they will afford. That it is his concern and interest so to do, we may imagine, upon these grounds:—

(1.) First, *Our consent must be gained.* This he cannot properly and truly force, but must entice and deceive us to a compliance with him.

(2.) Secondly, *If our condition speak for him, and lie fair for the furtherance of any device of his, our consent is upon the matter half gained.* It is much, if so powerful an advocate, as is our present state, do not influence us to an inclination.

(3.) Thirdly, *This doth his work easily and effectually.* He more generally prevails by this course, and with less labour.

Applic. This policy of Satan should advantage us by *suggesting fit memorials to us in our expectations of temptation.* Though we know not all

Satan's thoughts, yet may we know where and how he will usually make an onset. Our condition will tell us what to look for. The distressed and afflicted may expect a temptation suited to their condition, as of murmuring, repining, revenge, distrust, use of indirect means, despairings, &c. They that have peace and plenty may be sure they shall be tempted suitably, to pride, boasting, covetousness, oppression, contempt of others, security, or whatever may be fit to be ingrafted on that stock. The like may be said of any other different condition. How fairly are we forewarned, by an observation made upon Satan's proceeding upon these advantages, where to expect him, and how to provide against him.

Let us proceed to a further inquiry, *How the devil managed this advantage of Christ's hunger.* He plainly urgeth him with a necessity of providing supplies for himself, spreading before him his desire to eat, and the impossibility of help, in a barren and desolate wilderness: as if he had said, 'The want of the body is to be provided for; nature and religion consents to this; the wilderness affords no help, ordinary means fail; there is therefore a necessity that some extraordinary course be taken, therefore turn stones to bread; this is not unsuitable to the condition and power of him who is the Son of God.' At this rate he pleads.

Obs. 7. Observe then, *That Satan usually endeavours to run his temptations upon the plea of necessity, and from thence to infer a duty.*

When he cannot pretend a fair and direct way to irregular practices, he would break a door and force a way by necessity.

Under this notion of necessity, the devil marshals all those pretences that seem to be of more than ordinary force, in their usual prevalencies. Thus he teacheth men to think they are necessitated, if they be carried by a strong inclination of their own, or if there be an urgency and provocation from others, or if they be in straits and dangers; and sometime he goes so high as to teach men that a necessity is included in the very fabric of their natural principles, by which they presumptuously excuse themselves in being sinful, because by nature they are so, and cannot be changed without special grace. Scarce shall we meet any man with seasonable reproof for his iniquity, but he will plead such kind of necessities for himself, — I could not help it, I was strongly carried; or, I was compelled; I must do so, or else I could not escape such a danger, &c.

The reasons of this policy are these: —

(1.) First, *He knows that necessity hath a compulsive force,* even to things of otherwise greatest abhorrencies. A treasury of instances is to be had in famines and besieged places, where it is usual to eat unclean things, not only creatures that are vile, but even dung and entrails; nay, so tyrannical is necessity, that it makes inroads into, and conquests upon nature itself, causing 'the tender and delicate woman, which would not adventure the sole of her foot upon the ground for delicateness and tenderness, to have an evil eye towards the husband of her bosom, towards her son, and towards her daughter,' Deut. xxviii. 56. A like force doth it exercise upon the minds and consciences of men. It makes them rise up against their light, it engageth men to lay violent hands upon their own convictions, to stifle and extinguish them. How many mournful examples have we of this kind! How many have apostatized from truth, being terrified by the urging necessities of danger, contrary to the highest convictions of conscience!

(2.) Secondly, *Necessity can do much to the darkening of the understanding, and change of the judgment, by the strong influence it hath upon the affections.* Men are apt to form their apprehensions according to the dictates of necessity. What they see to be hazardous, they are inclinable to judge to be evil. Men in straits not only violate their reason, but sometime by insensible steps, unknown to themselves, slide into a contrary judgment of things, directly cross to what they have believed and professed. Which persuasion they owe not to any further accession of light, or new discovery of argument; for ofttimes the same arguments which, in the absence of trouble, they have contemned as weak, by the appearance of danger, put on another face and seem strong; but to the prevalency of their fears. And thus many in all ages have altered their judgments and thoughts, not because they knew more, but because they feared more.

The like necessities do men form to themselves from exorbitant and greedy hopes and expectations of a better condition, compared to that wherein they at present are; and the like influence it hath in the alteration of their judgments. Let the bishop of Spalato be an example of this, who loathed the Romish religion first, and in England, whither he came for refuge, writ against it; but saw a necessity, from the disappointment of expectation, to change his mind, returned to Rome again, and persuaded himself that that was true which he had formerly pronounced false; and so writ against the church of England, as before he had done against the church of Rome. To him we may add Ecebolius,385 of whom Socrates reports, that, according to the various appearings of hazards, he changed his religion several times. Under Constantine, he was a Christian; under Julian, a pagan; and under Jovinian, a Christian again.

(3.) Thirdly, Necessity offer's an excuse, if not a justification, of the greatest miscarriages.386 Lot offered to expose his daughters to the raging lust of the Sodomites for the preservation of his angel-strangers, which surely he would in no wise have done, but that he thought the present necessity might have excused him. Esau profanely sells his birthright, but excuseth the matter so, 'Behold, I am at the point to die; and what profit shall this birthright do to me?' Gen. xxv. 32. Aaron produceth a necessity, from the violent resolves of the people, in justification of himself in the matter of the golden calf, 'Thou knewest that this people are set on mischief,' [Exod. xxxii. 22.]

(4.) Fourthly, *Necessity is a universal plea*, and fitted to the conditions of all men in all callings, and under all extravagancies. The tradesman, in his unlawful gains or overreachings, pleads a necessity for it from the hardness of the buyer in other things; the poor man pleads a necessity for stealing, and the rich pleads the same necessity for revenge, and thus it serves all with a pretext.

These considerations, discovering this course so hopeful as to this design of the devil, he will be sure to put us to this pinch where he can. But, besides this, we may observe three cheats in this plea of necessity:—

[1.] First, *Sometimes he puts men upon feigning a necessity where there is none*. Saul sacrificed upon a needless supposal that, Samuel not coming at the time appointed, there was a necessity for him to do it. He spared also the cattle upon the like pretence, that it was a necessary provision for sacrifice. And thus would the devil have persuaded Christ, that there was an absolute necessity to turn stones to bread, when in truth there was no such need.

[2.] Secondly, *Sometimes he puts men upon a necessity of their own sinful procurement*. Herod sware to gratify the daughter of Herodias, and this is presently pleaded as a necessity for the cutting off John Baptist's head. Saul forbade the tasting of meat, and sealed the penalty by an oath and curse, and this is by and by made a necessity for the taking away of Jonathan's life,—who had tasted honey not knowing his father's curse,—had not the people rescued him, [1 Sam. xiv. 24, *seq.*]

[3.] Thirdly, *Sometime he stretcheth a necessity further than it ought*. He knows that God hath such a regard to real necessities, that upon that ground he will dispense with his Sabbath and the present performance of duty. These instances he lays before men, and endeavours to persuade them, that in like manner God will, upon a necessity, dispense with sins, as well as with the present opportunity of service. What a covering, in all ages, men have made of necessity for their highest outrages and extravagancies, and with what confidence they have managed such pleas, would be endless to relate.

Applic. This must warn us *not to suffer ourselves to be imposed upon by the highest pretences of necessity.* Whatever it may dispense with, as in some cases it will suspend a present service, and warrant the performance of a duty, besides the common rule and way wherein it ought ordinarily to be managed, it must never be pleaded to give warranty to anything in its own nature sinful. Necessity will not justify lying, stealing, covetousness, adulteries, &c., *Ferenda magis omnis necessitas quam perpetranda aliqua iniquitas.* — Aug[ustine.]

Besides, we must be wary in judging what is a necessity. Men are apt to plead a necessity where there is none; and if we give way to a facile admittance of excuses of this kind, we shall presently multiply necessities, and have them to serve us at every turn. Some would warrant sin by necessity, others would turn off duty and rule by pretending a necessity where none is; both are to be avoided as snares of Satan.

Once more, before we dismiss this rise of the temptation of Christ in hand, let us observe that, in persuading him to turn stones to bread, he seems to express a great deal of care and tenderness to Christ, with an invidious reflection upon the love and providence of God: as if he should say, 'I see thou art hungry, and this wilderness affords nothing to eat, and God hath not taken care to spread a table for thee; I therefore, pitying thy condition, as a friend, advise thee to turn stones to bread.'

Obs. 8. Note, *That Satan manageth his most cruel designs under the highest pretences of friendship.* He did so with Eve, 'The Lord knoweth that ye shall be as gods,' [Gen. iii. 5;] as if he had a greater regard to them than God himself. He tempted Christ in the mouth of Peter to 'spare himself,' under the show of great kindness, [Mat. xvi. 22;] and no less are his common pretences to all men. This is a deep policy, for by this means the mischief intended is the better concealed, and the less care and provision made against it; and besides, the affections and desires are stirred up to a hasty embracement of the motion, and an eager swallowing of the bait.

So great a subtlety is in this manner of dealing, that those who affect the name of great politicians in the world have learned from Satan to shew greatest respects and a most friendly countenance to those whom they most hate and intend to ruin. Thus our Richard the Third of England constantly dealt with those for whose blood he lay in wait; and the precepts of

Machiavel are fitted to this, that it is wisdom 'to hug those whom we desire to destroy.' Ehud's present made way for his dagger, [Judges iii. 22.] Joab's sword could not so well have despatched its errand upon Abner, if he had not ushered it in with a kiss, [2 Sam. xx. 9.]

Applic. This should make us most suspect those temptations that offer us most kindness and advantage, and such as are most gratifying to our humours and desires. For can it be imagined in good earnest that Satan intends us a real good? Can the gifts of enemies pass for courtesies and favours with any,387 but such as are bewitched into a blockish madness? Satan is more to be feared when he flatters than when he rageth; and though such offers may be looked upon by some as more benign, and less odious temptations, as some kind of familiar spirits are more kindly treated by some, under the notion of white devils, yet may we say of them, as Cornelius Agrippa speaks of some unlawful arts and ways of Thurgia,388 Eò sunt pernitiosiora, qùo imperitis diviniora, They have the greatest danger that pretend the highest friendship. Thus much for the rise of the temptation.

CHAPTER IX

Next follows the temptation itself, 'Command that these stones be made bread.' There is no great difficulty in the words. The Greek indeed hath a remarkable suitableness to the supposition, on which Satan insists, taking Christ to be the Son of God. It is very pertinently spoken, 'Say or speak' — εἰπε — that these stones be made bread; for if God speak, it must be done.

It is not worth the while to insist upon so small a variety of expression as is betwixt this evangelist, who hath it 'these stones,' and Luke, who speaks it in the singular number, 'this stone;' for besides that, as some suppose, this expression of Luke might, for anything that appears to the contrary, be Satan's lowering his request to one stone, when Christ had denied to turn many into bread upon his first asking; this one stone in Luke, taken collectively for the whole heap, will signify as much as these stones in Matthew; or the phrase 'these stones,' in Matthew, by an imitation of a common Hebraism, may be no more but one of these stones, or this stone, as it is in Luke; as it is said, Jephthah was buried in the cities of Gilead, that is, in one of the cities.389

The thing urged was the turning or changing the form of a creature, which is a work truly miraculous and wonderful, and such as had neither been unsuited to the power of Christ, nor unlawful in itself. It is from hence justly questioned where the sting of this suggestion lay, or in what point was the temptation couched.

(1.) First, It was not in *the unlawfulness or sinfulness of the thing mentioned.* For Christ did as much as would amount to all this when he turned water into wine, and when he fed multitudes by a miraculous multiplication of a few loaves and fishes.

(2.) Secondly, *It was not unsuitable to his condition, as hungry;* for so it seemed a duty to provide for himself, and which Satan took for granted.

(3.) Thirdly, Neither seemed it *any derogation to his power and divine nature, but rather an advantage and fit opportunity to give a full proof of it,* to the stopping of Satan's mouth for ever.

Notwithstanding these, there was poison and malignity enough in the suggestion, and under these green leaves of plausible pretences lay hid many snakes. For [1.] By this was he secretly tempted to admit of a doubting of the truth of the divine testimony, lately declaring him to be the Son of God. [2.] As also further to question his Father's providence and love; [3.] and unnecessarily to run out of the ordinary way of supply, and to betake himself to indirect means or extraordinary courses. [4.] And all this to the abuse and undervaluing of his power, in prostituting it to Satan's direction or persuasion; and the devil had gained a considerable advantage if he could have prevailed with him to do such a thing by his instigation. [5.] It may be he further thought this might entice to a high esteem of himself, and so make way for a vain ostentation of his power and interest in God. All or most of these seem to be the design that the devil was driving forward. Several things are hence observable.

Obs. 9. That where Satan doth not judge it his present interest to suggest to us things in their own nature sinful, he will move us to things good in themselves, in hopes thereby to lead us into evil. This way of tempting is from a more refined policy than downright motions to sin, and doubtless it is less suspected, and consequently more taking. The evils that Satan would introduce by this method are such as these:—

(1.) First, Sometime when he tempts us to that which is good, it is that he might *affright us from it*. His approbation is enough to put a discredit and disgraceful suspicion upon anything. Such a design had he when he gave testimony for Christ, 'that he was the Son of God,' Mat. viii. 29; or for the apostles, that they were the 'servants of the most high God,' Acts xvi. 17. It was not his intention to honour him or them by bearing them witness, but to bring them under suspicion and trouble.

(2.) Secondly, *There are a great many ways to miscarry in a lawful action,* either by propounding bad ends, or by failures in the manner of performance, or by a misimprovement of the whole. These miscarriages, and the possibility and probability of them, Satan carries in his mind; yet doth he not at first propound them, but moving us unto the thing, he hath an expectation that we will slide into them of ourselves, or be inclined by some suitable touches of suggestion upon our minds, together with the tendency or improvableness of the thing or action to such evils as are properly consequent to it. Satan did not here tempt Christ to these sinful ends directly, but to an action which he hoped might insensibly produce them.

(3.) Thirdly, Another evil hereby aimed at is *the hindrance of a greater good, not only as a diversion to turn us off a better or more profitable occasion, but also as an unseasonable interruption of something at present more concerning us.* Thus he makes the suggestion of good things the hindrance of prayer or hearing.

Quest. Some will say, This is a perplexing case, that in things good or lawful in themselves, men should be in such dangers, and will thereupon desire to know how they may distinguish Satan's contrivances and motions from those that have no dependence upon him, or are from the Spirit of God?

Ans. In answer to this:—

[1.] Let us, when we fear thus to be circumvented, look well *to what impressions are upon our spirit when we are moved to what may be lawful.* For together with the motion, if it be Satan's, we shall find either a corrupt reason and end privately rising up in our mind, or we may observe that our hearts are out of order and perversely inclined. This is oft unseen to ourselves. When the disciples moved Christ to bring down 'fire from heaven,' if they had considered the present revengeful selfish frame of their spirits, which our Lord tells them they were ignorant of, they might easily have known that the motion had proceeded from Satan.

[2.] Secondly, *The concurrent circumstances of the thing or action are to be seriously weighed,* for from thence we may take a right measure of the conveniency or inconveniency of the proceeding in it. What is from Satan it will be either unseasonable as to the time, place, and person, or some other thing will appear that may give a discovery. As here Christ refuseth to turn stones to bread, because not only the way and manner of the proposal doth sufficiently lay open the design, but also the circumstances of Christ's condition at that time shewed the motion to be unseasonable and inconvenient; for if Satan had urged the necessity of it for the satisfaction of his hunger, Christ could have answered, that the experience that he had of God's support for forty days together, was sufficient to engage him to rely yet further upon him. If he had urged further, that by this means he might have had a full proof of God's love and care, or of his sonship, it was at hand to tell him that it was needless to seek a further evidence when God had given one so full a little before. If again he had pleaded it to have been a useful occasion to give a testimony of his power to the satisfaction of others, he could have told him that it had been impertinent to have done it then, when he was in the wilderness, where none could have the benefit of it. So that nothing Satan could have propounded as a reason for that miracle, but it might have been repelled from a consideration of his present condition.

Applic. The instruction that may be gathered from this is, *that we must not entertain thoughts of doing lawful things without a due inquiry into the temper of our own hearts, and a full consideration of all circumstances round about, with the probable tendencies and consequences of it.*

Quest. But, may some say, if I judge such a motion to be a thing lawful, which doth proceed from Satan, what am I to do?

Answ. I answer, [1.] Consider whether the good be necessary or not. If it be necessary, it is a duty and not to be forborne, only the abuses are to be watched against and avoided.

[2.] Secondly, If it be a duty, consider whether it be seasonable or unseasonable, necessary or not, as to the present time; if it be not, it may be suspended, and a fitter opportunity waited for.

[3.] Thirdly, If it be only lawful and not necessary, we ought to abstain from it wholly, after the example of David, Ps. xxxix. 2, who 'abstained even from good,' that is, from lawful bemoanings of himself or complainings against Absalom, that had rebelled against him; because it was not necessary, and, the circumstances of his condition considered, very dangerous, lest vent and way being given, he might have been easily drawn to speak passionately or distrustfully against God, and foolishly against providences.

That the thing unto which Satan moved Christ was lawful, hath been noted. Next, let us consider *what end Satan might propound to himself in this motion*, and we shall see, as hath been said, that he did not so narrow and contract his design as that only one thing took up his intentions, but several. Hence have we this observation:—

Obs. 10. *That in one single temptation Satan may have various aims and designs.*

Temptation is a complicated thing, a many-headed monster. Satan hath always many things in his eye.

[1.] First, In every temptation there is *a direct and principal design, a main thing that the devil would have.*

[2.] Secondly, There are several things *subservient to the main design*, as steps, degrees, or means leading to it; the lesser still making way for the greater. If Satan design murder, he lays the foundation of his work in inward grudgings and hatreds; next he gives provocations, by reproachful words, or disdainful carriages and behaviours, as our Saviour notes in the expressions of *raca* and *fool*, Mat. v. 22, and so by degrees enticeth on to murder. The like we may observe in the lusts of uncleanness, and other things.

[3.] Thirdly, Besides these there are usually *reserves, something in ambushment to watch our retreats*; for Satan considers what to do in case we repel and refuse his motion, that so he may not altogether labour in vain. A contrary extreme watcheth those that fly from a temptation; pride, security, self-confidence, and boasting are ready to take them by the heel. So truly may it be said of Satan, that he knoweth the way that we take: if we go forward, he is there; if backward, we may also perceive him; on the left hand, he is at work; and on the right hand, he is not idle. All these we may particularly see in this temptation in hand. He had a main design, of which more presently; he prepares means and seconds to help it forward; such were those pleas of necessity and conveniency which the hunger and want of Christ did furnish him withal, and there wanted not the reserves of presumption and self-neglect in case he resisted the motion.

The reasons of this policy are these:—

(1.) First, *When Satan tempts, he is not certain of his prevalency, even when the probabilities are the greatest*; and therefore doth he provide himself with several things at once, that if the tempted party nauseate one thing, there may be another in readiness that may please his palate. God gives this advice to the spiritual seedsman, 'In the morning sow thy seed, and in the evening withhold not thine hand; for thou knowest not what shall prosper, whether this or that,' [Eccles. xi. 6.] Satan, that seedsman of the tares, imitates this; and because he knows not what shall prosper, therefore doth he use variety.

(2.) Secondly, *Where many things are at once designed, it is a hundred to one they will not all return empty.* It is much if many snares miss; he that hath broken one or two, may not only be enticed with a third temptation— as being either wearied out with the assaults, or made pliable with the allurements of the former, but may also sit down secure, as having, in his supposal, passed all the danger, and so unawares fall into an unseen or unsuspected trap.

Applic. This may [1.] by way of caution, assure us that we have no cause to think that all fear is over, when we have avoided the more obvious and conspicuous designments of a temptation, but rather to suspect some further train than we yet have discovered. [2.] That there is a necessity for us to be circumspect every way, and, Janus-like, to have an eye before and behind, that we may make timely discoveries of what Satan intends against us.

As we have taken a view of the various designments of Satan in one temptation, so it is also remarkable, that these various ways of his in this temptation, do give strength one to another, and have as close a connexion as stones in an arch. Christ was pleased to commend the wisdom of the unjust steward, though he intended not the least approbation of his dishonesty. So we may turn aside and observe the cunning artifice of the devil, in the management of this argument against Christ, which is to this purpose, as if he had thus proceeded: 'If thou art the Son of God,' as the voice from heaven lately testified, it can be no inconvenience, but every way an advantage to give a further proof of it. Thy present condition of want and hunger seem to contradict it; for how strange and unbeseeming is it for the Son of God to be in such straits! yet if thou beest what thou sayest thou art, it is easy for thee to help thyself. God, that made the world of nothing, by the power of his command, can much more change the forms of things that are made already; it is but speaking, and these stones that are before thee will be turned into bread; and besides that, in so doing thou mayest seasonably vindicate thyself from the eclipse of thy present condition. Necessity and duty—for it is duty to supply the want of the body, which cannot be supported without its proper nourishment—compel thee unavoidably to it, except thou fearest not to contract the guilt of self-destruction, especially seeing I do not urge thee to provide delicacies, but only bread, and such as is needful to keep in the lives of the poorest men, in the poorest manner.

Obs. 11. Hence note, *Satan in driving on a temptation, useth such an artificial contrivement of motives and things, that still one doth infer another, one strengthens another.* Temptations are like a screw, which if once admitted, will improve its first hold to draw in all the rest. By these arts doth Satan, like a cunning serpent, wriggle himself into the affections of men.

CHAPTER X

The various aims of Satan, and their close dependence one upon another, having contributed to us their several observations, it remains that we ask after the main and chief thing that Satan principally intended. And to make way to this, it must be noted, that in grand temptations especially, the main design of Satan comprehends these two: the chief end, and the chief means conducing to that end. About these, some authors conjecture variously, whose differences we have no great occasion to mention, seeing the text gives so great a satisfaction in this matter.

1. For first, The main end of Satan we have not obscurely expressed to us in these words, 'If thou be the Son of God,' which if we compare with Mat. iii. 17, 'This is my beloved Son, in whom I am well pleased,' we shall easily apprehend that here Satan doth but echo to that voice which came down from heaven; as he did with Eve. God had said, of the tree in the midst of the garden, ye shall not eat, [Gen. iii. 3.] Satan, having as it were the sound of this yet in his ears, in a clear reference to it saith, 'Yea, hath God said, Ye shall not eat?' ver. 1. So here is also an evident respect to God's testimony concerning Christ, as if he had said, 'Hath God said thou art his Son? If thou beest indeed such as he testified, give some proof of it,' &c. By which it appears that his design was to undermine this testimony, or some way or other to defeat it. Neither need it pass for an objection against this, that Satan doth not directly mention his doubt or distrust, nor positively suggest to Christ a questioning or misbelief of his sonship, for it was not suitable to his policy so to lay open his main end. That must have been expected afterward, as the last in execution, if it had taken effect, though it were first in intention.

2. Secondly, The chief means by which he would have brought this end about, may be understood from Christ's answer to the temptation; for it cannot but be imagined that Christ knew the bottom of Satan's policy, and that his answer must fully confront the means by which Satan endeavoured to ensnare him. His answer was, 'Man lives not by bread alone, but by every word that proceedeth out of the mouth of God.' If we can then come to a certain understanding of this scripture, which is not difficult, we shall evidently know the mind of the temptation, to which this is a direct answer.

These words are cited out of Deut. viii. 3, which some interpret to this sense,390 as if Christ had said, Man hath not only a life of the body—which is mentioned391 by bread—to look after, but another life of the soul, which is of so great concernment, that the bodily life is to be neglected, rather than that of the soul to be endangered. This is a truth in itself, but is apparently besides the meaning of Deut. viii. Neither doth it afford so full and particular an answer as doubtless Christ intended. But let us consider the text, and we shall find more in it; for Moses first sets down God's dealing with Israel in the wilderness, in that he suffered them to hunger, and took from them the ordinary means of life, which, as the latter part of the verse shews, is to be understood of ordinary bread; and then to supply that want, he fed them by an extraordinary means, such as they had never heard of before; this was by manna. Next he makes an inference from this way of God's proceeding, improving this particular to a general rule, 'That he might make thee know that man lives not by bread only, but by every word that proceedeth out of the mouth of the Lord doth man live;' which is clearly of this import, that man lives not by ordinary means only, but that God can provide for his life in an extraordinary way, by appointing anything to that end, through his mighty and powerful word and good pleasure. So that things never so unusual, or unfit in themselves for nourishment, will become strengthening to us, if he shall give out his command. Christ then applying this in this sense, did, as it were, thus say to Satan, 'Though I want ordinary means of life, which is bread, yet I know God can make anything which he pleaseth to nourish me instead of it. So that I will not cast off a dependence upon the providence of God in this strait, and without warrant run to an extraordinary course for supply.' Hence it is evident that to bring about his main end, which was to distrust of his relation to God, he used this means, that by reason of his strait in the failure of ordinary supply, he should distrust providence, and without warrant provide for himself. Observe,

Obs. 12. *That where Satan carries on a main design and end, he bestows most of his pains and skill in rendering the means to that end plausible and taking.* The end is least in mention, and the means in their fit contrivance takes up most of his art and care. The reasons whereof are these:—

(1.) First, *The end is apparently bad, so that it would be a contradiction to his design to mention it.* It is the snare and trap itself, which his wisdom and policy directs him to cover. His ultimate end is the destruction of the soul. This he dare not openly avouch to the vilest of men; he doth not say to them, 'Destroy your souls,' 'Bring eternal miseries upon yourselves,' but only tempts them to that which will bring this misery upon them; and as for those intermediate ends, which are the formal acts of sin, he useth also a kind of modesty in their concealment. He doth not usually say, Go and murder, or, Commit adultery; but rather puts them upon ways or means that will bring them up to those iniquities, except that he sometime have to deal with those that are so hardened in sin, that they make a sport to do wickedly, and then he can more freely discover his ends to such in the temptation.

(2.) Secondly, The means to such wicked ends have not only an innate and natural tendency in themselves, which are apt to sway and bias men that way, but are also capable *of artificial improvement, to a further enticement to the evils secretly intended; and these require the art and skill for the exact suiting and fitting of them.* The end cannot be reached without the means, and means so ordered, without the aid of grace, will scarce miss of the end.

(3.) Thirdly, The means are capable of *a varnish and paint.* He can make a shift to set them off and colour them over, that the proper drift of them cannot easily be discovered; whereas the ends to which these lead cannot receive, at least so easily with some, such fair shows. It is far easier to set off company-keeping, with the pleasurable pretences of necessity or refreshing divertisement, than to propound direct drunkenness, the thing to which company-keeping tends, under such a dress.

Query. If it be demanded, How and by what arts he renders the means so plausible? I shall endeavour a satisfaction to that query, by shewing the way that Satan took to render the means he made use of in this temptation, plausible to Christ, which were these:—

[1.] First, He represents it as *a harmless or lawful thing in itself.* Who can say it had been sinful for the Son of God to have turned stones into bread, more than to turn water into wine?

[2.] Secondly, He gives the motion a further pretext of *advantage or goodness.* He insinuated that it might be a useful discovery of his sonship, and a profitable supply against hunger.

[3.] Thirdly, He seems also to put *a necessity upon it,* that other ways of help failing, he must be constrained so to do, or to suffer further want.

[4.] Fourthly, He forgets not to tell him that to do this was but *suitable to his condition,* and that it was a thing well becoming the Son of God to do a miracle.

[5.] Fifthly, He doth urge it at the rate of *a duty,* and that being in hunger and want, it would be a sinful neglect not to do what he could and might for his preservation.

The same way doth he take in other temptations; in some cases pleading all, in some most of these things, by which the means conducing thereunto may seem plausible. If he presents to men occasions of sinning, he will tell them ordinarily that they may lawfully adventure upon them, that they are harmless, nay, of advantage, as tending to the recreating of the spirits and health of the body; yea, that it is necessary for them to take such a liberty, and that in doing so, they do but what others do that profess religion. And often he hath such advantage from the circumstances of the thing, and the inclination of our heart, that he makes bold to tell us it is no less than duty. Such did the outrage of Demetrius seem to him, when he considered how much his livelihood did depend upon the Diana of the Ephesians. Paul's zeal made him confident that persecution of Christians was his duty; neither is there anything which can pretend to any zeal, advantage, or colourable ground, but presently it takes the denomination of duty.

If any wonder that such poor and shallow pretences are not seen through by all men, they may know that this happens from a fourfold ignorance: —

(1.) First, *From an ignorance of the thing itself.* How easily may they be imposed upon, who know not the nature or the usual issues of things! As children are deluded to put a value upon a useless or hurtful trifle, so are men deceived and easily imposed upon in what they do not understand. And for this cause are sinners compared to birds, who are easily enticed with the bait proposed to their view as profitable and good for them, because they know not the snare that lies laid under it. This ignorance causing the mistake mentioned, is not only a simple ignorance, but also that ignorance which owes its rise to a wilful and perverse disposition, — for there are some that are willingly ignorant, — doth often lay those open to a delusion, who, through prepossession or idleness, will not be at pains to make full inquiries.

(2.) Secondly, This also comes to pass from *an ignorance of our spirits*: for while we either engage in the things proposed by Satan upon the general warranty of a good intention, or that we have no evil meaning in it, we are kept from a discovery of the intended design. Hence Paul saw nothing, in his persecuting the church of God, of what Satan aimed at; or while upon the pretence of a good intention, our secret corrupt principles do indeed move us underhand to any undertaking, we are as little apt to see the ends of Satan in what he propounds to us. Jehu and the disciples, Luke ix. 55, pretending a zeal for God, but really carried on by their own furious tempers, did as little as others see what the devil was doing with them.

(3.) Thirdly, The means of a temptation are rendered less suspicious, from *an ignorance of the circumstances and concomitants that do attend them.*

(4.) Fourthly, As also from *an ignorance of our own weakness and inclination.* While we are confident of greater strength to resist than indeed we have, of a greater averseness than is in us to the evil suspected, we contemn the danger of the means as below us, and so grow bold with the occasions of iniquity, as pretending no hazard or danger to us.

Applic. This may teach us a piece of wisdom in the imitation of the devil. We see his malice appears in the bloody and destructive aims or intendments which he discovers against us, but his skill and cunning in a suitable disposal and ordering of the means. So should we learn to employ all our care and watchfulness about those plausible ways or introductions to sin that Satan puts in our hand; and as his eager desire of gaining his end makes him industrious about the offering of means fit to compass it, so our fear of his design and end should make us jealous of every overture propounded to us. They that from wilfulness or neglect shall admit the means of evil, cannot expect to avoid the evil to which they lead, or if they may, unexpectedly, be rescued from the end, while they use the means,—by grace interposing, as between the cup and the lip,—it is no thanks to them, and often they come not off so clear, but that some lameness or other sticks by them.

Quest. I may suspect this will be retorted back as an advice scarce practicable: for if all means leading to sin are to be avoided, then can we use nothing, but rather, as the apostle saith in another case, 'we must go out of the world,' [1 Cor. v. 10,] seeing everything may lead to evil?

Ans. I answer, We are not by any command of God put into any such strait. Things that are or may be improveable against us, may be used by us with due care and watchfulness; yet all things are not alike neither, for we must look upon things under a threefold consideration.

[1.] First, If that which is propounded or laid before us as a means to sin, be in itself sinful, the refusal of both is an undoubted duty.

[2.] Secondly, We must look upon things under the consideration of the suspiciousness which they carry with them of a further evil. Some circumstances, or postures of an opportunity and occasion offered, are of such a threatening aspect, that they fairly warn us to hold off. To keep company with a friend may be admitted, when yet that society in a suspicious place, as tavern or whore-house, is to be avoided.

[3.] Thirdly, We must further consider things as we are free or engaged to them, and accordingly where there is appearance of danger or the fear of it, we must keep at a distance, if we are engaged to such things, either by the obligation of the law of nature, or lawful calling, or command of God, or unavoidable providence, or relation. Where these ties are upon us, we cannot avoid the thing or action, but are the more concerned to take heed of being overreached or overtaken by them.

CHAPTER XI

I have particularly insisted upon the aims of Satan in this temptation in their variety, and also the cunning connexion and coherences of them. I have also singled out his chief design. I am now in the last place to present you with the suitableness and respects that the subordinate means carry to the principal, and that proportion which may be found in all these to the end designed by them.

The chief means in reference to the end designed, was a distrust of providence, and the subordinate means to bring on that distrust, was the failure of ordinary means of supply: for so he endeavoured to improve his hunger and want in the wilderness, as a manifest neglect of providence towards him, for which, as he tacitly suggests, there was no ground to wait or rely upon it any further, but to betake himself to another course. Hence note,

Obs. 13. *That the failure of ordinary means of help is by Satan improved as his special engine to bring men to a distrust of providence, and from thence to an unwarrantable attempt for their relief in an extraordinary way.*

That the failure of ordinary and usual supplies hath by the devil's subtlety brought a distrust of providence, and run men beyond all hopes of help, is a thing commonly and notoriously known. When men are afflicted, and brought unto unusual straits, and the ordinary ways of relief are out of sight, they are soon tempted to distrust God and man; and to conclude they are cut off, and that their 'hope is perished,' and that 'their eye shall no more see good.' David distressed, proclaims 'all men liars:' concludes that he should at last 'be cut off,' Ps. cxvi. 11, xxxi. 22. Jonah, in the whale's belly, thought that all hope was gone, and that he was cast out of God's sight, chap. ii. 4. The church of Israel in captivity, 'forgot prosperity,' notwithstanding the promise of deliverance after seventy years, and thought no less than that 'her hope and strength was perished,' Lam. iii. 18. And from the scriptures mentioned, we may also see the strength and prevalency of the temptation, especially when it is reduced to particulars. As,

(1.) First, *It is not a thing altogether of no weight that such a temptation should prevail against such persons*; as David and Jonah, and the whole church of Israel, that the manifold experiences that some of them have had of God's faithfulness in delivering, and the seasonableness of help at times of greatest hazard, the particular promises that all of them have had—how dismal and black soever things have seemed—have given the fullest assurances imaginable, that what he had spoken should certainly be performed; the gracious qualifications of such persons as eminently holy and skilled in the duties of trust, and in the ways of providence, and the special advantage which some of them, as prophets, have had above others, to enable them to improve that skill, experience, knowledge, and grace, to a firm adherence to such special promises: that all these things should not be sufficient to keep them off distrust, though at present the ways of deliverence were hid from them, seems strange.

(2.) Secondly, It is wonderful to what a height such a prevailing temptation hath carried some of them. David seems to be a little outrageous, and did upon the matter call God 'a liar,' when he said, 'All men are liars;' which however that some interpret392 as if it had been David's trust in God, and his confident avouchment of his enemies' prognostications of his ruin, to be but lies, and that this he spake from his firm belief of the promise, 'I believed, therefore have I spoken;' yet the acknowledgment of his 'haste,' which, compared with Ps. xxxi. 22, is declared as his weakness, will force us to conclude it an ingenuous confession of his distrust at the first, when he was greatly afflicted, though he recovered himself afterwards to a belief of the promise; and that in that distemper he plainly reflected upon Samuel, and calls the promises of God given by him 'a very lie.'

(3.) Thirdly, It is strange also *that present instances of God's providences working out unexpected deliverances should not relieve the hearts of his saints from the power of such distrust;* that when they see God is not unmindful of them, but doth hear them in what they feared, they should still retain in their minds the impression of an unbelieving apprehension; and not rather free themselves from their expectations of future ruin by concluding, that he that hath and doth deliver will also yet deliver. David had this thought in his heart, that he should 'one day perish by the hand of Saul,' 1 Sam. xxvii. 1, even then when God had so remarkably rescued him from Saul, and forced Saul not only to acknowledge his sin in prosecuting him, but also to declare his belief of the promise concerning David. See chap. xxvi. One would have expected that this should have been such a demonstration of the truth of what had been promised, that he should cast out all fear; and yet, contrariwise, this pledge of God's purpose to him is received by a heart strongly prepossessed with misgiving thoughts, and he continues to think that for all this Saul would one day destroy him.

(4.) Fourthly, *The pangs of this distrust are also so remarkable, that after they have been delivered, and have found that the event hath not answered their fears, they have in the review of their carriage under such fears, recounted this their weakness among other remarkable things,* thereby shewing the unreasonableness of their unbelief, and their wonder that God should pass by so great a provocation, and notwithstanding so unexpectedly deliver them. David in the places before cited was upon a thankful acknowledgment of God's love and wonderful kindness, which be thought he could not perform without leaving a record of his strange and unworthy distrust; as if he had said, 'So greatly did I sin, and so unsuitably did I behave myself, that I then gave off, and concluded all was lost.'

To open this a little further, I shall add the reasons why Satan strikes in with such an occasion as the want of means to tempt to distrust, which are these:—

[1.] First, *Such a condition doth usually transport men beside themselves;* puts them, as it were, into an ecstacy, and by a sudden rapture of astonishment and fear, forceth them beyond their settled thoughts and purposes. This David notes as the ground of his inconsiderate rash speaking: 'It was my haste,' I was transported, &c. Now as passion does not only make men speak what otherwise they would not, but also to put bad interpretations upon actions and things beyond what they will bear, and hasten men to resolves exceedingly unreasonable; so doth this state of the heart, under an amazement and surprise of fear, give opportunity to Satan to put men to injurious and unrighteous thoughts of the providence of God, and by such ways to alienate their minds from the trust which they owe him.

[2.] Secondly, *Sense is a great help to faith.* Faith then must needs be much hazarded when sense is at a loss or contradicted, as usually it is in straits.

That faith doth receive an advantage by sense, cannot be denied. To believe what we see, is easier than to believe what we see not; and that in our state of weakness and infirmity God doth so far indulge us, that by his allowance we may take the help of our senses, is evident by his appointment of the two sacraments, where by outward visible signs our faith may be quickened to apprehend the spiritual benefits offered. Thomas, resolving to suspend his belief till he were satisfied that Christ was risen, by the utmost trial that sense could give, determining not to credit the testimony of the rest of the disciples till by putting his finger into his side he had made himself more certain, Christ not only condescended to him, but also pronounceth his approbation of his belief, accepting it, that he had believed because he had seen. But when outward usual helps fail us, our sense, being not able to see afar off, is wholly puzzled and overthrown. The very disappearing of probabilities gives so great a shake to our faith that it commonly staggers at it; and therefore was it given as the great commendation of Abraham's faith, that he, notwithstanding the unlikelihood of the thing, 'staggered not at the promise;' noting thereby how extraordinary it was in him at that time to keep up against the contradiction of sense, and how usual it is with others to be beaten off all trust by it. It is no wonder to see that faith, which usually called sense for a supporter, to fail when it is deprived of its crutch. And he that would a little understand what disadvantage this might prove to a good man when sense altogether fails his expectation, he may consider with himself in what a case Thomas might have been if Christ had refused to let him see his side, and to thrust his finger into the print of the nails. In all appearance, had it been so, he had gone away confirmed in his unbelief.

[3.] Thirdly, *Though faith can act above sense, and is employed about things not seen, yet every saint at all times doth not act his faith so high.* Christ tells us that to believe where a man hath not had the help of sight and sense, is noble and blessed, John xx. 29; yet withal, he hints it to be rare and difficult: 'he that hath not seen, and yet hath believed,' implies that it is but one amongst many that doth so, and that it is the conquest of a more than ordinary difficulty. Hence it is, that to love God when he kills, to believe when means fail, are reckoned among the high actings of Christianity.

[4.] Fourthly, *When sense is nonplussed, and faith fails, the soul of man is at a great loss.* Having nothing to bear it up, it must needs sink; but having something to throw it down, besides its own propensity downward to distrust, it hath the force of so great a disappointment to push it forward; and such bitterness of spirit, heightened by the malignant influence of Satan, that with a violence like the angel's throwing a millstone into the sea, it is cast into the bottom of such depths of unbelief, that the knowledge of former power and extraordinary providences cannot keep it from an absolute denial of the like for the future. Israel in the wilderness, when they came to the want of bread, though they acknowledged he 'clave the rock,' and gave them water in the like strait, yet so far did their hearts fail of that due trust in the power and mercy of God, which might have been expected, that though they confessed the one, they as distrustfully question and deny the other. 'He clave the rock, but can he provide flesh? can he give bread?' [Ps. lxxviii. 20.] Strange unbelief, that sees and acknowledgeth omnipotency in one thing, and yet denies it in another!

[5.] Fifthly, *Providence hath been an old question.* It is an atheism that some have been guilty of, to deny that God ordereth all affairs relating to his children here below, who yet have not so fully extinguished their natural impressions as to dare to deny the being of God. That God is, they confess, but withal they think that he 'walketh in the circuit of heaven,' and as to the smaller concerns of men, neither doth good nor evil. This being an old error, to which most are but too inclinable; and the more because such things are permitted—as the punishment of his children, and their trials, while others have all their heart can wish—as seem scarce consistent with that love and care which men look for from him to his servants, they are apt enough to renew the thoughts of that persuasion upon their minds—for which the failure of ordinary ways of help seems to be a high probability—that he keeps himself unconcerned, and therefore there seems to be no such cause of reliance upon him. The psalmist so expresseth that truth, 'Men shall say, Verily there is a God that judgeth in the earth,' [Ps. lviii. 11;] that it is discovered to be a special retrievement of it, by many and signal convincing evidences, from that distrust of God and his providences that men usually slide into upon their observation of the many seeming failures of outward means of help.

Secondly, The other branch of the observation, *that from a distrust of providence he endeavours to draw them to an unwarrantable attempt for their relief,* is as clear as the former. Sarah being under a distrust of the promise for a son, because of her age, gave her handmaid to Abraham, that in that way, the promise seeming to fail, she might obtain children by her, Gen. xvi. 2. David, because of the many and violent pursuits of Saul, not only distrusted the promise, thinking he might 'one day perish' by him, but resolves to provide for his own safety by a speedy escape into the land of the Philistines, 1 Sam. xxvii. 1; a course which, as appears by the temptations and evils he met with there, was altogether unwarrantable. That from a distrust men are next put upon unwarrantable attempts, is clear from the following reasons:—

[1.] First, *The affrightment which is bred by such distrusts of providences will not suffer men to be idle.* Fear is active, and strongly prompts that something is to be done.

[2.] Secondly, Yet such is *the confusion of men's minds in such a case, that though many things are propounded, in that hurry of thoughts they are deprived usually of a true judgment and deliberation,* so that they are oppressed with a multitude of thoughts, as David on the like occasion takes notice, 'In the multitude of my thoughts within me,' &c., [Ps. xciv. 19;] and, as he expresseth the case of seamen in a storm, 'they are at their wits' end.'

[3.] Thirdly, *The despairing grievance of spirit* makes them take that which comes next to hand, as a drowning man that grasps a twig or straw, though to no purpose.

[4.] Fourthly, Being once turned off their rock, and the true stay of the promise of God for help, *whatever other course they take must needs be unwarrantable*. If they once be out of the right way, they must needs wander, and every step they take must of necessity be wrong.

[5.] Fifthly, *Satan is so officious in an evil thing*, that seeing any in this condition, he will not fail to proffer his help; and in place of God's providence, to set some unlawful shift before them.

[6.] Sixthly, And so much the rather do men close in with such overtures, because a *sudden fit of passionate fury doth drive them, and out of a bitter kind of despite and crossness*—as if they meditated a revenge against God for their disappointment—*they take up a hasty wilful resolve to go that way that seems most agreeable to their passion*, saying with king Joram, 'What wait we upon the Lord any longer for?' [2 Kings vi. 33.] We will take such a course, let come on us what will.

Applic. The service which the observation, well digested, may perform for us, is very fully contained in an advice which David gives on the like occasion, Ps. xxxvii. 34, which is this, 'Wait on the Lord, and keep his way.' Failures of ordinary means should not fill us with distrust, neither then should we run out of God's way for help. He that would practise this must have these three things which are comprehended in it:—

[1.] First, *He must have full persuasions of the power and promise of God*. I do not mean the bare hearsay that God hath promised to help, and that he is able to deliver, but these truths must be wrought upon the heart to a full assurance of them, and then we must keep our eye upon them; for if ever we lose the sight of this, when troubles beset us, our heart will fail us, and we shall do no otherwise than Hagar, who, when her bottle of water was spent, and she saw no way of supply, sat down, gave up her son and self for lost and so falls a-weeping over her helpless condition. This was that sight of God, in regard of his power, goodness, faithfulness, and truth, which are things invisible, Heb. xi. 27, which kept up the heart of Moses, that it sunk not under the pressure of his fears, when all things threatened his ruin.

[2.] Secondly, He that would thus wait upon God *had need to have an equal balance of spirit in reference to second causes*. Despise or neglect them he may not, when he may have them, for that were intolerable presumption; and so to centre our hopes and expectations upon them, as if our welfare did certainly depend upon them, is a high affront to God's omnipotency, and no less than a sinful idolizing of the creature; but the engagements of our duty must keep carefully to the first, and the consideration of an independency of an almighty power, as to any subordinate means or causes, must help us against the other miscarriage. When all means visible fail us, we must look to live upon omnipotent faithfulness and goodness, which is not tied to anything, but that without all means, and contrary to the powers of second causes, can do what he hath promised or sees fit.

[3.] Thirdly, There is no waiting upon God, and keeping his way, without *a particular trust in God.* To this we are not only warranted by frequent commands, 'Trust in the Lord, I say, trust in the Lord,' but highly encouraged to it under the greatest assurances of help: Ps. xxxvii. 5, 'Trust in him, and he shall bring it to pass.' 'Trust in the Lord and do good, and verily thou shalt be fed,' ver. 3. The Lord shall help and deliver them, because they trust in him. And this we are to do at 'all times,' and in the greatest hazards, and with the highest security: 'I laid me down and slept; I will not be afraid of ten thousands of people that have set themselves against me round about,' Ps. iii. 5, 6.

Quest. But some, possibly, may say, Is it our duty to sit still in such a case? When all the usual ways of supply fail us, must nothing be attempted?

Ans. (1.) I answer, first, *At such times greater care and diligence is necessary in outward things.* That what one lawful course cannot help, another lawful course may; and as to spiritual diligence, it should be extraordinary. We should be more earnest and frequent in prayer, fastings, meditations, and the exercise of graces.

(2.) Secondly, While we are in the pursuit of duty, and where the substance of it may be preserved entire, if our straits and wants unavoidably put us out of the way, *we may be satisfied to go on, though some circumstances be necessarily waived and hindered.* Phinehas might kill Zimri and Cosbi upon the command of Moses, Num. xxv. 5; and consequently in prosecution of duty, though, other circumstances considered, it was in some respects extraordinary.

(3.) Thirdly, But let the strait be what it will, *we must not forsake duty;* for so we go out of God's way, and do contradict that trust and hope which we are to keep up to God-ward.

Quest. But, it may be further urged, must we, when all means fail, positively trust in God for those very things which we might expect in an ordinary way?

Ans. In some cases our duty is *submission to his will,* and the particular mercy neither positively to be expected not yet distrusted. Thus did David behave himself when he fled from Jerusalem upon Absalom's rebellion; 'Let him do what seemeth him good.'

But there are other cases wherein it is our duty to fix our trust upon the particular mercy or help. I shall name four; and possibly a great many more may be added. As,

[1.] First, *When mercies are expressly and particularly promised*: as when the kingdom was promised to David; when a son was promised to Abraham. Whatever had been the improbabilities of their obtaining the thing promised, it was their duty positively to believe. This is indeed not a general case.

[2.] Secondly, *When God leads us into straits by engaging us in his service*: as when Israel followed the Lord into the wilderness, in order to an enjoyment of a further mercy, which was the possession of the land of Canaan. When they had no water to drink, nor food to eat, and saw no natural possibility of supply in that wilderness, they ought positively to have expected supplies from God in an extraordinary way; and it is reckoned up against them as their sin that they did not believe. This was the very case of Christ under this temptation; the Spirit led him into the wilderness upon the prosecution of a further design. When there was no bread there to satisfy his hunger, he refuseth to work a miracle for his supply, but leans upon an extraordinary providence.

[3.] Thirdly, *When the things we want are common universal blessings, and such as we cannot subsist without*. If we have nothing to eat, and nothing to put on, yet seeing the body cannot live without both, we must positively expect such supplies from providence, though we see not the way whence they should arise to us. This kind of distrust, which reflects upon the general necessary providence of God, by which he is engaged to preserve his creatures in their stations, 'to clothe the grass of the field, to feed the birds of the air,' &c., Christ doth severely challenge, 'Shall he not much more clothe you, O ye of little faith?' Mat. vi. 30. He hath little or no faith, and in that regard a very prodigy of distrust, that will not believe for necessaries. Hence, Hab. iii. 17, the prophet resolves upon a rejoicing confidence in God, when neither tree, nor field, nor flock would yield any hope in an ordinary way.

[4.] Fourthly, *When God is eminently engaged for our help, and his honour lies at stake in that very matter*; so that whether God will help or no, or whether he is able, is become the controversy, upon which religion in its truth or the honour of God is to be tried; then are we engaged to a certain belief of help. The three children upon this ground did not only assert that 'God was able to deliver them,' or that their death and martyrdom they could bear, which is all that most martyrs are able to arise up to, but they asserted positively that 'God would deliver them,' and that the fire should not burn them. They saw evidently that the contest, whether the Lord was God, was managed at so high a rate, that God was more concerned to vindicate his honour by their preservation, than to vindicate their grace and patience by their constancy and suffering, [Dan. iii.] Another instance we have in Mat. viii. 26, where Christ rebukes his disciples for unbelief, in their fears of shipwreck in a great storm—not that every seaman ordinarily lies under that charge, that gives himself up to the apprehensions of danger—the ground of which charge was this, that Christ was with them, and consequently it had unavoidably contradicted his design, and reflected upon his honour, if he had suffered his disciples at that time to be drowned. Their not minding how far Christ was engaged with them, and not supporting themselves against their fears by that consideration, made Christ tax them for their little faith.

CHAPTER XII

Lastly, we are to consider the suitableness of the means to the end. He had, as we have seen, fitly proportioned the subordinate means to the chief and principal. The failure of ordinary means of help was shrewdly proper to infer a distrust of providence. Now let it be noted how fitly he improves this distrust of providence to bring about the end he aimed at, which was a distrust of his filial interest in God, as if he should have thus reasoned: 'He that in straits is forsaken, as to all the usual supplies that may be expected in an ordinary way, hath no reason to rely on providence; and he that hath no reason to rely on providence for the body, hath less cause to expect spiritual blessings and favours for the soul.' Hence note,

Obs. 14. *That it is Satan's endeavour to make men proceed from a distrust of providence to a distrust of their spiritual sonship, or filial interest in God.* First, I shall evidence that this is Satan's design, and next I shall give the reasons of it. The former I shall make good by these several considerations:—

(1.) First, *We see it is a usual inference that others make of men whose heart fails them, under an absence or disappearance of all means of help in their distresses.* If providence doth not appear for them, they conclude God hath forsaken them. Bildad thus concludes against Job, chap. iv. 6, 'Is not this thy fear, thy confidence, thy hope, and the uprightness of thy ways?' Which must not only be understood as an ironical scoff at the weakness of his confidence and hope, as not being able to support him against fainting in his trouble, but as a direct accusation of the falseness and hypocrisy of his supposed integrity, and all the hopes and confidence which was built upon it; and ver. 7 doth evidence, where he plainly declares himself to mean that Job could not be innocent or righteous, it being, in his apprehension, a thing never heard of, that so great calamities should overtake an upright man, 'Who ever perished, being innocent?' The ground of which assertion was from ver. 5, 'It is now come upon thee, and thou faintest.' That is, distresses are upon thee, and thou hast no visible means of help, but despairest ever to see a providence that will bring thee out; therefore surely thou hast had no real interest in God, as his child. Eliphaz also seconds his friend in this uncharitable censure, 'If thou wert pure and upright, he would awake for thee,' Job viii. 6; that is, because he doth thus overlook thee, therefore thou art not pure and upright.

If men do thus assault the comforts of God's children, we have reason enough to think that Satan will; for besides that we may conclude they are set on work by the devil, and what he speaks by them, he will also by other ways promote, as being a design that is upon his heart; we may be confident, that this being a surmise so natural to the heart of man, he will not let slip so fair an advantage, for the forming of it in our own hearts against ourselves.

(2.) Secondly, *The best of God's children, in such cases, escape it very hardly, if at all*; which declares not only the depth and power of that policy, but also how usual it is with Satan to urge the servants of God with it. Job, chap. xix. 25, recovered himself to a firm persuasion of sonship, 'I know that my Redeemer liveth,' &c.; but by the way his foot had well-nigh slipped, when, ver. 10, 11, he cries out, 'He hath destroyed me on every side, and I am gone; he hath also kindled his wrath against me, and he counteth me unto him as one of his enemies.' His earnest resolve not to give up his trust in God, and the confidence of his integrity, is sufficient to discover Satan's eager endeavours to have him bereaved of it.

(3.) Thirdly, *Satan's success in this temptation over the saints of God, who sometime have actually failed*, shews how much it is his work to cast down their hopes of interest in God, by overthrowing their trust in his providences. If he attempts this, and that successfully, on such whose frequent experiences might discourage the tempter, and in probability frustrate his undertaking; we have little cause to think that he will be more sparing and gentle in this assault upon those that are more weak, and less acquainted with those clouds and darknesses that overshadow the ways of providence. David, for all the promises that he had received, and notwithstanding the manifold trials that he had of seasonable and unexpected deliverances, yet when he was distressed, he once and again falls into a fear of his soul, and a questioning of God's favour. He complains as one utterly forsaken, 'Why hast thou forsaken me?' Ps. xxii. 1. In Ps. lxix., he expresseth himself, ver. 1, 'sinking in the deep mire,' as a man that had no firm ground to stand upon, and that his troubles had brought him to fear the state of his soul, not only as deprived of God's favour—and therefore, ver. 17, begs that his face may be no longer hid—but also as suspecting the loss of it; ver. 18, 'draw nigh unto my soul, and redeem it.' Ps. lxxvii., upon the occasion of outward troubles, Asaph falls into such a fit of fear about his spiritual condition, that no consideration of former mercies could relieve him, 'He remembered God,' ver. 3, 'but was troubled;' he 'considered the days of old,' called to remembrance his 'songs in the night;' but none of these were effectual to keep him from that sad outcry of distrust, ver. 7, 'Will the Lord cast off for ever? is his mercy clean gone for ever? hath God forgotten to be gracious?' &c. Which upon the review, in the composing of the psalm, he acknowledged an unbelieving miscarriage; I said, 'This is mine infirmity.'

(4.) Fourthly, It is also a common and ordinary thing with most, *to entertain misapprehensions of their spiritual condition, when they meet with disappointments of providence.* Hence the apostle, Heb. xii. 5, 6, when he would quiet the hearts of men under the Lord's chastening, doth of purpose make use of this encouragement, that God speaks to them in the rod as to children, and such as are under his care and love, 'My son, despise not the chastening of the Lord;' 'whom the Lord loveth, he chasteneth,' &c. Which certainly tells us thus much, that it is ordinary for men to doubt their sonship because of their afflictions. We may conjecture what the malady is, when we know what is prepared as a medicine. This would not have been a common remedy, 'that we may be children, though we be scourged,' if the disbelief of this had not been the usual interpretation of afflictions, and a common distemper.

(5.) Fifthly, We may further take notice, *that those disquiets of mind, that were only occasioned by outward things, and seem to have no affinity, either in the nature of the occasion, or present inclination of the party, with a spiritual trouble; yet if they continue long, do wholly change their nature.* They that at first only troubled themselves for losses or crosses, forget these troubles and take up fears for their souls.

Sometime this ariseth from a natural softness and timorousness of spirit. Such are apt to misgive upon any occasion, and to say, Surely if I were his child, he would not thus forsake me; his fatherly compassions would some way or other work towards me.

Sometime this ariseth from melancholy, contracted or heightened by outward troubles. These, when they continue long, and pierce deep, put men into 'a spirit of heaviness,' which makes them refuse to be comforted. Here the devil takes his advantage. Unlawful sorrows are as delightfully improved by him as unlawful pleasures; they are Diaboli balneum, his bath in which he sports himself, as the leviathan in the waters. When for temporal losses or troubles men fall into melancholy, if they be not relieved soon, then their grief changeth its object, and presently they disquiet themselves, as being out of God's favour, as being estranged from God, as being of the number of the damned; such against whom the door of mercy is shut, and so cry out of themselves as hopeless and miserable. The observations of physicians afford store of instances of this kind. Felix Platerus gives one, of a woman at Basle who first grieved for the death of her son, and when by this means she grew melancholy, that changed into a higher trouble; she mourns that her sins would not be pardoned, that God would not have mercy for her soul. Another, for some loss of wheat, first vexeth himself for that, and then at last despairs of the happiness of his soul; with a great many more of that kind.393

Sometimes a desperate humour doth, from the same occasion, distract men into a fury; of which Mercerus gives one instance from his own knowledge, of a person who, upon the distresses which he met with, fell into a rage against God, uttering speeches full of horror and blasphemy, not fit to be related.394

If there be such an affinity betwixt distrust of providence and distrust of sonship, that the one slides into the other naturally; if this be common to all men under troubles, to suspect their souls; if the best do here actually miscarry; if those that do not, yet hardly escape; and if bystanders commonly give this judgment of men in straits, that there is no help for them in their God; we cannot but collect from all this, that it is an advantage which Satan will not neglect, and that he doth very much employ himself to bring it about.

The reasons of it are these:—

(1.) First, Distrust of providence hath in it the very formal nature of distrust of sonship. If the object of distrust were but changed, it would without any further addition work that way. He that trusts providence acknowledgeth that God knoweth his wants, that he is of a merciful inclination to give what he sees he hath need of; that he hath manifested this by promise, that he is so faithful that this promise cannot be neglected, and that he hath power to do what he hath promised.395 He that distrusts providence disbelieves all these, consequentially at least; and he that will not believe that God takes any care of the body, or that he is of a merciful disposition toward him, or thinks either he hath made no such promise, or will not keep it, if any such were made; cannot believe, if that doubt were but once started, that God is his Father, or that he hath interest in the privilege of a son, seeing it is impossible to believe a sonship, while his care, mercy, promises, and power are distrusted. In this then Satan's work is very easy. It is but his moving the question about the Lord's mercy to the soul, and presently, as when new matter is ministered to a raging flame, it takes hold upon it, and with equal, nay greater, force it carries the soul to distrust spiritual mercies, as before it disbelieved temporal kindnesses.

(2.) Secondly, *The same reasons, which any man doth gather from the seeming neglect or opposition of providence, upon which he grounds his distrust of the Lord's kindness in reference to outward things, will also serve as arguments for a distrust of spiritual favours.* The distresses of men seem to argue—[1.] That there is sin and provocation on their part; [2.] And that there is a manifestation of anger on God's part; [3.] And from these apprehensions ariseth bitterness, anxiety, fear, and dejection of spirit, which intercepts all the help and consolation which might arise from other considerations of the Lord's promise or mercy, for the quieting of the heart and fortifying it against such apprehensions. These same grounds, with the prevailing fears and perplexities arising from them, are enough to make us suspect that we are not yet under any such peculiar favours as may bespeak us his children by adoption; so that from the same premises Satan will conclude, that as he hath no care for our bodies, so no love to our souls; that we neither love God nor are beloved of him. Betwixt the one conclusion and the other there is but a step, and with a small labour he can cut the channel, and let in that very distrust to run with all its force against our spiritual interest in God.

(3.) Thirdly, *To trust God for the soul is a higher act than to trust him for the body.* The soul being of greater excellency than the body, and the mercy necessary for the happiness of it being more precious and less visible, it must require a higher confidence in God to assure of this than satisfy us in the other. It is more easy to believe a lesser kindness from a friend than a singular or extraordinary favour. He, then, that cannot trust God for temporal mercies, shall be more unable to believe eternal blessings. 'If we run with footmen, and they have wearied us, shall we be able to contend with horsemen? If the shallow brooks be too strong for us, what shall we do in the swellings of Jordan?' [Jer. xii. 5.]

(4.) Fourthly, *When faith is weakened as to one object, it is so tainted and discouraged that it is generally weakened as to all other.* If the hand be so weakened that it cannot hold a ring, it will be less able to grasp a crown. When we are baffled in our trust for temporal mercies, if Satan then put us to it not to believe for spiritual blessings, how can we expect but to be much more at a loss in them? So that he is sure of the victory before he fights, and he that is so sedulous to take advantage against us will not lose so considerable a conquest for want of pursuit. There is indeed one thing that may seem fit to be objected against this, which is, that men may retain their faith in one thing when yet they distrust in another, as the Israelites distrusted the power and goodness of God for bread and flesh in the wilderness, when yet they believed that as he had given water out of the rock, so he could do it again if there were need: Ps. lxxviii. 20, 'He smote the rock, and the waters gushed out; but can he give bread?' as if they had said, We believe he can give water, but it is impossible he should provide bread. But they that would thus object may consider that the reason of men's confidence in one thing, while distrust is in other things prevailing, is not from any real strength of their faith, but a present want of a temptation. If such a confidence were put to it, it would quickly be seen that it were truly nothing. As confident as the Israelites were that they could believe for a supply of water, we find that neither that experience, nor the other of supplying them with manna and quails, were sufficient to keep up their trust in God, but that at the next strait all was to seek: ver. 32, 'For all this they sinned still, and believed not for his wondrous works.'

(5.) Fifthly, Besides all the forementioned advantages that Satan hath in raising this temptation, of distrusting sonship out of a distrust of providence, we may suppose him the more earnest in this matter, because it is so provoking to God to distrust his providence, that he often, as a just chastisement of that evil, punisheth it by giving them up to distrust him for their souls. The height of the provocation may be measured by this, that it is not only a denial of God that is above, but usually a vesting some mean and contemptible thing with those attributes which only suit a God infinite and eternal. As Israel did not only forsake the Almighty by their distrust, but place their hopes upon Ashur, upon their own horses and warlike preparations, and at last upon the works of their hands, which they called their gods, Hosea xiv. 2, 3. How offensive this is to the Lord, we may observe by that notable check which the prophet gave Ahaz, Isa. vii. 8, 13, notwithstanding his compliment of refusing a sign, which God offered him for the strengthening of his hope, upon a pretence that he would trust without it, — though indeed he absolutely distrusted him, as appears by 2 Chron. xxviii. 20, — that it was a weaning396 and tiring out the patience of a long-suffering God: 'Is it a small thing for you to weary men, but will you weary my God also?' God is so active and jealous of all encroachments of this kind, that they may expect he will give up such offenders to be punished by the terrors of a higher distrust. He that is not owned as a God in his providences, will not be owned as a Father for spiritual mercies; they that will not own him for the body, shall not be able to lay hold upon him or his strength to be at peace with him for their souls; and by this piece of just discipline he often cures the distrust of providence in his children, who when they see themselves plunged into terrors and fears about their everlasting welfare, do not only call God just, and accept of the punishment of their iniquity in distrusting him for smaller matters, but now wish with all their hearts that they might have no greater thing to trouble them than what relates to the body or this life.

To sum up all these reasons in one word: Satan hath from the forementioned considerations *a certain expectation of prevalency*. For not only in this case doth God, as it were, fight for him, by giving them up to distrust their filial interest that have provoked him by a distrust of providence, and our faith is also so weakened by the former overthrow that it is not able to maintain its ground in a higher matter; but also this distrust carries that in the nature and grounds of it that will of itself work up to a disbelief of spiritual mercies. He knows, then, that this piece of the victory is an easy consequence of the former; and we may say of it as the prophet Nahum, chap. iii. 12, of the strongholds of Nineveh, It is like 'a fig-tree with the first ripe figs, if they be shaken, they shall even fall into the mouth of the eater.' This temptation of distrusting our sonship falls into Satan's mouth with a little labour, when once he hath prevailed so far as to make us distrust the providence of God in outward matters.

Applic. This must warn and caution us against any unbeseeming unbelieving entertainment of jealousy against the Lord's providence. We are but too apt in our straits to take a greater liberty to question his mercy and power, not foreseeing how closely this borders upon a greater evil. We may say of it, as the apostle speaks of 'babbling in controversies,' that they 'lead to more ungodliness,' and that such words 'eat as a canker,' [2 Tim. ii. 17;] so doth this distrust usually carry us further, and when we fall out with God for small matters, he will be angry in earnest, and withdraw from us our consolations in greater. In the depth of your distresses, when your fears are round about you, and God seems to compass you about with his net, — when lover and friend forsakes, and when there is no appearance of help, endeavour, for the keeping hold of your interest in God, to behave yourselves according to the following directions: —

[1.] First, *Look upon the providences of God to be as a great deep, the bottom of whose ways and designs you cannot reach.* Think of them as of a mystery, which indeed you must study, but not throw away, because you cannot at first understand it. Providences are not to be dealt with as Alexander did by Gordius his knot, who when he could not loose it he cut it. If you see not the end of the Lord, or cannot meet with a door of hope in it, yet 'lay your hand upon your mouth,' speak not, think not evil of things you know not, but wait till the time of their 'bringing forth.'

[2.] Secondly, *You must keep up in your hearts high and honourable thoughts of God,* yea, of his mercy and goodness, and where you cannot see your way, or God's way, before you, yet, as it were by a kind of implicit faith, must you believe that he is holy and good in all his ways.

[3.] Thirdly, Though you may read your sins or God's displeasure in them, and accordingly endeavour to humble yourselves and call yourselves vile, yet must it be always remembered that *eternal love or eternal hatred is not to be measured by them.*

[4.] Fourthly, *Restrain complainings*. It is indeed an ease to complain; 'I will speak,' saith Job, 'that I may be refreshed,' chap. xxxii. 20; notwithstanding a vent being given, it is difficult to keep within bounds. Our complainings entice us to distrust, as may appear in Job, who took a boldness this way more than was fit, as chap. x. 3, 'Is it good unto thee that thou shouldest oppress, and that thou shouldest despise the work of thine hands?'

All this hath been said in the opening of the temptation itself. Now must I consider the motive that Satan used to bring on the temptation by, 'If thou be the Son of God,' &c.

The question that is here moved by some is, whether Satan really knew or truly doubted Christ to be the Son of God. Several learned men think that he was in doubt,397 and the reasons are variously conjectured. Cyprian conceives that the unity of the two natures in one person did blind him; he knew it to be impossible that the divine nature should hunger, and might think it strange that the human nature should fast so long.398 Cornelius a-Lapide thinks that Satan knew that there should be two natures united in one person, and that this occasioned Satan's fall, while he proudly stomached the exaltation of the human nature; but he imagines Satan's doubt arose from a doubtful sense of that phrase, 'This is my beloved Son,' as not knowing whether Christ were the natural or an adopted son of God.

But notwithstanding these apprehensions, others conceive that Satan knew very well who Christ was, and that being privy to so many things relating to him, as the promises which went before and directly pointed out the time, the angel's salutation of Mary at his conception, the star that conducted the wise men to him, the testimony from heaven concerning him, with a great many things more, he could not possibly be ignorant that he was the Messias and the Son of God by nature. Neither doth that expression, 'If thou be the Son of God,' imply any doubting, seeing that that is usually expressive of the greatest certainty and assurance, as in the speech of Lamech, 'If Cain shall be avenged sevenfold,' that is, as certainly he shall be avenged; so Satan might use it to this sense, 'If, or seeing thou art the Son of God.' Now, whereas it may seem strange that he should set upon Christ, if he knew who he was, I have answered that before, and shall here only add that though Satan did believe Christ to be the Son of God, yet so strongly did the power of malice work in him, that he would have had him to have doubted that he was not so. From all this we have this observation,

Obs. 15. That the great design of Satan is to weaken the assurance and hopes of the children of God in their adoption.

This is the masterpiece of his design, the very centre in which most of his devices meet. We may say of him as Esau said of Jacob, 'Is he not rightly called Jacob, a supplanter?' [Genesis xxvii. 36;] he first stole away our birthright at the creation, and now he seeks to take away our blessing in Christ the Redeemer.

The reasons of this undertaking I shall not here insist on. It is sufficiently obvious that the greatest perplexity and sorrow ariseth to the children of God from hence, and that a troop of other spiritual evils, as impatience, fury, blasphemy, and many more, doth follow it at the heels, besides all that inability for service, and at last plain neglect of all duty. All I shall further do at this time shall be to shew in a few particulars, from Satan's carriage to Christ in this temptation, how and after what manner he doth manage that design, in which note:—

(1.) First, *That it is his design to sever us from the promise, and to weaken our faith in that*. When Eve was tempted, this was that he aimed at, that she should question the good earnest of the prohibition, 'Hath God said so?' Was he real in that command, that you should not eat at all? &c. The like he doth to Christ, 'Is it true? or can it be so as that voice declared, that thou art the Son of God?'

(2.) Secondly, *Though this be his design, yet his way to come to it is not at first to deny it, but to question and inquire*; yet after such a manner as may imply and withal suggest a doubting or suspicion that it is not so. He doth not come to Christ thus, 'Thou art not the Son of God; or that voice that gave thee that testimony was but a lie or a delusion;' but he rather proceeds by questioning, which might seem to grant that he was so, yet withal might possibly beget a doubt in his mind.

(3.) Thirdly, *Next he more plainly suggests something that may seem to argue the contrary*; for thus he aggravates Christ's present condition of want, 'Can it be that God would leave thee to these oppressing straits, if thou wert his Son?' At this rate he deals with us, improving the failure of outward means of help, the permission of temptation, the want of comfort, the continuance of affliction, notwithstanding prayers, &c., as probabilities that we belong not to God.

(4.) Fourthly, *After this he urgeth Christ to a sinful miscarriage, to distrust providence, and to rely no longer on the care of his Father*. If Christ had been prevailed with in this, he would have made use of it as an argument to prove that he was not the Son of God indeed. It is usual in his disputings with us about adoption, to put us upon something which may be as an argument out of our own mouths against us. Christ might have answered him in this as the man answered Joab, 'If I should do so, then thou thyself wouldst set thyself against me.'

(5.) Fifthly, When at last he hath gradually ascended to that confidence as to deny our adoption, then, at a very great disadvantage, he puts us upon the proof, in which he puts by the ordinary evidences, and insists on extraordinary proofs as necessary. The servants of the Lord that are under this exercise, do find that in this case the ordinary evidences of repentance, mortification, love to the brethren, &c., do nothing for them. Satan puts their spirit upon clamouring for higher evidences. Nothing will serve except they may view the records of eternity, and read their names enrolled in the everlasting decrees, or except God will speak from heaven in an extraordinary way, to testify of them, as Thomas resolved that no less should satisfy his doubt than the feeling and seeing of the print of the nails. To this purpose some stand upon no less than a miracle for proof of sonship. Of which we have two instances of later years, the one Mrs Honywood, the other Mrs Sarah Wight,399 who in their distresses for their souls were tempted by Satan to make a hasty experiment, the one by throwing a Venice glass, the other by throwing a cup against the wall, with this or the like expression, 'If I must be saved, then let not this glass break'—a desperate temptation! Their manner of desiring satisfaction is so provoking, that it cannot be expected God will give an answer by it, but rather the contrary; and if he should not condescend, as he is not bound—though he strangely preserved the cup and glass fore-mentioned from breaking—what a dangerous conclusion would Satan draw from it! Of this nature and design was that proposal of Satan's to Christ, 'Command that these stones be made bread,' that is, do it as a proof of thy sonship.

Applic. By this we must learn this skill, *not too easily to give up our hopes, or to be prodigal of our interest in Christ, so as to part with it slenderly.* If Satan would chiefly rob us of this, we may learn thence to put a price upon these jewels, and to account that precious, and of singular concernment, which he useth so much cunning to bereave us of. Many of the Lord's servants may justly blame themselves for their lavish unthriftiness in this matter, who, as if it were a necessary piece of humility or modesty, will readily conclude against themselves that they are not God's children, that they are not yet converted, &c. Thus, at unawares, they give up to Satan without a stroke all that he seeks for.

Quest. But you will say, Must all men be confident of adoption?

Ans. No, I mean not so; yet all men must be wary how they cast away their hopes. Particularly,

[1.] First, Though it be a dangerous arrogancy for a sinful, wicked creature to bear himself up in a belief that he is converted and actually instated into the adoption of sons; yet it is as dangerous, on the other hand, for that man to cast off all hope, and to say he is reprobated, and such a one as cannot expect pardon and grace.

[2.] Secondly, Those that are converted, though they may and ought to humble themselves deeply for their sinful miscarriage, and sincerely acknowledge that they deserve not to be called his children, yet must they be careful not to renounce their filial interest. They may say they are prodigal, yet keep to this, that they are sons; though they are wandering sheep, yet must they stick here, that they are sheep still, and that God is still a Father, though a provoked Father, otherwise their folly will give more than all his fury could get, at least so quickly and easily.

CHAPTER XIII

I omit Christ's answer to the first temptation at present, purposing to handle his answers to all the temptations together. And now the second temptation is before us, in which, first, I shall observe a few things in Satan's preparation to the temptation, which takes in [1.] The time; [2.] The manner of his carrying him; [3.] The place where he acted it.

(1.) First, For the time. That is noted in the word 'then,' which [1.] Points at the immediate succession of this to the former assault. The evangelist Luke puts this temptation last, but he only had respect to the substance of the temptation in his narration; not regarding the order of them, which Matthew hath punctually observed, as appears by his close connecting of them, with the particles 'then' and 'again,' ver. 5, 8. Besides, whosoever shall consider that in the first, Satan tempted Christ to distrust, which he repelled by telling him that it was his duty, in the failure of outward means, to rely upon divine providence, seeing man lives not by bread alone, &c., he will see so much of connexion in the matter of the temptations that he will easily persuade himself that the second place belongs to this, for this is but, as it were, a fit and pertinent reply to Christ's refusal; as if Satan had said, 'Since thou wilt rely upon the help and providence of God in an extraordinary way of working, give an experiment of that by casting thyself down, which thou mayest with greater confidence do, because he hath promised an extraordinary help, and hath given his angels charge concerning thee,' &c. Hence observe,

Obs. 1. *That Satan is not discouraged easily, nor doth he always desist upon the first repulse, but frequently renews the assault when he is strongly and resolutely resisted.*

This word, 'then,' doth also [2.] Tell us of Satan's nimbleness in catching a present advantage for a new temptation from Christ's answer. He declared his trust in providence; this he presently lays hold on as a fit opportunity to tempt him to presumption. Here note,

Obs. 2. *That when Satan is upon any design, if an occasional advantage occur from our way of refusal, he will not let it slip, but improves it to what it may lead to, though it be contrary to that which he was first labouring for.*

This was the policy which Benhadad's servants used in their address to Ahab, 1 Kings xx. 33; the men did diligently observe whether anything would come from him, and did hastily catch it. If anything come from us we are under his temptation, he is diligent to observe it, and prosecutes it accordingly; which may serve to satisfy the wonder that some have concerning the contrariety in the temptations to which they are urged. They admire how it comes to pass that their temptations should so suddenly alter, that when Satan seems to be so intent upon one design, he should so quickly change, and urge them presently to a different or contrary thing; but they may know that the devil watcheth the wind, and spreads his sail according to the advantage which ariseth from our answer or repulse. So that if we would but plough with our own heifer, and observe our frame of spirit, we should easily find out this riddle. For as it is in disputings and arguings of men, replies beget new matter for answer, and so do they multiply one another; thus are temptations altered and multiplied, and out of the ashes of one assault repelled, another doth quickly spring up.

The second circumstance of preparation is, Satan's taking him up and setting him on the temple. That this was not a visionary or an imaginary thing, hath been proved before. Yet granting it to have been real, as in truth it seems to have been, it is disputed what was the modus, the way and manner of it. Some think this was no more than Christ's voluntary following of Satan, who guided and conducted the way;400 partly because the words παραλαμβάνειν and ἄγειν are in Scripture accommodated to a man's taking of any as a companion under his guide and conduct of the way, and to a disposal of them in any kind of station. Thus, where it is said, 'Joseph took Mary and the young child to go to Egypt,' Mat. ii. 13, the same word is used; and when Christ tells his disciples that they shall bring the ass and the colt which they should find tied, the same word which expresseth Christ being set on the temple is there used, Mat. xxii. 2. Partly also, they think it below the dignity of Christ to be thus violently hurried.

Others think that Satan was permitted to take up the body of Christ, and by his power to have conveyed him in the air; and indeed the whole series of the narration, with all the circumstances thereof, are evident for it. The distances of places, the quickness and speediness of the removals, the more proper applications of the words, 'taking' and 'setting,' to Satan as the actor, and the declaration of his power therein, as able to do great things; these make the matter so clear, that it seems to be an unnatural forcing of the text to give it any other interpretation. Besides, the former opinion of Satan's taking of Christ, as a manuductor or guide, seems every way unreasonable; for if Christ only followed Satan, then it must have been either by a land journey on foot or in the air. This latter it could not be;

for if Christ had supported himself in the air by his own power, he had anticipated the temptation, and it would have been folly and madness for Satan to have urged him to fly in the air, after such an evidence of his power; and who can imagine that Christ followed Satan on foot from the wilderness to the temple, or that his access to the roof of the temple was so easy, in such a way when the temple was always so strictly guarded? Note, hence,

Obs. 3. That Satan is sometime permitted to exercise his power upon the bodies of those that are dear to God. That he hath power to carry the bodies of men in the air, is sufficiently confirmed by what he doth frequently to witches, who are usually carried, if we can give any credit to the stories that are writ of them, in the air, to places far remote from their dwellings, equitatio cum Diana aut Herodiade. And that this power is permitted him upon others, than such as are in compact with him, is as evident from what is testified of those whose forward curiosity hath led to imitate witches in their anointings, who have thereupon been conveyed after them to their assemblies, and when the company hath been suddenly dismissed, they have been found many miles distant from their dwellings; such instances we have in Bodin, and among other things that of Domina Rossa mentioned by him, whom Satan would sometime bind to a tree, sometime to a table, or to a bed's-foot, or to a manger, sometime one hand bound to another; the devil thus molested her from eight years old, a long time.401 This power of conveying persons in the air is not usual, yet there are some in this place— Newcastle—that have known one frequently molested by Satan at this rate. However, if we take notice of his power to abuse the bodies of holy persons more generally, we shall find it frequent. Mary Magdelene was possessed; Christ mentions a daughter of Abraham bowed down by him many years; Job was filled with botches and sores; and there are many diseases wherein Satan hath a greater hand than is commonly imagined. Physicians frequently conclude so much, while they observe some distempers to elude such remedies as are usually successful upon other persons under the same diseases.

Applic. From this we may infer, [1.] The great power of Satan; who can tell the extent of it? doubtless, if he were permitted, we should see sad instances hereof daily. [2.] This discovers the wonderful care and providence of God over us in our preservation from his fury. [3.] We may further note that the abuse of the bodies of men by Satan, will be no evidence that therefore God doth disregard them, or that they are not precious to him. Christ did undergo this abuse, to give such as shall be so molested, some comfort in his example.

The third circumstance, which is that *of place,* is set down first in general, 'the holy city,' that is Jerusalem, for so Luke speaks expressly, Luke iv. 9.

Jerusalem was so called, because of God's worship there established, and his peculiar presence there; but that it should be called so at this time may seem strange, seeing it might now be lamented as of old, 'How is the faithful city become an harlot! Righteousness lodged in it, but now murderers,' [Isa. i. 21.] In answer to this, we must know that God having not yet given her a bill of divorce, he is pleased to continue her title and privilege. This might be profitably improved; but I will not suffer myself to be diverted from the matter of temptation, which is the only thing I propound to prosecute from hence. I shall here only observe,

Obs. 4. *That the holiness or sanctity of a place will be no privilege against temptations.* He is not so fearful, as many imagine, as that he dares not approach a churchyard or a church; neither place nor duty can keep him off. I do not believe the popish fiction of their St Bennet's vision, wherein they tell of his seeing but one devil in a market, and ten in a monastery; yet I question not the truth of this, that the devil is as busy at a sermon or prayer as at any other employment.

But to search a little further into this matter, it seems undeniable that Satan had a design in reference to the place, of which afterward; and I see no reason to exclude our suspicion of a design from the name and title which the evangelist here gives to Jerusalem. It is an expression which, to my remembrance, we meet not with oft in the New Testament. At the suffering of Christ, when the bodies of the saints arose out of their graves, it is said 'they went into the holy city,' Mat. xxvii. 53; but it is evident that it is there so styled upon special design, as if the evangelist would by that point at the staining of their glory, and that in a little time their boast of the temple and holy city should cease, and that all should be polluted with the carcases of the slain. And by the same reason may we suppose that Satan, intending for Christ a temptation of presumption, and backing it with the promise of a guard of angels, had in his eye the usual confidence that the Jews had of that city, as a place where the presence of angels might be more expected than elsewhere. So that it seems Satan intended to impose upon Christ a confidence in order to presumption. From the privilege of the place, here observe,

Obs. 5. *That Satan is willing to gratify us with nominal and imaginary privileges and defences against himself.* He will willingly allow us such defences as are altogether insignificant and delusive, and his policy here is centred upon these two things: —

(1.) First, He doth industriously prompt us to self-devised inventions, such as were never appointed or blessed of God to any such use; but only found out by the bold superstitions of men. Of this we have an instance in Balak, who carried Baalam from place to place in his prosecution of his design cf cursing Israel; neither can we imagine that a commodious prospect of Israel was all he aimed at, seeing he discovers his mind in this variation of places, 'Peradventure it will please God that thou mayest curse them from thence,' Num. xxiii. 27; clearly implying that he had a confidence that the place might contribute something to his design, and that there was some inherent virtue in those consecrated places; and therefore did he begin with the high-places of Baal, and then to the held of Zophim, and then to the top of Peor, Num. xxii. 27, xxiii. 14, 28. Among the papists we find too much of this. What power they attribute to holy water, blessed salt, sign of the cross, hallowed earth, consecrated places, relics, baptized bells, exorcisms, and abundance of such stuff, may be seen in many of their writings, too tedious to be related.402

(2.) Secondly, He is also willing *that men use those real defences and helps which God hath commanded, so that they use them in a formal manner*, which indeed deprives them of all the life and efficacy that might be expected from an instituted means. Thus he readily permits ignorant persons, without any disturbance or molestation, to use the repetition of the Lord's prayer, ten commandments, and creed, or any other prayer, while they persuade themselves that the very saying of the words is a sufficient defence against the devil all that day.

The reasons of Satan's policy in such gratifications are these: —

[1.] First, *While we are kept doing with these, we are diverted from that which might be really helpful*. He puts a broken reed into our hand, that we might be deprived of a staff. Experience confirms this. Those that, with greatest devotion, use these empty inventions, are usually careless in the use of God's own appointments.

[2.] Secondly, *Besides that he thus betrays them by these lying helps, he doth by this means cast them on a further iniquity of idolising these foolish calves of their own invention*. In this case men have a presumptuous expectation from such usages of that which God never promised to do by them, neither ever entered into his heart so to do, seeing he answers them all with this, 'Who hath required these things at your hands?' [Isa. i. 12.] And accordingly their consciences are more concerned for the omission of one of these fooleries, than for the neglect of the greater things of the law. Such are more troubled for the neglect of the sign of the cross or holy water, than for their constant carelessness and want of faith, by which their hearts should be guarded against their enemy.

[3.] Thirdly, In the meantime he makes work for his own triumph over them that dote upon these sottish inventions. If we can suppose Satan to have pleasure or mirth at anything, we may be sure he will laugh at such preparations for a spiritual welfare,403 it being as truly ridiculous for any man to go out with these weapons against Satan, as for a combatant to assail a giant with a paper helmet, a wicker shield, and a wooden dagger. And indeed when Satan counterfeits a flight or fear of such matters, as for his advantage he sometimes doth, it is but in design to beget or confirm in men a confidence of a virtue or strength in these usages against his power, that so they may fix upon them to the neglect of God's own institutions, which he most dreads. Thus we read that he cunningly ceased his oracle at Daphne upon a pretence of the silencing power of the bones of the martyr Babilas, which were buried near the place, on purpose to lead unwary Christians to the adoration of saints and their relics.404 Many such instances we have in Sprenger, of the devil's feigned flight at the sign of the cross, the sprinkling of holy water, the angelical salutation, St Bernard's staff, or certain words and verses hung about the neck.405 And a great deal of such stuff we may meet with in most of their writers, all which are but cunning contrivances of Satan, to advance a belief of the virtue of these things; and so to stop men there, to the neglect of those spiritual weapons which the Scripture recommends.

These we have observed from the place in general, 'the holy city.' Let us go on to the place in particular where Satan acted all this, 'the pinnacle of the temple.' Various are the conjectures of men about this, whether it were some fane, or the top of some spire, or the place whence the apostle James was thrown down, or the top of the king's porch, which was erected to a great height over a deep valley, or some battlement, &c. But we are not concerned in such inquiries; only here shall I take notice of Scultetus, who, supposing the place to be the top of a fane or spire, and reading in Josephus that the points of such broaches were so sharp that a bird could not rest upon them without piercing its foot, was therefore willing to conclude that these temptations were not really and historically acted, but in vision only.406 All this ariseth from a wrong interpretation of πτερύγιον, which our English renders pinnacle, whereas it properly signifies any battlement or angular prominency, jutting out over the rest like a wing, which would afford a sufficient footing and support.407

It is more profitable to inquire after Satan's reason for the choice of such a place. No question but it was upon design, for else he might with equal convenience have tempted Christ to cast himself down from some tree or precipice in the wilderness; but then what that design was, is not so easy to determine. It seems plain that he might suppose that Christ might be the rather animated to the undertaking of flying in the air by the hopes of glory which might be expected from such a performance before so many spectators. But some think that he had a design also upon the men of Jerusalem, and intended some delusion to the Jews,408 which I am not unwilling to close with, partly because the experiences that we have of his devices assure us that in one temptation his ends are oft manifold; and I cannot but think that Satan would make all things sure, and provide, in his projecting mind, against all events. For if Christ should have yielded and evidenced so great a power in the sight of all the people, it might have been a conviction general that he was the Messiah, about that time universally expected; and partly I am ready to think so, because, in case Christ had done so, it lay so fair to confirm the Jews in a misapprehension of the personal coming of Elias, of whom they understood the prophecy of Mal. iii. 1, 'Behold, I will send my messenger; and he shall prepare the way before me; and the Lord whom ye seek shall suddenly come to his temple, even the messenger of the covenant.'409 If the Jews expected Elias to come from heaven to the temple, how strongly would they have been confirmed in this opinion if they had seen a man fly from the temple in the air; and by this means John the Baptist, who was the Elias that was to come, should have been neglected, and Christ himself, though honoured as Elias, not owned for the Messiah.

Obs. 6. Observe then, *That Satan's designs are large, and that he projects the ensnaring or deluding of others by such temptations as seem only to concern those that are under the immediate trouble of them.* He tempts Christ to cast himself down, and also by it, at least, intends a delusion to the Jews. He tempts one man upon the back of another. One is tempted to error; another by that man's temptation is tempted to atheism and rejecting of all religion. One man is tempted to profaneness, another is tempted by that to an uncharitable disrespect of him. It is easy to multiply instance of this.

CHAPTER XIV

Next to the preparation which Satan made for the second conflict, already explained, the temptation intended offers itself to our view, which is this, 'Cast thyself down.' What Satan chiefly intended by it, we may collect from Christ's answer, as well as from the thing itself; for he thus replies, 'It is written, Thou shalt not tempt the Lord thy God.' Christ doth not use this scripture to any such sense as this, that he should hereby prohibit Satan to tempt him because he was Satan's Lord and God; but he mentioned this scripture as a rule of obedience: as if he should say, 'I may not cast myself down, and so rely on extraordinary help, seeing I can go down another way;' for the neglect of ordinary means, when we have them, is a tempting of God, which may not be done. So that it appears by this, that Satan here tempted Christ to presumption. There is only this objection in our way, that Deut. vi. 16, the place by Christ cited, refers to the temptation of the Israelites in Massah, mentioned Exod. xvii. 2, where they chide with Moses for water; and there it would seem their tempting the Lord was rather in despairing of his power and help than presuming in the neglect of the ordinary means. I answer, though the occasion and matter of that temptation be different from this of Christ's, yet the presumptuous experiment that they there made of God's presence and power was the same with this which Satan designed; for ver. 7, where the account of that tempting is given, it is said, 'because they tempted the Lord, saying, Is the Lord among us or not?' they put it to this issue, that the being and power of God should be tried by the giving or not giving of water. The manner, then, of that temptation being so agreeable to this, Christ very pertinently applies that command to it, presumption being the thing which Christ was tempted to. It might occasion some wonder in us to see Satan take such strange steps. He was before tempting him to despair, now to presumption; but it is no argument of his lightness or uncertain roving in his way of tempting, but rather of his depth and subtlety. Note then,

Obs. 7. That it is Satan's policy in tempting, to run from one extreme to another. The Corinthians were first tempted to a sinful compliance with the adulterous person, and were averse to his excommunication; afterwards they were tempted to the contrary severity, and were as backward to receive him again. The same men that have been overcome by prodigality and excess, when they begin to see the evil of that, are oft tempted to worldliness or covetousness, the contrary disposition. Reasons of this policy are:—

(1.) First, *The avoiding of one extreme gives the soul such a swing, if care be not used to prevent it, that they are cast more than half way upon the other.* Peter, in an extreme of modesty, refused the washing of his feet by Christ; but when he understood the danger, then he runs as far wrong another way—'Not my feet only, but my hands and my head,' John xiii. 9. Thus some are so for purity of churches, that they exclude the weak; others so for unity, that they admit the open scandalous and profane.

(2.) Secondly, *While men avoid one extreme by running into another, they carry with them such strong impressions of the evil they would avoid, and such fierce prejudices, that it is not an ordinary conviction will bring them right, but they are apt to be confident of the goodness of the way they take, and so are the more bold and fixed in their miscarriage.*

Presumption being the great design of Satan in this temptation, we may further observe:—

Obs. 8. *That as distrust on the one hand, so presumption on the other, is one of his grand designs.* Of these two, we may say as it was said of the sword of Hazael and Jehu, that of all those that are slain by the devil, whosoever hath escaped the sword of distrust and despair, the sword of presumption hath slain. To explain this I shall,

1. First, Shew what presumption is. It is in the general a confidence without a ground. [1.] First, It is made up of audacity—which is a bold and daring undertaking of a thing—and security. [2.] Secondly, The ground of it is an error of judgment. A blind or a misled judgment doth always nourish it; and this is either a mistake of the nature of such means on which we rely for assistance, as when a man lays as much stress upon a thread as upon a cable, or expects as much nourishment from a stone as from bread;410 or a mistake of the will of others, from whom we expect aid and help, without a warrant for such a confidence. [3.] Thirdly, In its way of working it is directly opposite to distrust, and is a kind of excessive though irregular hope; not that in this case a man believes or hopes overmuch, for there can be no excess properly in the exercise of divine graces, but that he hopes too rashly or lightly, without a solid foundation or reason.411 Hope hath for its object that which is good under the considerations of futurity, possibility, and difficulty. On the one side, desperation looks upon that good as future, but under so great a difficulty that it forgets the possibility of it, and thereupon surceaseth all endeavours. Presumption, on the other hand, is so keenly apprehensive of the possibility, that it never regards the difficulty, and so thrusts forward into irregular endeavours or expectations. The nature of this will be better understood when the particular instances of presumption are before us.

(1.) First, Then it is presumption, *when from external or subordinate means men expect that for which they were never designed nor appointed of God.* To expect 'grapes of thorns or figs of thistles,' would be a presumption, because God never designed them for such fruits; and no less is it when in any other case men look for high and extraordinary things from any created good above what God hath put into it by the law of creation.

(2.) Secondly, *When men do expect those fruits and effects from anything unto which it is appointed, in neglect or opposition to the supreme cause, without whose concurrent influence they cannot reach their proper ends*—that is, our hopes are wholly centred upon means, when in the meantime our eye is not upon God. Thus 'to make gold our hope,' Job xxxi. 24, 'to make flesh our arm,' Jer. xvii. 5, 'to make Ashur a saviour,' Hosea xiv. 3, or to trust to any creatures whatsoever, is in Scripture condemned as a presumptuous reliance, and, in regard of the necessary disappointment, 'a trusting in a lie;' in which sense it is said that 'every man is a liar,' Ps. lxii. 9. The like presumption it is when we boast great things of ourselves, and, as Peter, make confident engagements, in our own strength, that we will avoid such a sin or perform such a duty; for we are but frail, and all our sufficiency is from the Lord, so that it can be no less than intolerable arrogance to promise anything of ourselves without him; neither can men promise to themselves the continuance of that good or advantage which they have already received from second causes, if their confidence builds itself upon that sole consideration, without a just blame. Job had said he should 'die in his nest,' [chap. xxix. 18,] and David that 'he should never be moved,' [Ps. xvi. 8,] but both of them afterward noted these confidences to have been no other than deceitful presumptions.

(3.) Thirdly, It is a presumption *to expect things above the reach of our present state and condition;* as for a mean man to beg of God authority and rule, or to expect to be set with princes; or for ordinary Christians to look for miracles, signs from heaven, visions, revelations, extraordinary answers to prayers, and thē like, all which expectations are groundless, and the issue of a presumptuous pride: *sperare non speranda.*

(4.) Fourthly, *When men expect things contrary to the rules that God hath set for his dispensations of mercy, they boldly presume upon his will.* God hath promised preservation to his children while they are in God's way, but if any shall go out of that way, and sinfully put himself into dangers and hazards, it would be presumption in him to expect a preservation. It is the same in spiritual things. God promiseth eternal life and the blessings of his covenant to such as give up themselves to him and his laws; will it not be intolerable presumption for men 'to bless themselves in their heart' with expectations of reigning with him in glory, while in the meantime they contradict his own rule and neglect his order, walking in profaneness and living to themselves?

This is a high presumption of mercy against his express will. Hence are such courses called 'presumptuous sins,' Ps. xix. 13, and such sinners transgress 'with a high hand.'

(5.) Fifthly, It is also a presumption *to expect any mercy, though common and usual, without the ordinary means by which God in providence hath settled the usual dispensations of such favours*; as when men look for his aid and help for supply of corporal wants, while they throw off all care, and refuse their own endeavours, which are the ways of God's appointment, in the conscientious use whereof such mercies are to be expected. The heathen, upon the consideration of the necessary connexion of means and the end, have usually judged such sluggish expectations to be no better than solemn mockings of a deity: *admotâ manu invocanda est Minerva*. In spiritual things it is no less presumptuous to expect conversion, and an interest in Christ and heaven, while they refuse the careful use of his ordinances; and therefore we are commanded to pray for such blessings, 'to cry after knowledge, and to lift up the voice for understanding,' Prov. ii. 3-5, and to second these prayers with our own utmost endeavours 'to seek for it as for silver, and to search for it as for hid treasures,' and in so doing to expect the finding of the knowledge of God.

(6.) Sixthly, *When ordinary or extraordinary mercies are expected for an unlawful end*; as when the Israelites at Massah called for water,—which they ought to believe God would supply them withal, their condition considered,—but for a test and proof of the being of God; for they said, 'Is God among us, or not?' Exod. xvii. 7. It is by James made a piece of spiritual unfaithfulness and adultery to ask anything of God with a design 'to spend it upon a lust,' [chap. iv. 3.] Ahaz his refusing a sign when God offered it, however he made a show of modesty and believing, argued no other thing but that he was conscious to himself that, in case he had accepted it, he should have abused that favour to an unlawful end, and have tempted God by it, as putting it upon this experiment whether there was a God or not. This is also another act of presumption. When a man becomes guilty of any of these miscarriages, he is presumptuous.

2. Secondly, I further add to this discovery of the nature and kinds of presumption, that this is one of Satan's grand engines; which I prove by two demonstrations:—

(1.) First, *By Satan's common practice in this kind upon all sorts of men, in most occasions.* That which is his frequent practice upon most men, and on most occasions, must of necessity be understood to be chiefly designed. Some men may possibly be free from the trouble of some particular temptations, as Hieronimus Wallerus saith of Luther his master, that he heard him often report of himself that he had been assaulted and vexed with all kind of temptations, saving only that of covetousness; but none can say they have not been assaulted with this. I shall make it out by an induction of particulars:—

[1.] First, *The generality of men that live in the profession of religion are presumptuous, nay, the greatest part of the blind world are so.* They presume of mercy and salvation. The devil preacheth nothing else but all hope, no fear, and in these golden dreams they slide down to hell. If we look into their way of sinning, and then into their hopes, we can judge no less of them. They stick not at the most grievous abominations, the works of the flesh, and in these they continue. It is their trade, their life; they make provisions for them, they cannot sleep except they do wickedly; he that reproveth is derided by them; they make but a mock and sport of those things which, as the shame and reproach of mankind, should rather fly the light and hide themselves as things of darkness. These things they practise without regret or sorrow of heart, without smiting upon the thigh, and in all this they have the confidence to say, 'Is not the Lord among us?' They can call themselves Christians, and have as bold expectations of eternal happiness, as if the committing of these evils were made by God the necessary qualifications to everlasting happiness. What is more common, and yet what more presumptuous? For (1.) These men audaciously hope and expect mercy, expressly contrary to the peremptory threatenings of God. God saith, 'There is no peace to the wicked;' they say, 'We shall have peace.' (2.) These run upon the greatest hazards of ruin and woe, with the least fear, in the contempt of all danger, 'as the horse rusheth into the battle, who mocketh at fear, and is not affrighted, neither turneth his back from the sword,' Job xxxix. 22. (3.) They dare God to do his worst, they provoke God to jealousy, and that to his face; hence was it that Nimrod was said to be a mighty hunter before the Lord, [Gen. x. 9;] and Er, the son of Judah, that he was wicked 'before the Lord,' [Gen. xxxviii. 7,] because such audacious sinners will not, as we may say, go behind his back to sin.

[2.] Secondly, *Hypocrites whose carnage is more smooth, they also are presumptuous*; for while they hide their sin, they do against dictates of conscience presume 'that he that made the eye doth not see,' and that there is a possibility to cheat God as well as men: besides, their boastings and hopes have a special mark set upon them in Scripture as audaciously false; 'the hope of the hypocrite shall be cut off,' [Job viii. 13;] their confidence of the temple of the Lord is but a lie, and so termed expressly by the prophet.

[3.] Thirdly, *Even despairing persons are not always free of presumption.* The act of self-murder is a terrible presuming upon infinite justice. Spira's desire to know the worst was of the same kind. These are indeed extraordinary;

but there are some other kinds of despair that come nearer to presumption, as that sensual despair which ariseth out of an excessive love of carnal delights, and a secure contempt of spiritual things; for when sensuality prompts them to eat and drink while they may, despairing and hopeless of a future happiness, 'for to-morrow they shall die,' [Isa. xxii. 13,] and their pleasure cease, they highly presume against the patience and goodness of God.

[4.] Fourthly, *The best of men are too frequently overcome by it.* (1.) Not only while they are overtaken with sins more grievous, and above the rate of sins of infirmity, to which how liable the holiest saint may be upon temptation, may be gathered from David's prayer, 'Keep thy servant from presumptuous sins, that they have not dominion over me,' [Ps. xix. 13.] (2.) But by their earnest prosecutions of their own wills when contradicted by providence. It is by the prophet, Isaiah ix. 9, called 'a pride and stoutness of heart,' to contend with providence, to attempt to build with 'hewn stone when the bricks are fallen,' or to 'strive for cedars when divine wrath hath cut down the sycamores.' (3.) How frequently are they guilty of presuming upon their privileges, their strength, their graces, and upon that score venture themselves upon occasions of sin, or bear high above others upon a conceit of their higher attainments, or when they boldly put themselves upon suffering, or upon doing, while they want that due humility and care that should balance them. (4.) There is also a presumptuous rashness, upon which the zeal and good intentions of holy men may sometimes precipitate them. Such was Uzziah's putting forth his hand to hold the ark, for which the Lord smote him. All these instances put together will sufficiently demonstrate that presumption is one of Satan's master designs.

The second demonstration of this truth is from the general subserviency of other things to this. Most of Satan's endeavours and temptations aim at this point, and this is the result and consequence of most sins. That must needs be chief, to which so many things do but serve and minister. In this centre do most of the lines of his policy meet, — pride, vainglory, conceited privileges, supposed advantages, and many things more were but under-agents to this temptation which the devil attempted upon Christ, as hath in part, and presently shall be further, evidenced.

3. Thirdly, Having thus proved that presumption is one of the great things he aims at, I shall next *discover the reasons of his earnestness and industry in his design*, which are these: —

(1.) First, *It is a sin very natural, in which he hath the advantage of our own readiness and inclination.* However that some from a melancholy temper are inclinable to fears and distrust at some time, when these black apprehensions are exalted, yet, these excepted, hopes are more predominant than fears; and self-love, which provides fuel to these hopes, is a natural principle in all. When so many things give him such advantages and promise him a success, we may well suppose he will not miss such an opportunity.

(2.) Secondly, *As it is easy for Satan's attempt, so it is remote from conviction, and not rooted out without great difficulty.* It is a sin that is covered with a pretext of a higher degree of hope. Men in many ways of this iniquity are under persuasions of duty, and by reason of that confidence, fear, which is the soul's sentinel, is asleep. Hence do they not lie so fairly open to counsel or reproof. The Israelites, Deut. i. 27, 28, being under discouragement, refuse to go up to Canaan, when they were upon the border of the land; but being convinced of their sin in distrusting the arm of the Lord, by God's declared wrath and threatening against them, they fall upon the contrary extreme of presumption, and then, ver. 41, 'they would go up and fight;' and the conviction of their former sin made them so confident that this was their present duty—for thus they argue, 'We have sinned against the Lord, we will go up and fight, according to all that the Lord our God commanded us'—that though they were expressly forbidden from God, ver. 42, 'Go not up, neither fight, for I am not among you;' yet were they so strangely carried by their former persuasion, that they refused to be convinced, 'and went presumptuously into the hill.' By which instance we see what great pretences lead on presumption, and how difficultly they are removed, which two things do no less than tempt Satan to lay out himself to the uttermost in that design.

(3.) Thirdly, *The greatness of the sin when it is committed, is another reason of his diligence in the pursuit of it.* It is not only from a simple error or mistake, but that error ariseth from intolerable pride; they say and do such things from the pride and stoutness of their heart, Isa. ix. 9. He that is presumptuous is self-willed, 2 Pet. ii. 10. Hence these sins, which we translate presumptuous, are in the original called prides or arrogancies, Ps. xix. 13; Deut. xvii. 12. Besides, they are contradictions to Gods order, separating those things that God hath joined together, as the means from the end, or the end from the means, as if the 'earth should be turned out of its place' for us. And in some cases it is no less than the open affronting of God by abusing his own favours against himself; for thus they deal with him, who are opinionated in sin because of his mercy, concluding, by an irrational consequence, that they ought to be wicked because God is good, or that they may freely offend because he doth not punish.

(4.) Fourthly, *The dangerous issues and consequences of this way of sinning, do not a little animate Satan to tempt to it.* In some cases it was to be punished by death: Deut. xvii. 12, 'The man that doth presumptuously, even that man shall die;' and most usually it is plagued with sad disappointments, by a severe engagement of God's displeasure against it. 'The hypocrite's hope shall perish, it shall be as the giving up of the ghost,' Job viii. 13, and xi. 20. And generally, 'He that thus blesseth himself in his heart, when he heareth the words of the curse,' Deut. xxix. 19, 20, 'the Lord will not spare him, but then the anger of the Lord and his jealousy shall smoke against that man, and all the curses that are written in this book shall lie upon him, and the Lord shall blot out his name from under heaven.'

4. Fourthly and lastly, I shall lay before you *the deceitful contrivance of Satan in bringing this sin about*, by shewing the particulars of his craft against Christ herein. As,

(1.) First, *He takes advantage from his resolve to rely upon providence, contrary to the former temptation of turning stones to bread.* Christ had refused that, telling him it was duty to trust him, who not only by the ordinary means of bread could feed him, but also by any other appointment. To this Satan rejoins, by offering an irregular opportunity of such a trust, in casting himself from the pinnacle of the temple: as if he should say, 'If thou wilt thus rely upon providence, do it in this.' Wherein we may note, that from an obediential dependence, he would draw Christ to an irregular presumption. He retorts Christ's argument back again upon him thus, 'If God is to be relied upon by a certain trust for food, by the like trust he is to be relied upon for preservation; if the belief of supply of bread can consist with a neglect or refusal of ordinary means for the procurement thereof, then may the belief of preservation in casting thyself from the pinnacle of the temple consist also with a neglect of the ordinary means.' Thus, like a cunning sophister, he endeavours to conclude sin from duty, from a seeming parity betwixt them, though indeed the cases were vastly different. For, though it be duty to depend upon providence, when God, in the pursuit of service and duty, brings us out of the sight and hopes of outward means, yet it can be no less than sinful presumption for us to make such experiments of providences, when we need not, and when ordinary means are at hand. After the same manner doth he endeavour to put fallacies upon us, and to cheat us into presumptuous undertakings, by arguing from a necessary trust, in some cases, a necessity of presuming in others, upon a seeming likeness and proportion.

(2.) Secondly, *It was no small piece of Satan's craft to take this advantage, while the impression of trust in the want of outward means was warm upon the heart of Christ.* He hoped thereby the more easily to draw him to an excess. For he knows that a zealous earnestness to avoid a sin, and to keep to a duty, doth often too much incline us to an extreme, and he well hoped that when Christ had declared himself so positively to depend upon God, he might have prevailed to have stretched that dependence beyond its due bounds, taking the opportunity of his sway that way, which, as a ship before wind and tide, might soon be overdriven. And this was the design of his haste in this second temptation, because he would strike while the iron was hot, and closely pursue his advantage, while the strength and forwardness of these resolves were upon him.

(3.) Thirdly, *He endeavours to animate him to this presumption by popular applause, and to tickle him into a humour of affecting the glory and admiration, which by such a strange undertaking might be raised in the minds of the spectators;* and therefore did he bring him to the most conspicuous place of a great and populous city, not thinking the matter so feasible if he had tempted him to it in a solitary desert.

(4.) Fourthly, *He propounds to him a plausible end, and a seeming advantage,* viz., the clear and undoubted discovery of his divine nature and near interest in God; urging this as a necessary duty, for his own satisfaction, and the manifestation of his sonship to others.

(5.) Fifthly, To drive out of his mind those fears of miscarrying in his attempt, which otherwise might have been a block in his way, *he is officious in strengthening his confidence by propounding treacherous helps and preservatives,* suggesting a safety to him from the privilege of the place where this was to be acted, a holy city and temple, producing more of a divine presence for his safety than other places.

(6.) Sixthly, To make all sure, *he backs all this with a promise of preservation,* that nothing might be wanting to his security.

By this method applied to other things and cases, he endeavours to bring us to presumption.

Applic. The consideration of this should *put us upon a special care and watchfulness against presumption.* It is more designed, and hath a greater prevalency than men are aware of. Two things I shall only at present propound for our preservation, out of Ps. xix. 12, 13.

[1.] First, *He that would be kept from presumptuous sins must make conscience of secret sins, to search for them, to mortify them, to beg pardon for them.* With what face or hope can we expect from God help against these, when we provoke him to leave us to ourselves, by indulging ourselves in the other?

[2.] Secondly, He that would avoid them *must be under the awe and fear of being overcome by them.* He that slights and contemns such visible hazards shall not long be innocent. David here first shews his conscience to be concerned with secret sins, and then begs to be kept from presumptuous sins, and by such earnest begging he next shews how much he dreaded such miscarriages. [Dickson, *in loc.*]

CHAPTER XV

We have seen and considered the main end of Satan in this temptation. Let us further consider whether this was the sole end that he propounded to himself. We have little reason to think that he would confine himself to one, when the thing itself doth so clearly suggest another, which might possibly have followed. In most cases, the ends of the devil are manifold. We may therefore easily suppose—and several have noted it412—that the devil, that great murderer, had herein a secret design against the life of Christ, and that he tempted him here indirectly to self-murder. And indeed, supposing that Christ had attempted to fly in the air, and had failed in the enterprise, what else could have followed but death and ruin? Hence let us note,

Obs. 9. That Satan seeks the ruin of our bodies as well as of our souls, and tempts men often to self-murder. That the devil goes about seeking how he may destroy men, by putting them upon attempts against their own lives, is evident, not only from the experience and confessions of such as have suffered under Satan's suggestions to that end—and it is a temptation more common than we think of, because most men are unwilling to lay open themselves to others in this matter—but also from those many sad instances of men over whom Satan so far prevails, that they execute upon themselves this design by destroying themselves. Yet by the way we may note, that such thoughts are often in the minds of men where Satan is not industriously designing their destruction; for he often casts in such thoughts, not only to try how men take with them, but to affright and disquiet them; and it is usual with men of sad and melancholy tempers to mistake their own fears of such a temptation, for Satan's endeavours against them, when indeed their fear and trouble lest they should be so tempted, makes them think they are tempted indeed.

Satan drives on the design of self-murder two ways:—

1. First, *Directly, when in plain terms he urgeth men to destroy themselves.* This because it is directly repugnant to the law of nature, which vehemently urgeth them to self-preservation, he cannot effect but by the help of some advantages; yet some ways and methods by experience he hath found to be so available to such an unnatural resolve, that he frequently puts them in practice. As, (1.) first, He works upon *the discontents of men*, and improves

the disquiet of their minds, upon the occasion of any loss, vexation, disappointment, or disgrace, to as great a height as he can, and when their lives are made bitter to them, and they are sufficiently prepared by the uneasiness of their condition, then he propounds death as the only remedy to set them at quiet; wherein, besides his officiousness to provide them with instruments of cruelty and opportunity for their use, he follows them with arguments drawn from the sense of their present condition; the great intendment whereof is to aggravate their smart, and to make their burden seem intolerable, and then self-ruin is but a natural consequence. We may see enough of this in the discontents of good men, and that they naturally work this way. Job speaks the general apprehensions of men in trouble, chap. iii. 20, 21, 'The bitter in soul value not life; they long for death, and dig for it more than for hid treasures; they rejoice exceedingly, and are glad when they can find the grave.' Jonah in his discontent prefers death before life: 'It is better for me to die than to live,' [chap. iv. 3.] Elias doth the like; and Job seems impatient for it. All this is from the power and working of this temptation, though God held their hand that it did not fully prevail. In Ahithophel the ground of discontent was more a fancied than a real disgrace; his counsel was rejected—which was in itself no great dishonour—and this works up such a perplexing resentment in his mind, that Satan prevails with him to hang himself very deliberately.

(2.) Secondly, He most frequently draws on men to destroy themselves by terrors and despairing troubles of conscience. These, as they afford greater disquiet and distress of mind than other kind of discontentments, so doth he more prevail by them; for a wounded spirit is above ordinary strength, and hard to bear; only it may seem strange that those who so experimentally feel how 'fearful a thing it is to fall into the hands of the living God,' [Heb. x. 31,] should entertain such a temptation as, to their apprehensions and knowledge, will certainly plunge them into the very ocean of everlasting vengeance. This no doubt Satan finds tō be no small obstruction to his design; but here he useth his skill to open a way for them that would outrun their lives on the one hand, as he labours to pursue them with sense of wrath and indignation on the other hand. To this purpose he tells them, [1.] That all the hell they are to meet with is in their consciences, and that death will free them from all, or at least that death will give a present ease, and that till the resurrection they shall be in quiet. Those that are willing to receive these apprehensions may easily be prevailed with to hasten their own death, seeing they have already fixed this conclusion with themselves, that there is no hope nor pardon for them, that they are reprobates and cut off; for their thoughts can meditate nothing but the terrors of such conclusions. [2.] He sometimes endeavours to persuade them, that by executing this revenge upon themselves, they may make some kind of satisfaction and amends for the sins they have committed; which though most false, yet it is a wonder how far such ungrounded surmises may possess the minds of the desperate. That Judas might have some such thought when he destroyed himself, is conjectured by some;413 but that must be but a conjecture, seeing none can pretend to know his thoughts; but we may speak with greater freedom of those who have declared the working of such apprehensions upon their minds. [3.] A more plausible pretext he useth when he endeavours to persuade them that they may kill themselves, and yet go to heaven for all that. To this purpose the subtle adversary is not backward to tell them what have been the charitable expressions of some men who have supposed a possibility of repentance inter pontem et fontem, as we say, betwixt the stroke or halter and the death. Capel is so apprehensive of the mischievous improvement of this charity, for an encouragement to self-murder, that he with great earnestness cautions all ministers against such liberal expressions.414 I have known some, and heard of others, that have been so possessed with this imagination of being saved, notwithstanding that having purposed to destroy themselves—though God prevented them that they did it not—they have first by prayer recommended themselves to God, and so prepared themselves to die. [4.] Sometime, though such afflicted ones have no such persuasion but that from death they go immediately to hell, yet are they pushed forward by a certain fearful curiosity of knowing the worst. At that rate did Spira express himself, when he desired to be freed of his life that he might know the utmost of those torments which he feared; as if the affrightments of his fearful expectations were worse than the real feeling of them. [5.] But most of all doth he prevail against that objection of greater misery after death, by running men up to a desperate distraction in their terrors. Their present anguish is made insupportable, so that they hasten out of life, without care or consideration of what shall follow.

(3.) Thirdly, He tempts men directly to destroy themselves from a principle of heroic boldness and seeming fortitude of mind—a thing very common among the Romans, who impatient of injuries, and from pride of heart, not willing to subject themselves to affronts, chose rather to tear their own bowels than to live to see themselves abused. Lucretia being forced by Tarquinius, and not willing to outlive her disgrace, stabbed herself. Cato, not being able to endure the victory of Cæsar, puts an end to his days. Innumerable instances of this kind histories do everywhere afford. These, though they consulted their own passions, and knew of nothing that prompted them but their own generosity or magnanimity, yet were they not without a tempter to such cruel actions. Satan undoubtedly pleased himself by exercising his cruelty upon them so easily, by the help of such a humour, which passed among these blind heathens for the highest proof of virtue and fortitude. To this height it came, insomuch that we find Seneca highly applauding Cato415 for procuring his liberty by his own death; and setting forth that fact as the most delightful spectacle to the gods. Though indeed, as Augustine notes,416 it is not fortitude but weakness, and a clear evidence of impatience, which cannot bear other men's insolencies or their own hardships. And if we examine the matter to the bottom, though there be audacity in it to undertake their own death, yet is this led on by no better principles than pride, impatience, and despair: which may the better be discovered if we consider such kind of attempts as they arise from more ignoble and base occasions. Paterculus tells us of a Tuscan soothsayer, who being carried to prison with his friend Fulvius Flaccus, and despairing of pardon, desperately runs his head against the prison door and dashed out his brains; and yet this man was moved to attempt his destruction upon the same general principles by which Cato destroyed himself.

(4.) Fourthly, It is also sufficiently known that Satan by the force of custom in several countries, doth as it were necessitate men to cut off their own lives. In some barbarous places, at the death of the husband, the wife, in a brutal affection of the praise of love and loyalty, casts herself to be devoured by the same flame in which the dead body of her husband is consumed.417 And there are found in other places customs of self-destruction for the avoiding the tedious inconveniences of old age, where it is usual for old persons with joy to prepare their own funeral pile, and to make a quick despatch of their lives, and rather to die at once than by piecemeal, as Seneca expresseth it.418 Calanus, an Indian philosopher, being dysenterical, obtained leave of Alexander to burn himself for more quick despatch.

(5.) Fifthly, There is yet another way by which men are tempted sometime, though rarely, to hasten themselves out of the world, and that is by a pretence of an earnest and impatient desire of happiness to come. That longings for such enjoyments do become the best of saints, and is indeed their excellency, cannot be denied; but to make such a preposterous haste must be a cheat of Satan. That there is a possibility of this, may appear in the story of Cleombrotus, mentioned also by Augustine, who reading Plato's 'Phædo, of the Immortality of the Soul,' that he might hasten thither, threw himself headlong from a wall, and died.419 Now, though it be hard to find such an instance among Christians, yet we have reason to believe that where Satan perceives such a temptation may take place, he will not be wanting in the prosecution. And if we may conjecture Augustine's thoughts by that question which he propounds—viz., Whether it be lawful for a man to kill himself for the avoiding of sin, which he solidly confutes,420 we may conclude that such thoughts were the usual temptations of good men in his time, and the rather because in the close of that chapter he applies that discourse particularly to the servants of Christ, that they should not think their lives a burden. Non itaque vobis, O fideles Christi, sit tœdio vita vestra.

2. Secondly, Satan promotes the design of self-murder, not only directly, as we have heard, but also *by some indirect ways he undermines the life of man.* That is, when he doth not formally say to them, Destroy yourselves, but tempts them to such things as he knows will let in upon death. This way of subtle malice I shall explain under these heads:—

(1.) First, Upon highest pretexts of zeal for Gods glory, he sometimes lays a snare for our lives. I cannot believe but Satan had a hand in that forwardness of ancient Christians, who by an open profession of their faith before persecuting judicatures, did as it were court a martyrdom; and I have the same persuasion of the painful earnestness of many holy preachers, who lavish out their strength in a prodigality of pains for the good of souls, which, like a thief in the candle, wastes them immediately; whereas a better husbanded strength might be truly more advantageous, as continuing the light the longer; and yet so sincere are their ends, so pleasant is their work, that they seldom observe, as they ought, that Satan, when he can do no better, is glad of the opportunity to destroy them with their own weapon; and therefore in this case they may expect he will do all he can to heighten and forward their zeal, not only by adding all the fuel he can to their inward propensity of laboriousness, but also by outward encouragement of the declared acceptations and expectations of their hearers.421

(2.) Secondly, *Upon baser pretences of the full enjoyment of sensual pleasures and carnal delights, he doth unawares push men forward to death and dangers.* Thus the voluptuous, the glutton, the drunkard, dig their own graves, and invite death to cut them off before they have lived out half their time. While Satan tempts men to such excesses of riot, he labours not only the destruction of the soul, but also of the body; not only that they be miserable, but that they may be so with all expedition.

(3.) Thirdly, Besides all these, he hath other subtle ways of contriving the death of men, by putting them upon ways and actions that are attended with hazard. Thus he sought the death of Christ, not directly but indirectly, by urging him to an action which he thought would unavoidably bring him to death, for a fall from so great a precipice would easily have bereaved any man of life. And sometimes when men are besotted with enthusiastical delusions, he can more easily beguile them with such stratagems. That instance of Stuker422 is famous, who cut off his brother's head upon a foolish persuasion that God would magnify his great power in giving him life again. If Satan can befool such bewitched slaves into such absurd and unreasonable apprehensions in regard of others, what hinders but that he may so far impose upon them, that they may be willing to practise upon themselves? I remember something to this purpose, of one whom the devil had well-nigh prevailed with to make a hole in his breast, which of necessity must have let out his life, upon a pretended promise of giving him eternal life, and was accordingly forced to take up a knife and to carry it to his throat.423 In anno 1647, in Yorkshire, a company of people were seduced to sacrifice certain creatures to God, among the rest they sacrificed their aged mother, persuading her she should rise the third day, and for this they were executed at York.

Applic. This may awaken all to be aware of this temptation. Some are sadly concerned in it. Many are the complaints which some of us have met withal about it in private, and the apprehensions of such hazards are sadly disquieting. Through such fears thousands of God's dear children have passed, and many, too many, have been overcome by this weapon. Those of us that have not yet known temptations of this nature, do not know how soon we may be assaulted in this kind. It is necessary for all to stand upon their guard, and for that end it behoves us to have at hand these defences against it:—

[1.] First, It is useful to consider *that this is one of Satan's great plots;* and when we meet with it clothed with never so many pretexts, enforced with never so many seeming necessities, yet must we look upon it as the counsel of an enemy, who certainly intends us no kindness, let him pretend what he will; and therefore may we be sure it will be our sad inconvenience and disadvantage.

[2.] Secondly, It must be fixed in our minds that the thing in itself is a high iniquity, a most grievous provocation. No instance of self-murder, properly such, can be met withal in Scripture, as practised by any holy person. The command is directly against it, 'Thou shalt not kill.' If we may not murder another, as Austin argues, we may not murder ourselves; for he that kills himself kills no other than a man; nay, we may much less lay hand upon our own life.424 It is a greater violation of the law of nature and of love. Every man is nearest to himself; and his love to himself is the pattern of his love to another. Self-murder must then be a sin of higher aggravations by far than the murder of another person. And the wiser heathens were far from countenancing any such cruelty. If Plato had thought it best, for an immediate enjoyment of immortality, which is the highest pretence of self-murder imaginable, to make an end of life violently, he would certainly have practised it himself, or recommended it to others, but he is so far from this, that he speaks against it as a great wickedness.

[3.] Thirdly, It is necessary that men keep in mind *the danger that follows such an act*. Death brings God's unalterable *mittimus*, and seals up the condition of every man, so that in the same posture he comes to judgment, it puts an end to all hopes and endeavours. Suppose then such tempted creatures to have fears and terrors as great as you can imagine them to be, yet there is a possibility that they may be deceived in them, that their case is not so bad as they fear, or if it be bad enough at present, that it may be better afterwards; for many that have in their anguish resolved against themselves, have been prevented of the execution of their resolves, and have lived to see the Lord and his salvation. And who is able to determine that secret, that their name is not in the book of life? Who can say he is certainly excluded out of God's decree? What madness is it then to rush into certain ruin, when our fears that distress us may be but mistakes! It is not so certain that men shall be damned, because of what they feel or fear at present, as it may be if they destroy themselves.

[4.] Fourthly, To prevent occasions to this temptation, *it must be our care not to give way to discontents for outward things, nor to distressing fears, such as are despairing and hopeless, for our spiritual estate*; or if we have a burden either way upon our mind, we must avoid as much as may be impatient fretfulness, 'lest Satan get advantage of us.' Discontented moods and casting away hope are sad occasions for this temptation. If we find ourselves thus burdened, we must look to it betimes, and not suffer it to go too far. And if this temptation come, we must take heed we keep not the devil's counsel, but discover the matter to some that are wise and faithful, able to advise and pray for us; remembering still that if only outward things trouble us, we have a better way of ease and remedy, by submitting to a chastising providence. If spiritual troubles move this way, we should not run from him, but rather resolve to perish at his foot as humble suppliants for mercy and pardon.

[5.] Fifthly, The temptation must also be opposed with *fasting and prayer*. If this be sincerely practised, it will go away at last.

[6.] Sixthly, Something may also be said for caution against unnecessary thrusting ourselves, while under such temptations, into places of danger, or into a converse with instruments of death. This may be too great a daring of the temptation, and in the consequence a mischief. Yet on the other hand, we must not be so cowardly as to be afraid of such places and things, unto which our callings and lawful employments do engage us; not to dare to go over a bridge, or to walk by a river or a pit, if it be our necessary way, is but to give an advantage to Satan to keep us under continual affrightments; and therefore I subscribe to Capel's advice, 'We must abide by it, and fight it out by faith; we must not fly the way, the place, the employment, but go on and look to God, and at last we shall make Satan fly.'425

Obj. But if some object to this, that their weakness is great, and their fears are strong, and Satan never idle, and that therefore they have little ground to expect an escape, I shall desire they would consider seriously the instance of Christ in this particular. When he was upon the pinnacle of the temple, a small push might have overthrown him, and yet it was not in Satan's power to do it himself, though he tempted Christ to cast himself down: which may sufficiently satisfy us, that there is a sure hedge of providence about us, and that Satan cannot do us the least hurt by pushing us into a pit or river, or any such danger.

CHAPTER XVI

The aims of Satan in this temptation being thus explained, I must now offer to your consideration the means by which he sought to bring his end about, which we have noted already, was pride: this he endeavoured to raise up in him two ways:—

(1.) First, By urging to him the privileges of his condition, as taking himself to be the Son of God.

(2.) Secondly, By offering him the occasion of popular applause; to which purpose he brought him into the holy city, where he might be sure of many spectators. I shall hence note,

Obs. 10. *That pride is Satan's proper engine to bring men on to presumption.*

If we should trace the history of presumptuous sins, we shall ever find it to have been so. Adam's first sin was a high presumption against God's express command, but pride was the stair by which he knew they must ascend to it; and therefore he used this argument to corrupt the hearts of our first parents, 'Ye shall be as gods.' The presumption of Uzziah in burning incense upon the altar, was from his pride, 2 Chron. xxvi. 16, 'His heart was lifted up, because he was become strong.' David's presumption in numbering the people was from hence. Thus might we run through many instances. But Satan's own case may be instead of all. His first sin, though we have but conjecture what it was particularly, is concluded by all to have been highly presumptuous, and the Scripture expressly asserts that it was his pride that brought him to it. 1 Tim. iii. 6, 'He that is lifted up with pride, falls into the condemnation of the devil.' And in the general we are told by the prophet, Hab. ii. 4, 'that the soul that is lifted up,' cannot be so upright as patiently to wait upon God in a way of believing, but it will be presuming to evade a trouble by indirect contrivances.

To explain the observation, I shall do no more but shew what pride is, and how fit it is to beget presumption.

Pride is a self-idolising, an over-valuation or admiration of ourselves, upon a real or supposed excellency, inward or outward, appertaining to us. It is in Scripture frequently expressed by the lifting up or exaltation of the soul. And this is done, upon the consideration of any kind of thing, which we apprehend makes us excel others; so that inward gifts of mind, as knowledge, humility, courage, &c., or outward gifts of the body, as beauty, strength, activity, &c., or additional advantages of riches, honour, authority, &c., or anything well done by us, &c., may all be abused to beget and nourish pride, and to fill us with high and lofty thoughts concerning ourselves; and being thus blown up, we are fitted for any presumptuous undertaking. For,

(1.) First, *The mind thus corrupted begets to itself apprehensions of a self-sufficiency*: and therefore, as it is not apt to remember from what fountain all those excellencies come, and to what ends they are to serve; so it brings them to a contempt of others, and to a confidence of themselves. Thus are men by degrees so intoxicated by their own humour, that they mount up to irrational and absurd conceits, fancying that they are more than they are, and that they can do far more than is possible for them to accomplish, till at last they become apparently foolish in the pursuit of their imaginations. I need not instance in the follies of Alexander, who being elated in mind, would be Jupiter's son, and go like Hercules in a lion's skin. Or in the mad frenzies of Caius, who as he would need fancy himself a god, so would he change his godship when he pleased: to-day he would wear a lion's skin and club, and then he must be Hercules; to-morrow in another garb he conceits himself Apollo; a caduceus made him Mercury, a sword and helmet made him Mars, &c. Or in Xerxes, who would whip the seas, and fetter Neptune. The Scripture affords enough of this nature, as the boast of Nebuchadnezzar; 'Is not this great Babel that I have built?' In the insolency of Nineveh, Zeph. ii. 15, 'I am, and there is none besides me.' The blasphemy of Tyre, Ezek. xxviii. 2, who set her heart 'as the heart of God, saying, I am a god, I sit in the seat of God.' The arrogancy of Sennacherib, Isa. xxxvi. 19, 20, 'Where are the gods of Hamath ... that the Lord should deliver Jerusalem out of my hand?' Though all pride in all men ariseth not to so great a height of madness, yet it is the nature of it, and none have any of it without this humour of conceiting themselves above themselves, which strangely prepares them for any presumption.

(2.) Secondly, He that is proud, *as he looks upon himself in a flattering glass, and measures himself by the length of his shadow; so doth he contemn and undervalue things that lie before his attempts as easy and small.* Hence doth he put himself upon things that are far beyond him. David notes the working of a proud heart, Ps. cxxxi. 1, in this particular, 'Neither do I exercise myself in great matters, or in things too high for me,' shewing that it is the guise of pride to outbid itself in its attempts.

(3.) Thirdly, *It is not only forward to attempt, but also desperate to execute without consideration of hazard.* Difficulty and danger, when they stand in the way, should usually deter men from their enterprise; but pride hardens the heart, and, in a blind rage, engageth it to contemn all inconveniencies. If sin and the breach of God's law be set before a person, whose pride engageth him to an unlawful undertaking, he overlooks it as a thing of nought: 'Through the pride of his countenance he will not seek after God: God is not in all his thoughts,' Ps. x. 4.

(4.) Fourthly, Pride ariseth up *to a scornful competition with anything that opposeth it*; and the more it is opposed, the more it rageth, for the contest is for having its will. This was the voice of pride in Pharaoh, 'Who is the Lord, that I should serve him?' [Exod. v. 2.] Hence men are said to 'despise the commandments of God,' [Lev. xxvi. 15,] when in the strength of their pride they are carried on to an open contest for their own ways and desires against peremptory commands and threatenings.

(5.) Fifthly, All this is done by *a pleasing allurement*. It is a witchcraft that strongly holds men, *Amabilis insania mentis gratissimus error*; and they think they are sufficiently rewarded if they be but gratified. Though other things go to wreck, yet they apprehend, if credit and honour be kept up, it is enough. Saul, when Samuel had declared that God would forsake him, yet sought to please himself by keeping up his esteem and authority. 'Honour me,' saith he, 'before the people,' [1 Sam. xv. 30.]

If all these particulars be weighed, what presumptuous act can be propounded by Satan which pride may not lead to? He that swells himself to a conceit of absoluteness, that will needs be attempting things too high, that contemneth all hazards, and is made more forward by opposition, and yet pleaseth himself in all, as in a golden dream, he is as much prepared for any figure or shape that Satan is ready to impress upon him, as melted metals for their mould or stamp.

Applic. Hence must we be warned against pride, as we would avoid presumption. If we admit this, we cannot well escape the other. And we are the more concerned to resist pride,

[1.] First, *Because it is a natural sin*. It was the first sin, and our natures are so deeply tainted with it, that it is a sin that first shews itself in our infancy; for children will express a pride in their clothes very early, and it is a general infection, from which none are exempted in some degree or other. The apostle's phrase, 1 John ii. 16, shews that our whole life, and all the concerns thereof, is but the sphere in which pride acts; and therefore, whereas he restrains other lusts to some particular ends or peculiar instruments, he calls this iniquity the 'pride of life,' implying how impossible it is to confine it in a narrow compass.

[2.] Secondly, *It is a subtle sin, and often lies where it is least suspected*. Every man sees it, as it is expressed in 'haughty looks,' in 'boasting speeches,' in 'gorgeous apparel,' in 'insolent behaviour;' but often men are insensibly possessed with this sin and know not of it. Under an affected contempt of honours and fine clothes they secretly hug themselves in their private conceits, and raise up in their own thoughts imaginary trophies of honour and victory, for despising what others so much dote upon. It was observed of Diogenes that he did *intus gloriari*, inwardly boast, and with greater pride contemned honour, riches, plenty, &c., than they were troubled with that enjoyed them. Some decry pride in others, vehemently declare against it as a sin, recommend humility as an ornament of great price in the sight of God, and yet are proud that they are above others in a fancied humility; and, in the management of themselves in their reproofs and exhortations, express such sad symptoms of an insulting humour, that the latent pride of their heart doth appear by it. It is possible for men to give thanks to the Almighty for all they have, and yet to be proud of what is in them. The Pharisee was proud, for so Christ calls him, that 'he was not as other men,' and yet he could 'thank God,' as ascribing all to him; nay, he that is truly sensible of the working of this pride in himself, and dares not approve it, yet he shall find in his heart such a delight when he is stroked or praised; and when some actions, praiseworthy, are not taken notice of, the best shall find that, without great watchfulness, they shall not be able to hold from giving some hints to others, as a memorial to them, of observing their excellency, or from some insinuations of their own commendation.

[3.] Thirdly, Pride is a sin *no less dangerous than subtle*. There are no attempts so strange, unreasonable, monstrous, or absurd, but it may prompt to them. It was a strange arrogancy in Herod to deify himself in his own thoughts, and yet the acclamations of the people swelled him into such a blasphemous imagination, that God thought fit to chastise him, and instruct others by so dreadful a judgment, as clearly baffled his insolency, and made him and his flatterers confess he was but a poor, frail man. Ordinarily pride is attended with a judgment, it is the very prognostic of ruin: 'Pride goeth before destruction, and a haughty spirit before a fall,' Prov. xvi. 18. But these judgments have something in them peculiar, which other judgments for other sins do not always express, to a manifestation of a special abhorrency in God against pride; as, (1.) He commonly smites the thing for which they are proud. Staupitius boasted of his memory, and God smote it; Hezekiah boasted of his treasure, and for that God designed them for captivity; David glorified [himself] in the multitude of his people, but God lessened them by pestilence; Nebuchadnezzar is proud of his Babel, and God drove him from the enjoyment of it. Men are proud of children or relations, and God oft removes them, or makes them a shame and sorrow. (2.) He doth not only this, but also orders the judgment so that it shall bring a shame and contempt upon men in that thing wherein they prided themselves. He will not only punish, but also stain their pride. The haughty daughters of Zion were not only plagued by removing their ornaments, bracelets, and the rest of their bravery, but over and above he 'smites with a scab the crown of their head, and discovers their secret parts, and brings a stink and baldness upon them instead of a sweet smell and well-set hair, and burning instead of beauty,' Isa. iii. 17, 24.

So sad a distemper stands in need of a special care; and for that end we should,

[1.] First, *In all things we have or do, not so much consider what is excellent, or wherein we excel, as what we have not, and wherein we come short.* We should be strange to ourselves, and design that the 'right hand should not know what the left hand doth,' which must be by having our eye upon the imperfections that attend us at the best.

[2.] Secondly, *It must be our care to be suspicious of the working of pride in us;* and also by an industrious watchfulness to give a stop or check to thoughts of this nature when they arise.

[3.] Thirdly, *The conquest of this cannot be expected without a serious and constant labour herein.* A humble soul is compared by David to a weaned child, Ps. cxxxi. 2. But a child is not weaned easily. Wormwood must be laid on the breast, and time allowed, before the child will forget it. He only that is content to exercise a discipline upon himself, and by frequent practices to habituate himself to low and careful thoughts, is likely to overcome it.

Pride, we have seen, was Satan's great engine to bring on presumption. The means by which he endeavoureth to beget pride, as was before noted, were,

[1.] First, *The consideration of privileges,* as being 'the Son of God.' For this expression, 'If thou art the Son of God,' is now urged in a sense different from that which it had in the first temptation. There he propounded it as unlikely that he should be the Son of God, and yet be under such a disregard of providence. In this sense it notably suited his design of drawing him to a distrust of God's care, and consequently of his sonship. Here he is upon a contrary temptation, and therefore propounds this as a thing of which Christ was assured, and from that assurance he thus disputes: 'Thou believest thou art the Son of God, and dost well depend on his care; therefore needest thou not to distrust thy preservation, if thou castest thyself down.'

[2.] Secondly, To help his confidence forward to the undertaking, he suggests *what credit and honour it would be to him, in the sight of all the people, to be so miraculously kept from hurt.* Hence note,

Obs. 11. *That Satan doth usually kindle and nourish pride, by a perverse confidence of our privileges.*

It is very hard for Christians to carry their assurance *even*: not but that grace in its proper working begets humility, and a watchful care against sin and folly; but such is our infirmity that we are easily drawn to be proud of our mercies, and to persuade ourselves that we may make bold with God because we are his children. Hence was that paradox of Mr Foxe, 'That his sins did him most good, and his graces most hurt;' he means, sins occasioned his humility, whereas his graces were apt, through his weakness, to make him proud. And to hide this pride from man, God is forced to keep them sometime from the sight of their assurance, or to discipline them by other temptations, as he did with Paul, lest they should be 'exalted above measure.'

Note further, *Obs.* 12. *That popular applause Satan finds, and useth accordingly, to be a great instigator to pride.*

The great thing that moved the Pharisees in their often fastings and large charity, was that they might have praise of men, and therefore took they care to be seen of men.426 The heathens noted this to be the great feeder of that humour which animated them, as a drum or trumpet animates soldiers to adventurous acts.427 And some good men have found no small difficulty to carry steadily, when they have been hoisted up by the breath of men's praise; which hath also occasioned those serious cautions against the danger of flattery and high commendations, 'A flattering mouth worketh ruin,' Prov. xxvi. 28.

CHAPTER XVII

The ways of Satan, hitherto insisted on, to engage Christ in this act of presumption, were secret insinuations and underhand contrivances: but that which he openly and expressly urged to this purpose, was an argument drawn from the promise of God, though sadly abused and misrepresented, 'He shall give his angels charge concerning thee,' &c. This we are next to consider, in which, as cited by him, we may easily see, (1.) That Satan affected an imitation of Christ, in the way of his resistance. Christ had urged Scripture before, and now Satan endeavours to manage the same weapon against him. (2.) It is observable that Scripture is the weapon that Satan doth desire to wield against him. In his other ways of dealing he was shy, and did but lay them in Christ's way, offering only the occasion, and leaving him to take them up; but in this he is more confident, and industriously pleads it, as a thing which he could better stand to and more confidently avouch. (3.) The care of his subtlety herein, lay in the misrepresentation and abuse of it, as may be seen in these particulars: [1.] In that he urged this promise to promote a sinful thing, contrary to the general end of all Scripture, which was therefore written 'that we sin not.' [2.] But more especially in his clipping and mutilating of it. He industriously leaves out that part of it which doth limit and confine the promise of protection to lawful undertakings, such as this was not, and renders it as a general promise of absolute safety, be the action what it will. It is a citation from Ps. xci. 11, 12, which there runs thus, 'He shall give his angels charge over thee, to keep thee in all thy ways.' These last words, 'in all thy ways,' which doth direct to a true understanding of God's intention in that promise, he deceitfully leaves out, as if they were needless and unnecessary parts of the promise, when indeed they were on purpose put there by the Spirit of God, to give a description of those persons and actions, unto whom, in such cases, the accomplishment of the promise might be expected; for albeit the word in the original, which is translated 'ways'— מיכרד —doth signify any kind of way or action in the general, yet in this place it doth not; for then God were engaged to an absolute protection of men, not only when they unnecessarily thrust themselves into dangers, but in the most abominably sinful actions whatsoever; which would have been a direct contradiction to those many scriptures wherein God threatens to withdraw his hand and leave sinners to the danger of their iniquities; but it is evident that the sense of it is no more than this, 'God is with you, while you are with him.' We have a paraphrase of this text, to this purpose, in Prov. iii. 23, 'Then shalt thou walk in thy way safely, and thy foot shall not stumble:' where the condition of this safety, pointed to in the word 'then,' which leads the promise, is expressly mentioned in the foregoing verses, 'My son, let them' — that is, the precepts of wisdom — 'not depart from thine eyes.... Then' — not upon other terms — 'shalt thou walk in thy way safely.' The ways then in this promise, cited by Satan, are the ways of duty, or the ways of our lawful callings. The fallacy of Satan in this dealing with Scripture is obvious, and Christ might have given this answer, as Bernard hath it, That God promiseth to keep him in his ways, but not in self-created dangers, for that was not his way, but his ruin; or if a way, it was Satan's way, but not his.428 (3.) To these two, some add another abuse, in a subtle concealment of the following verse in Ps. xci., 'Thou shalt tread upon the lion and adder.' This concerned Satan, whose cruelty and poisonous deceits were fitly represented by the lion and the adder, and there the promise is also explained to have a respect to Satan's temptations — that is, God would so manage his protection, that his children should not be led into a snare.

Hence observe, *Obs. 13. That Satan sometimes imitates the Spirit of God by an officious pretence of teaching the mind of God to men.*

This our adversary doth not always appear in one shape. Sometime he acts as a lion or dragon, in ways of cruelty and fierceness; sometimes as a filthy swine, in temptations to bestial uncleanness and sensual lusts; sometime he puts on the garb of holiness, and makes as if he were not a spiritual adversary, but a spiritual friend and counsellor. That this is frequent with him, the apostle tells us: 2 Cor. xi. 14, 'Satan himself is transformed into an angel of light.' Angels of light are those blessed spirits sent forth to minister for the good of the elect, whose ministry God useth not only for our preservation from bodily hurts, but also for prevention of sin and furtherance of duty. Satan, as wicked as he is, doth counterfeit that employment, and takes upon him to give advice for our good, pretending to teach us in the truth, or to direct and further us in our endeavours.429

That he designs an imitation of God and his Spirit, may be discovered by expressing a great many particulars of God's ways and appointments, wherein Satan, as God's ape, partly out of mockery and scorn, partly upon other grounds of advantage to his intendments, doth counterfeit the current coin of the Lord's establishments by a very close imitation. But I shall here confine myself to the point of teaching and instruction, wherein how he proceeds, we shall the better understand by considering how many ways God hath of old, and now still doth use in declaring his mind to his people. The sum of all we have, Heb. i. 12. Heretofore he signified his mind in 'divers manners' by the prophets, and 'in these last days by his Son,' in all which we shall trace the steps of Satan.

(1.) First, God revealed himself sometime by voice; as to Abraham, Moses, and others. The devil hath dared to imitate this. There want not instances of it; in the temptation, which is now under explanation, he did so; and his confessing Christ, 'I know thee who thou art,' [Mat. i. 24,] &c., doth shew that he is ready enough to do it at any time for advantage. Sprenger tells us a story of the devil's preaching to a congregation in the habit and likeness of a priest, wherein he reproved sin, and urged truth, and seemed no way culpable for false doctrine; but I suspect this for a fabulous tale. However, it is undeniable that he sometime hath appeared to men with godly exhortations in his mouth, of living justly, and doing no man wrong, &c.,430 except we resolve to discredit all history, and the narrations of persons, and some such are known to some in this auditory, who solemnly affirm they have met with such dealing from him.

(2.) Secondly, *God hath sometime revealed himself to men in ecstasies and trances*; such as was that of Paul: Acts xxii. 17, 'I was in an ecstasy or trance,' γενέσθαι με ἐν ἐκστάσει. This also hath the devil imitated. Mohammed made this advantage of his disease, the epilepsy or falling-sickness, pretending that at such times he was in an ecstasy, and had converse with the angel Gabriel. But what he only in knavery pretended, others have really felt. The stories of Familists and deluded Quakers are full of such things. They frequently have fallen down and have lain as in a swoon, and when they have awaked, told wonderful stories of what they have heard and seen.

(3.) Thirdly, *Visions and dreams were usual things in the Old Testament, and famous ways of divine revelation*; but Satan was not behind in this matter. His instruments had their visions too. In Ezek. xiii. 7 we have mention of vain visions and lying divinations; and such satanical dreams are also noted, Deut. xiii. 1, 'If there arise among you a dreamer of dreams.' Those days of confusion, that are not yet out of memory, afforded store of these. While unstable, giddy-headed people began to dote on novelties and questions in religion, they gave opportunity to Satan to beguile them; for he taking advantage of their nauseating of old truths, and their expectation of sublime discoveries, which had sufficiently prepared them for any impression, did so overwork their fancies that they easily conceived themselves to have had divine revelations, and nothing was more ordinary than to hear stories of visions and dreams. And this spread further by a kind of infection, for it grew into a religious fashion; and he was not esteemed that had not something of this nature to experience. And though the folly and impertinences of such things generally, and sometime the apparent wickedness of them, as contradicting truth and the divine rules of holiness, were sufficient discoveries that Satan's hand was in them, yet until time, experience, and the power of God had cooled the intemperate heat of this raving humour, it continued in the good liking and admiration of the more inconsiderate vulgar. And sometime those from whom more seriousness and consideration might have been expected fell into a reverence for these pretences in others, and helped forward this spiritual witchcraft by their countenance and arguings, often abusing that text in Acts ii. 17, 'Your young men shall see visions, and your old men shall dream dreams,' by applying it to a justification of these apparently foolish dotages. And indeed the effect hath discovered they were no better, for many of those things which with great confidence were avouched as certain, were by time proved to be false. Many things were useless, vain, ridiculous, and some were brought to lament and confess their folly after they proceeded far in these ways; and at last, when the former opportunities were worn out, Satan grew weary of that design as being no longer proper to be insisted on. There is now a great calm, so that it is but seldom that we hear of such things talked of. It were needless to give particular instances, when you may at your leisure fetch them from hundreds of pamphlets commonly known.

(4.) Fourthly, One of the most noted ways by which God discovered his mind was that of inspiration, by which some eminent persons, called therefore prophets, spake the will of God 'as they were moved or acted by the Spirit of God,' [2 Peter i. 21.] The devil had also his false prophets. Such are frequently taxed in the Old Testament, and foretold in the New: 'False Christs, and false prophets shall arise,' Mat. xxiv. 24; 'There were false prophets among the people, as there shall be false teachers among you,' 2 Peter ii. 1. Many false teachers are gone out into the world. Such a one was Montanus in Tertullian's time, David George, John of Leyden, Hacket, our countryman, were such, and a great many such there have been in all ages. It is notoriously known that Satan hath thus inspired poor, possessed wretches, who have uttered threatenings against sin and woe to sinners. The sayings of such possessed creatures have not long since been gathered into a volume and published, as containing very persuasive arguments to repentance and amendment of life.431 Besides these, our own times afford too many examples of this kind. Many have put on the guise of the old prophets in a foolish though adventurous imitation of their actions and prophecies. Some have in our streets resembled Jonah in Nineveh, 'Yet forty days,' &c. Some fancied to walk naked like Isaiah; others have come with their earthen pitchers and broken them, imitating these and other types by which God in his true prophets foresignified his judgments to come; in all which actions and garbs, with much earnestness, and in an affected tone, they have called out for repentance in a confident denunciation of woes and miseries, with a bold limiting of the time of forty days, that the same might carry a parallel to Jonah's prophecy, and sometime giving—which is the surest way—an unlimited, uncertain time. How the devil acts in these matters, and by what ways he seduceth them to believe they are inspired of God, or have real visions and revelations, it is not my business now to inquire; only let those that think such things strange, consider that the devil hath the advantage of deep fanciful apprehensions and a working melancholy in such persons, by which he can easily work them to conceit anything, and confidently believe what they have conceited.

(5.) Fifthly, Sometime God notified his mind *by signs and miracles*. Satan hath also his 'lying signs and wonders;' a power God hath permitted him this way, which is very great, and the delusions wrought thereby are strong, hazarding the deception of the elect. This power of doing wonders the devil usually applies to false doctrines, to strengthen and countenance errors. The apostle testifies, 2 Thes. ii. 9, that Satan shall employ this power for the advancement of the 'man of sin, whose coming shall be with signs and lying wonders.' The beast arising out of the earth, Rev. xiii. 14, 'he shall deceive by the means of those miracles which he hath power to do.' And accordingly the popish legends are full of stories of miracles, whereof, though most be lies, forgeries, and the false contrivements of those who sought to bring the people to receive their doctrines, the credit and advancement of which they sought by such ways; some notwithstanding, though not true miracles, yet were truly acted, to countenance those errors which are pretended to be established by them.

(6.) Sixthly, God doth teach and lead his people by impulses. Christ was thus 'led of the Spirit into the wilderness;' and Paul was 'bound in spirit to go to Jerusalem,' [Acts xx. 22.] It is common for Satan to imitate such impulses. We have clear instances of diabolical impulses to sin in Scripture. A strong impulse was on Ananias, 'Satan filled his heart,' [Acts v. 3;] a strong impulse on Judas, 'Satan entered into his heart,' [Luke xxii. 3;] and what then more easy to apprehend, than that Satan can counterfeit better impulses, and violently stir up the hearts of men to actions seemingly good or indifferent? Some hypocrites are moved strongly to pray or preach,— Satan therein aiming at an increase of pride or presumption in them;—and they know no other, but that it is the Spirit of God. God's children may have impulses from Satan, upon pretences of zeal, as the disciples had, when they called for fire from heaven. In these impulses Satan doth not so act the heart of man as the Spirit of God doth, whose commands in this case are irresistible; but he only works by altering the disposition of our bodies in a natural way; and then having fitted us all he can for an impression, he endeavours to set it on by strong persuasions. Some memorable instances of these impulses might profitably illustrate this. Math. Parisiensis takes notice of a boy, in anno 1213, of whom also Fuller makes mention,432 who, after some loss which the Christians had received in the war against the Turks, went up and down, singing this rhyme—

'Jesus Lord, redeem our loss:

Restore to us thy holy cross.'

And by this means he gathered a multitude of boys together, who could not by the severest menaces of their parents be hindered from following him to their own ruin. Another instance of a strange impulse we have in Josephus:433 one Jesus, the son of Ananus, about four years before the destruction of Jerusalem, at the feast of tabernacles, begins to cry out, 'Woe, woe, to the east and west, to men and women,' &c., and could by no means be restrained night or day; and when his flesh was beaten off his bones, he begged no pity nor ease, but still continued his usual crying.

(7.) Seventhly, God doth also by his Spirit teach his people in *bringing things to their remembrance*, John xiv. 26. Satan also in imitation of this, can put into the minds of men, with great readiness and dexterity, promises or sentences of Scripture, insomuch that they conclude that all such actings are from the Spirit of God, who, as they conclude, set such a scripture upon their heart. Thus dealt Satan with Christ. He urgeth the promise upon him, wherein upon the matter he doth as much, as when he secretly suggests such things to the heart without an audible voice. In this way of craft Satan doth very much resemble the true work of the Spirit; [1.] In the readiness and quickness of suggesting; [2.] In seeming exact-suiting scripture suggested, with the present occasion; and [3.] In the earnestness of his urging it upon the fancies of men. Yet when all this is done, they that shall seriously consider all ends, matter and circumstances, will easily observe it is but the cunning work of a tempter, and not from the Holy Spirit.

Obs. 14. Observe also, *That whatever be the various ways of Satan's imitation, yet the matter which he works and practiseth upon is still Scripture.* To this he confines himself:—

[1.] First, *Because the Scriptures are generally, among Christians, received as the undoubted oracles of God, the rule of our lives and duties, and the grounds of our hope.* It would be a vain and bootless labour to impose upon those that retain this belief, the sayings of the Turkish Alcoran, the precepts of heathen philosophers, or any other thing that may carry a visible estrangement from or contradiction to Scripture. He could not then possibly pretend to a divine instruction, nor could he so 'transform himself into an angel of light:' but by using this covert of divine command, promise, or discovery, he can more easily beget a belief that God hath said it, and that there is neither sin nor danger in the thing propounded, but duty and advantage to be expected; and this is the very thing that makes way for an easy entertainment of such delusions. Poor creatures believe that is all from God, and that they are acted by his Spirit, and that with such confidence that they contemn and descry those, as ignorant of divine mysteries, and of the power of God, who are not so besotted as themselves.

[2.] Secondly, *The Scriptures have a glorious irresistible majesty in them, peculiar to themselves, which cannot be found in all that art or eloquence can contribute to other authors.* It is not play-book language, nor scraps of romances that Satan can effect these cheats withal; and therefore we may observe that in the highest delusions men have had pretences of Scripture; and their strong persuasions of extraordinary discoveries have stricken men into a reverence of their profession, because of the Scripture words and phrases with which their boldest follies are woven up. For let but men inquire into the reason of the prevalency of Familism of old, upon so vast a number of people as were carried away with it, and they shall find that the great artifice lay in the words they used, a language abstracted from Scripture, to signify such conceits as the Scripture never intended. Hence were their expressions always high, soaring, and relating to a more excellent and mystical interpretation of those divine writings. This may be observed in David George, Hen. Nicholas, and others, who usually talk of being consubstantiated with God, taken up into his love, of the angelical life, and a great deal more of the same kind. The Ranters at first had the like language, and the Quakers after them affected such a canting expression. And we may be the more certain of the truth of this observation, that such a kind of speaking, which borrows its majesty from the style of the Scripture, is of moment to Satan's design; because we find the Scripture itself gives particular notice of it. The false teachers in 2 Pet. ii. 18, are described, among other things, by their 'swelling words of vanity,' which the Syriac renders to be 'a proud and lofty way of speaking.' The original signifies no less — ὑπέρογκα, — they were words swelled like bladders, though being pricked, they be found to be empty sounds, and no substance. There are indeed swelling words of atheistical contempt of those who, as the psalmist speaks, 'set their mouths against heaven,' Ps. lxxiii. 9, 11; but this passage of Peter, as also the like in Jude 16, signify big swollen words, from high pretensions and fancies of knowing the mind of God more perfectly; for they that use them pretend themselves prophets of God, ver. 1, and as to their height in profession, are compared to clouds highly soaring; and in 2 Cor. xi. 14, they are said to be 'transformed into the apostles of Christ,' and to the garb of the ministers of righteousness.' And that which is more, this particular design of Satan is noted as the rise of all; 'No marvel, for Satan himself is transformed into an angel of light.'

Having seen the reasons why Satan chooseth Scripture as his tool to work by, I shall next shew to what base designs he makes it subserve.

[1.] First, He useth this artifice *to beget and propagate erroneous doctrines*. Hence no opinion is so vile, but pretends to Scripture as its patron. The Arians pretend Scripture against the divinity of Christ. The Socinians, Pelagians, Papists, yea, and those that pretend to inspirations for their rule, and disclaim the binding force of those antiquated declarations of the saints' conditions, as they call them, yet conform all their sayings to the Scripture expression, and endeavour to prove their mistakes by its authority.

[2.] Secondly, *He makes abused Scripture to encourage sinful actions.* He can cite passages of God's patience and long-suffering, of his pardoning grace and readiness to forgive, and a thousand more, upon no other design than the 'turning of the grace of God into wantonness,' [Jude 4.] When professors turn loose and negligent, when they adventure too far upon sinful pleasures, they lick themselves whole by an overforward grasping at such passages of Scripture, which Satan will with great readiness set upon their hearts; and then they pretend to themselves that their peace is made up with God, and that they have no less than a sealed pardon in their bosoms; which notwithstanding may be known to have only Satan's hand and seal at it, by their overly and formal sorrow for such miscarriages, and their readiness to return to the same follies again.

[3.] Thirdly, By this imitation of the commands and promises of God, he doth strangely engage such as he can thus delude unto desperate undertakings.434 The Familists of Germany were persuaded by this delusion, to expose themselves unarmed to the greatest hazards, upon vain pretences of promises set home upon them, as that God would fight for them, that they must 'stand still and see the salvation of God,' [Exod. xiv. 13.] Some of later times have paid their lives for their bold misapplication of that promise, 'One shall chase a thousand,' [Deut. xxxii. 30.] Judas of Galilee and Theudas were prompted by Satan to gather multitudes together, though to their own ruin, upon a vain persuasion that they were raised up of God, and that God would be with them.435

[4.] Fourthly, He sometimes *procures groundless peace and assurance in the hearts of careless ones by Scripture misapplied.* Many you may meet with who will roundly tell you a long story how they were cast down and comforted by such a scripture brought to their minds, when, it may be much feared, they are but deceived, and that as yet God hath not spoken peace to them.

Lastly, This way of Satan's setting home scriptures proves sadly effectual to beget or heighten *the inward distresses and fears of the children of God.* It is a wonder to hear some dispute against themselves, so nimble they be to object a scripture against their peace, above their reading or ability, that you would easily conclude there is one at hand that prompts them, and suggests these things to their own prejudice. And sometime a scripture will be set so cross or edgeway to their good and comfort, that many pleadings, much time, prayers, and discourses cannot remove it. I have known some that have seriously professed scriptures have been thrown into their hearts like arrows, and have with such violence fixed a false apprehension upon their minds, as that God had cut them off, that they were reprobate, damned, &c., that they have borne the tedious, restless affrightments of it for many days, and yet the thing itself, as well as the issue of it, doth declare that this was not the fruit of the Spirit of God, which is a spirit of truth, and cannot suggest a falsehood, but of Satan, who hath been a liar from the beginning.

Observe lastly, *Obs.* 15. *Though Satan useth Scripture in these deceitful workings, yet he never doth it faithfully.*

(1.) First, Because it is against his nature, as it is now corrupted by his fall. There is no truth in him: 'When he speaketh a lie he speaketh of his own, for he is a liar,' John viii. 44; not that he cannot speak a truth, but that he usually is a liar, and that he never speaks truth but with a purpose to deceive.436

(2.) Secondly, *To deal faithfully in urging scriptures upon the consciences of men, is also contrary to his interest.* He hath a kingdom which he endeavours to uphold. This kingdom, being directly contrary to that of Christ's, which is a kingdom of light, is therefore called a kingdom of darkness, being maintained and propagated only by lies and deceits. He cannot then be supposed to use Scripture faithfully, because that is the true sceptre of Christ's kingdom, for then should Satan, as Christ argues, Mat. xii. 26, 'cast out Satan, and be divided against himself.'

This unfaithful dealing with Scripture is threefold.

(1.) First, The unfaithfulness of his *design*. Though he speaks what is true, yet he doth it with an evil mind, aiming at one of these three things: —

[1.] First, *To deceive and delude.* If he applies promises, or insists upon the privileges of God's children, it is to make them proud or presumptuous. If he urge threatenings, or stir up the conscience to accuse for sin, it is to bring them to despair; if he object the law, it is to enrage lust; and that 'sin by the commandment might become exceeding sinful,' [Rom. vii. 13.]

[2.] Secondly, His design is sometime to bring the Scripture under suspicion or contempt. He puts some weak Christians upon unseasonable or imprudent use of Scripture, and then tempts others to laugh at them, and to despise in their hearts those ways of religion which some zealots with too much weakness do manage. Men are apt enough to scoff at the most serious and weighty duties of holiness, even when performed in a most serious manner. If David put on sackcloth, and afflict himself with fasting, it is presently turned to his reproach, 'and the drunkards make a song of it,' [Ps. lxix. 12;] but much more advantage hath the devil to raise up scorn and loathing in the minds of debauched persons, by the affected and unskilful use of Scripture. Some by a narrow confinement of the words brother and sister to those of their own fellowship, as if none else were to be owned by them, have occasioned the scoff of holy brethren—a phrase notwithstanding used with a grave seriousness by the apostle—in the usual discourses of those who wait all occasions to harden themselves against the power of religion. The like observations they make of other ways and forms of speaking, which some have accustomed themselves unto, in a conscientious conformity to Scripture phrase: in all which the devil observing the weakness and injudiciousness of some on the one hand, and the scornful pride of others on the other hand, is willing to provide matter for their atheistical jeers, by putting all the obligations he can upon the consciences of the weak, to continue in the use of these expressions. For some proof of this matter we may note the secret deceit of Satan, in that liberal profession of Christ to be 'the Son of God,' [Mark i. 24; Luke iv. 34], 'I know thee who thou art; the Holy One of God.' Here was truth spoken by him, and one would have thought with great ingenuity;437 but yet he cunningly insinuated into the minds of the hearers a ground of suspicion that he was not the Son of God; and for that end calls him Jesus of Nazareth, as if Christ had been born there. He knew well that the Jews expected no Messiah from Nazareth, and therefore on set purpose used he that expression, that he might draw him into contempt. And accordingly we find this very mistake, that Christ was born at Nazareth, became an argument against him: John vii. 41, while some were convinced, and said, 'This is the Christ,' others said, 'Shall Christ come out of Galilee?'

[3.] Thirdly, Another part of his design in the use of scriptures is to *put a varnish upon hypocrisy*. He is ready to serve men by putting Scripture expressions in their mouths, and inuring them to a constant use of the phrases of those divine writings, that they may less suspect themselves of the pride, formality, and secret wickedness of their hearts; and to help on their mistakes concerning their spiritual condition, he can urge upon their consciences those scriptures that serve to engage them in external observances of religion. It may appear by the Pharisee's boast of fasting 'twice a week,' of 'paying tithes,' of 'giving alms,' Luke xviii. 11, that their consciences were someway concerned in these things, so that though they were left without check of conscience 'to devour widows' houses,' yet were they urged to make 'long prayers.' Suitable to this is that which Solomon speaks of the harlot, who, to colour over her wickedness, had her offerings and vows; and when her conscience is appeased with these performances, she can excuse herself in her way of sinning, 'She eats and wipes her mouth, and saith, I have done no wickedness,' Prov. xxx. 20. Satan doth but hereby help to paint a sepulchre, or gild a potsherd, and to furnish men with excuses and pretexts in their way of sinning. Not unlike to this was that service which the devil with great readiness performed—as I was informed from some of good credit—to a young student who had fallen upon some books of magic in a college library, into which having stolen privately one night in pursuit of that study, was almost surprised by the president, who, seeing a candle there at an unseasonable time, suddenly opens the door to know who was up so late, in which strait the devil—to gratify his pupil with a ready excuse—snatcheth away his book, and in a moment lays Montanus his Bible before him, that he might pretend that for his employment.

(2.) Secondly, Another point of Satan's unfaithful dealing with Scripture is *his false citation of it*. It is nothing with him to alter, change, or leave out such a part as may make against him. If he urge promises upon men, in order to their security and negligence, he conceals the condition of them, and banisheth the threatening far from their minds, representing the mercy of God in a false glass, as if he had promised to save and bring to heaven every man upon the common and easy terms of being called a Christian. If it be his purpose to disquiet the hearts of God's children, to promote their fears, or to lead them to despair, then he sets home the commands and threatenings, but hides the promises that might relieve them, and, which is remarkable, he hath so puzzled some by setting on their hearts a piece of Scripture, that when the next words, or next verse, might have eased them of their fears, and answered the sad objections which they raised against themselves from thence, as if their eyes had been holden, or as if a mist had been cast over them, they have not for a long time been able to consider the relief which they might have had. This hiding of Scripture from their eyes, setting aside what God may do for the just chastisement of his children's folly, is effected by the strong impression which Satan sets upon their hearts, and by holding their minds down to a fixed meditation of the dreadful inferences which he presents to them from thence, not suffering them to divert their thoughts by his incessant clamours against them.

(3.) Thirdly, He unfaithfully handleth scriptures, *by wresting the true import and sense of them*. We read of some, 2 Pet. iii. 16, who 'wrest the Scripture.' The word in the original—στρεβλοῦσι—signifies a racking or torturing of it, as men upon a rack are stretched beyond their due length, to a dislocation of their joints, and sometimes forced to speak what they never did nor intended; so are the Scriptures used. Those that do so are Satan's scholars, and taught of him, though in regard of the Spirit's true teaching, they are called unlearned, which is sufficient to shew Satan's deceitful dealing. He often lays his dead and corrupt sense—as the harlot did with her dead child in the room of the living infant—in the place of the living meaning of the scripture. This may be seen evidently:—

[1.] First, *In heresies or errors*. These are Satan's brood, and there are none so vile, that pretend to Christian religion, but they claim a kindred to Scripture, and are confident on its authority for them. Now seeing truth is but one, and these errors not only contradictory to truth, but to each other, Satan could never spin out such conclusions from the divine oracles, but by wresting them from their true intendments; and he that would contemplate the great subtlety of Satan in this his art, need but consider what different strange and monstrous shapes are put upon the Scripture by the several heresies which march under its colours. The Quakers in their way represent it like an old almanack out of date, and withal, in the use they make of it, they render it as a piece of nonsensical furious raving. The Socinians take down the sublime mysteries of Christ's satisfaction and justification by faith, with external rewards and punishments, to a strain as low as the Turkish Alcoran. The papists make it like a few leaves of an imperfect book, wanting beginning and end, and so not fit to be set up as a sufficient rule. The Ranters make it seem rather like language from hell than the commands of the pure and holy God. Some will have it to countenance most ridiculous inventions in worship; others will have it to discharge all outward observations and ordinances, as childish rudiments. Some raise it all to the pitch of enigmatical unintelligible mysteries; others can find no more in the precepts of it than in Aristotle's ethics. Thus by distorting and wresting, Satan hath learned these unskilful ones to make it serve their vilest lusts and humours.

[2.] Secondly, The same art of wresting Scripture is observable in his *secret suggestions*. If he would encourage any in sin, he can wrest Scripture for that, and tell him that God is merciful, that Christ died for sinners, that there is hope of pardon, that saints have done the like: things very true in themselves, but perverted by him to another sense than ever they were intended to by God, who hath spoken these things that we sin not. If he would discourage a saint, he can tell him when he finds him doubting his estate, that the 'fearful and unbelieving have their part in the lake which burns with fire and brimstone,' Rev. xxi. 8; when he finds him under a known sin, he tells that of the apostle, 'If we sin wilfully after we have received the knowledge of the truth, there remains no more sacrifice for sins,' [Heb. x. 26.] When he observes them discomposed and wandering in duty, then he objects, 'They draw nigh me with their lips, but their heart is far from me,' [Isa. xxix. 13.] If he sees them dull and without consolation at the Lord's supper, then to be sure they hear of him, 'He that eats and drinks unworthily, eateth and drinketh damnation to himself,' 1 Cor. xi. 29. If he find him bemoaning that he is not so apprehensive of mercies or judgments as he would be, then he sets home some such scripture as this, 'This people's heart is waxed gross, and their ears are dull of hearing,' Mat. xiii. 15, &c. These scriptures are frequently perverted by Satan from the true and proper meaning of them. I have had complaints from several dejected Christians of these very scriptures urged upon them to their great trouble, when yet it was evident that none of these were truly applied, by Satan's temptation against them.

Applic. These things give us warning not *to take anything of this nature upon trust.* If Satan can so imitate the Spirit of God in applications of Scripture, and bringing it to our remembrance, we have great reason to beware lest we be imposed upon by Satan's design clothed in Scripture phrase; not that I would have men esteem the secret setting of Scripture upon their minds, to be in all cases a delusion, and to be disregarded as such. Some indeed there are that so severely remark the weaknesses of professors of religion, that they raise up a scorn to that which is of most necessary and serious use. Because the devil prevails with some hypocrites to gild themselves with Scripture phrase, and others through imprudent inadvertency are, unknown to themselves, beguiled by Satan, to misapplications of Scripture to their own estate, or to other things; they therefore decry all the inward workings of the heart, as fancy or affected singularity; these do but the devil's work. But that the Spirit of God, whom Satan treacherously endeavours to imitate, doth set home Scripture commands, threatenings, and promises upon the hearts of his people, is not only attested by the experience of all that are inwardly acquainted with the ways of God, but is one of the great promises which Christ hath given for the comfort of his people in his absence: John xiv. 26, 'But the Comforter, which is the Holy Ghost, whom the Father shall send in my name, he shall teach you all things, and bring all things to your remembrance, whatsoever I have said unto you.' This then being granted as a firm unshaken truth, our care must be in discovering and avoiding Satan's counterfeit using of Scripture, and in this we should be more wary;

[1.] First, *Because we are not so apt to suspect what we meet with in such a way, when it is brought to us in the language of Scripture.*

[2.] Secondly, *And those that are not exercised in the Scripture, will be at a sad loss, as not knowing how to extricate themselves from such difficulties as may arise to them from Satan's sophistry.*

[3.] Thirdly, Wariness is also more necessary, *because we are inclinable to believe what suits our desires, and conscience awakened is averse to the rejecting of that which answers its fears.*

Quest. You may say, What is there of direction for us in this case?

Ans. The answer is ready. Two things are given us in charge. (1.) That we be wisely suspicious. A facile hasty credulity is treacherous. Christ forbids, when he foretells the rising of false Christs, Mat. xxiv. 26, the forwardness of a sudden belief, taxing thereby those that are presently taken with every new appearance. It is childish to be carried with every wind. We are warned also of this: 1 John iv. 1, 'Believe not every spirit.' (2.) We are commanded to bring all pretences whatsoever to trial. Though immediate revelation or vision be pretended, or extraordinary commission, yet must all be brought to the touchstone. 'We must prove all things,' 1 Thes. v. 21, 'and try those that say they are apostles,' Rev. ii. 2; nay, 'the spirits are to be tried whether they be of God,' 1 John iv. 1.

Quest. You will say, How must we try?

Ans. I answer, God hath given a public, sufficient, and certain rule, which is *the Scripture, and all must be tried by that;* so that if there be impulses or discoveries or remembrances of Scripture upon any, it must not be taken for granted that they are of God, because they pretend so high, for so we shall make Satan judge in his own cause; but lay all to the line and plummet of the written word, and if it answer not that, call it confidently a delusion, and reject it as accursed, though it might seem in other regards to have been suggested by an angel from heaven.

Obj. But it will be said, Satan pretends to this rule, and it is Scripture that is urged by him.

Ans. I answer, Though it be so, yet he useth not Scripture in its own intendment and sense. For the discovery of his unfaithful dealing;—

[1.] First, Compare the inference of the suggestion with other scriptures. If it be from a dark scripture, compare it with those that are more plain, and in every case see whether the general current of the Scriptures speak the same thing; for if it be from Satan, he either plays with the words and phrases, from doubtful and equivalent terms making his conclusion, or his citation will be found impertinent, or, which is most usual, contrary to truth or holiness. If any of these appear by a true examination of the import of the scripture which he seeks to abuse, or by comparing it with the scope and genius of other scriptures, you may certainly pronounce that it is not of God, but Satan's deceit.438

[2.] Secondly, *Consider the tendency of such suggestions.* Let no man say that this will come too late, or that it is an after-game. I do not mean that we should stay so long as to see the effects, though this is also a certain discovery of Satan's knavery in his highest pretences. The fanatic furies of the German enthusiasts do now appear plain to all the world to have been delusions, by their end, fruits, and issue. But that while these conclusions are obtruded upon us, we should observe to what they tend, which we shall the better know if all circumstances round about be considered. Sometimes Satan doth covertly hint his mind, and send it along with the suggestions; sometimes our condition will enough declare it, and there is no case but it will afford something of discovery if seriously pondered. If he either prompt us to pride, vainglory, or presumption, or that our condition sway us that way, it will be sufficient ground of suspicion that it is Satan that then urgeth promises or privileges upon us. If we are of a wounded spirit, inclined to distrust, or if we be put on to despair, it is past denial that it is Satan that urgeth the threatenings, and presseth the accusations of the law against us. He that gathers stones, timber, lime, and such materials together, as are usually employed in building, doth discover his intention before he actually build his house, and thus may Satan's end be known by his preparations, compared with the sway and inclination of our present temper.

[3.] Thirdly, *It must be remembered that with these endeavours, we often seek the face of the Lord for help and counsel;* and that we apply ourselves to such of the servants of God, as being more knowing than ourselves, and less prepossessed in their judgments, because not concerned, are better able to see into the nature of our straits, and to help us by their advices.

CHAPTER XVIII

Again the devil taketh him up into an exceeding high mountain, and sheweth him all the kingdoms of the world, and the glory of them. —Mat. iv. 8.

This is the preparation to the third temptation; in which we have, (1.) The place where it was acted; (2.) The object set before him there.

1. First, The place was an 'exceeding high mountain.' What mountain it was, Nebo, Pisgah, or any other, it is needless to inquire. It is of more use to ask after the reasons of Satan's choice of such a place. The text doth clearly imply one; that was the commodiousness of prospect. Satan intending to give him a view of the kingdoms of the world, chooseth a mountain as fittest for that end. But that this was not all the reason, is not only intimated by some,439 but positively affirmed by others,440 who think that Satan in this imitated the like in God to Moses, who was called up to Mount Nebo to view the land which God promised to Israel. Whether these circumstances of the mountain, and the view of the kingdoms of the world, were of purpose contrived to affront God by such an imitation, I will not be positive in it; but we may with greater evidence affirm that in offering the kingdoms of the world as things altogether in his disposal, he doth directly outbrave God by an insolent comparison of his power with that of the Almighty's, whose is 'the earth and the fulness of it,' [Ps. xxiv. 1,] and to whom the sovereignty of the disposal of it doth belong.

2. Secondly, That which Satan sheweth Christ from the mountain is said to be 'the kingdoms of the world, and the glory of them.' Here some busy themselves to conjecture what kingdoms were thus pointed at. Some keep so strictly to the word 'all,' that they are forced to take up with that opinion, that all these temptations were only in vision,441 for they consider that no one mountain in the world can give a prospect over one whole hemisphere, or if it could, yet no eye would be able to discern at so great a distance. But the inconveniences of this surmise have been pointed at before, and it is enough to shew that the text may admit of an interpretation which shall not be encumbered with this supposed impossibility.

Others restrain this to the land of Canaan, as if Satan only shewed this as a famous instance of the glory of all kingdoms. Some think the Roman empire, which was then most flourishing, and lifted up its head above other kingdoms, was the great bait laid before Christ, as if he had a design to divert Christ from the business of his office, by offering him the seat and power of Antichrist.442 But the text runs not so favourably for any of these opinions as to constrain us to stay upon them. 'Kingdoms of the world' seem to intend more than Canaan or the Roman empire; the word κόσμος used here, and οἰκουμένη in Luke, which we translate 'the world,' do so apply to one another in a mutual accommodation, that we cannot stretch the 'world' to the largest sense of the whole globe of the earth, because it is expressed in Luke by οἰκουμένη, which signifies such a part of the world which is more cultivated and honoured by inhabitants; nor can we so restrain it to the Roman empire-though when they spake their apprehensions of their own empire, they seem to engross all, Luke ii. 1—because Matthew useth the word κόσμος, a word of greater freedom. It seems then that many kingdoms, or the most considerable kingdoms of the then known world, were here exposed to his sight. But then the difficulty still remains, how the devil could shew them to his eye. That it was not a visionary discovery to his mind, hath been said. Some think he shewed these partly by ocular prospect of those cities, castles, towns, vineyards, and fields that were near, as a compend of the whole, and partly by a discourse of the glory, power, and extent of other kingdoms that were out of the reach of the eye; but because the expression which Luke adds, 'in a moment of time'—ἐν στυγμῇ χρόνου—intimates, that the way which Satan took was different from common prospecting or beholding, others are not satisfied with that solution of the difficulty, but fly to this supposition, that Satan used only juggling and delusion, by framing an airy horizon before the eyes of Christ, shewing not the kingdoms themselves, but a phantasm of his own making. But seeing this might have been done in any place, and that a high mountain was chosen for furthering the prospect, I think it is safest to conclude that the prospect was ocular, and not fantastical but real, only helped and assisted by Satan's skill and art, as a great naturalist and as a prince of the power of the air, by which means, in reflections or extraordinary prospectives, he might discover things at vast distances; which we may the rather fix upon, because we know what helps for prospect art hath discovered by glasses and telescopes, by which the bodies of the sun, moon, and planets, at such unspeakable distance from us, have in this latter age been discovered to us beyond ordinary belief.443 And we have reason to think that Satan's skill this way far exceeds anything that we have come to the knowledge of, and so might make real discoveries of countries far remote, more than we can well imagine.

These things thus explained, I shall note several observations.

Obs. 1. First, If we consider this great preparation that Satan makes as introductory to the temptation to follow, we may observe, *that where*

Satan hath a special design, he projects and makes ready all things relating to the temptation before he plainly utter his mind. He provides his materials before he builds, and lays his train before he gives fire. What is his method we may learn from the practice of those that are trained up in his service. They, in Rom. xiii. 14, are said to 'make provision for the flesh' — πρόνοια — to fore-contrive their sins, and to project all circumstances of time, place, occasion, and advantage for their accomplishment. This is not to be understood of all sins, for in some that are inward in the mind, as vain thoughts, pride of heart, &c., there needs not such provisions. We may say of them their times are always, and in many cases 'the house is swept and garnished' [Mat. xii. 44] to his hand; he finds all things ready by the forwardness of those who are free in his service, and the sudden accidental concurrence of things. But where the temptation is solemn, and where the thing designed, in the perfecting of it, relates to exterior acts, there he useth this policy, to have all in readiness, though it cost him the labour of 'compassing sea and land' for it, before he expressly speak his purposes. His reasons are these: —

(1.) First, If things necessary for the encouragement and accomplishment of a temptation *lay out of the way, and were not at hand, his suggestions would perish as soon as they were born, and would be rejected as impossible or inconvenient.* To tempt a man to steal when he knows not where nor how, or to revenge when he hath no enemy nor provocation, seem to be no other than if they should be commanded to remove a mountain or to fly in the air, which would quickly be declined as motions affording no ground of entertainment. And therefore that his temptations may not bring a reason of refusal with them as being unseasonable, he takes care to fit his servants with all things requisite for the work he puts them upon.

(2.) Secondly, As temptations of this kind would be no temptations, because not feasible, *without their preparations, so must we not think that it is the bare suggestion of Satan that makes a temptation to pierce.* The reason of its prevalency is not barely because Satan breaks such a motion to us, but because such a motion comes accomplished with all suitable preparations. When it prevails, it is the sinful motion that wounds; but preparations are as the feathers that wing his arrows, without which they would neither fly nor pierce.

Applic. Let this, (1.) First, *Renew our caution and suspicion in everything and every place that Satan is at work against us, though we see no visible snare.*

Let it put us upon such a watchful carefulness in every of our ways, that we may resolve to undertake nothing for which we have not a good and warrantable reason at hand, that if our conscience say to us, What dost thou here? we may be able to give a good account.

(2.) Secondly, If we mind the behaviour of Satan in these preparations and offers, *we see him act after the pattern of highest sovereignty, disposing of earthly kingdoms at such a rate as if all power were in his hand.* Hence we may observe,

Obs. 2. That when Satan tempts to sin of highest contempt and insolency against God, he then thinks it concerns him to bear himself out by confronting the Almighty in imitating his authority and power.

This carriage of Satan is not to be found in all his temptations. For in most cases he acts with greatest secrecy; and as a thief that is afraid of discovery, he useth all ways possible for concealment; but when he sets up himself as 'the god of the world,' and stands in competition with the Lord, claiming an interest in the fear and devotion of men, then he boldly avoucheth himself, and labours to outvie God in point of greatness, that he might possess them with a belief that he only ought to be feared. This arrogancy of Satan against God may be seen in three things: —

[1.] First, In imitating divine ordinances and institutions. There is not any part of divine worship, the observation whereof God hath enjoined to men, but Satan hath set up something like it for himself. As God appointed his temple, priests, altars, sacrifices, offerings, tithes, sanctuaries, sacraments, &c., so hath Satan had his temples, priests, altars, sacrifices, offerings, sanctuaries, sacraments, &c. This is sufficiently known to any that read his histories; and I could give a full account of it from heathen authors, but that I have done already when I spoke of Satan's subtlety in promoting idolatry in the world. I shall only add here that which Varro relates444 of the books of Numa Pompilius, which were casually cast up by the plough of one Terentius coming too near the sepulchre of Numa, where these books had been buried. This Numa was the second king of the Romans, who instituted the rites and ceremonies of pagan worship for his subjects, and in these books, which he thought fit to conceal by burying them with him, he had laid open the bottom of these devilish mysteries, so that when they were brought to the senate, they, judging them unfit to be known, adjudged them to the fire; which is a clear ground of suspicion that he had there discovered so much of the causes of these rites, or of the way whereby he came to be instructed in them, that the public knowledge thereof consisted not with the interest of their heathenish religion. This conjecture Austin hath of the matter,445 who also notes that Numa pretended familiar converse with the nymph Ægeria as a plausible cover to that devilish art of Hydromantia, by which he was instructed in ordering the ceremonies of idolatry which he established.

[2.] Secondly, Satan, with no less arrogancy, takes upon him to imitate God in his acts of power for the countenancing of his worship in the world. He had his miracles frequently, of which I have spoken elsewhere; so had he his oracles, as at Delphos and other places. Here it shall suffice to note that, as the sending the Lord Jesus into the world, furnished with such power of doing miracles for the confirmation of that office and authority which he had received from God for the redemption of man, was the highest instance that can be given of the mighty power, wisdom, and goodness of God; so Satan set himself with greatest industry to imitate that. Christ was almost no sooner ascended to the Father, but we hear of Simon Magus, Acts viii. 9, who was cried up as an instance of 'the great power of God;' and after that at Rome he gave out that he was God, confirming the people in such a belief, by the strange things which he there did among them, that a statue was erected for his honour, with this inscription, 'To Simon, a great god.'446 Long after this the devil raised up Apollonius Tyanæus, a man of an abstemious and commendable life. Him the devil did design to match Christ in his miracles, which were so many and so strange, that Philostratus doth not only compare him to Christ, but prefer him as the more honourable person. Christ himself foretold this stratagem of Satan, that he should raise up 'false Christs' with 'lying signs and wonders.' And to omit instances of former days, it is not beyond the memory of most of you, that the devil renewed this policy in James Nayler, who, in a blasphemous imitation of Christ's riding to Jerusalem, rode to Bristol with a great company before him, crying, 'Holy, holy,' and 'Hosanna to the son of David,' and strewing the way with branches of trees. The authority that was then, taking notice of this and other blasphemous outrages, sentenced him to exemplary punishment; but here also the devil renewed his mockery, for a certain citizen of London of good note, being overcome with delusion, printed a book of Nayler's sufferings, wherein the devil had opportunity to vent his malice more fully, for he compared all the parts of his punishment to the sufferings of Christ; his whipping, he said, was that it might be fulfilled which was spoken by Matthew, 'And Pilate delivered him to be scourged;' his stigmatizing, he said, was that it might be fulfilled which was spoken by the prophet, 'His visage was marred more than any man's;' the boring of his tongue with a hot iron, he said, was the fulfilling of that, and they 'crucified him;' and after other particulars of comparison, in all which he equalled him to Christ, he at last takes notice that the multitude of spectators held off their hats while his tongue was bored through, a thing common in a crowd to give opportunity of sight to those that are behind, and to this act he applies that of the evangelists, 'The vail of the temple was rent from the top to the bottom.'

[3.] Thirdly, *In acts of empire and sovereignty he imitates God*, that is, as God propounds himself as the only Lord God, and enjoins himself to be worshipped accordingly by promises of advantage in case of obedience, and threatenings of miseries and plagues in case of disobedience; so doth Satan set up himself in the world as god to be adored and worshipped, and him do all idolaters worship, as God testifies: Deut. xxxii. 17, 'They sacrificed unto devils, not to God:' Ps. cvi. 37, 'They sacrificed their sons and daughters unto devils:' 1 Cor. x. 20, 'The things which the Gentiles sacrifice, they sacrifice to devils, and not to God.' And though it be true that many of these blind worshippers did not formally worship the devil, but thought they had worshipped God, yet by such cunning did he engage them to take up with ways of worship of his prescribing, that it was in reality a service done to him. But, besides this, in those places of the world where he hath greater power, he formally propounds himself to be worshipped, and doth accordingly often appear to them in a visible shape; so that many of these blind heathens acknowledge two gods, one good and another cruel and hurtful, which latter they say they must worship, lest he destroy or harm them. By this Satan contests with God for an empire in the world; and to promote it the more he sometimes deals by fair promises of riches, advancement, pleasure, and such other baits, to allure men to his professed service. Thus are witches drawn to a compact with him. Thus Sylvester the Second gave up himself to the devil for the popedom, and so did several others. When this is not enough to prevail, he adds menacings, and breathes forth cruel threatenings, by which means many heathens are kept in awe by him and worship him, *ne noceat*, for no other reason but to preserve themselves from hurt by him. In this temptation he propounds himself to Christ as the object of divine worship, and boasts of the kingdoms of the world as things of his disposal; by which he seeks to draw him to fall down before him.

This course Satan takes for these reasons: —

First, *As this proud and malicious ostentation of his power is some kind of satisfaction to his revengeful humour against God*; so, Secondly, *He doth hereby raise up himself and his wicked institutions of idolatry into credit and esteem with men.* Thirdly, *As this is a mockery to true religion, and a scorn cast upon the ways of God's service, to bring it into disgrace and discredit*; so, Fourthly, *By this means he hardens the hearts of men against God.* This was the consideration by which Pharaoh hardened his heart. When Moses turned his rod into a serpent, changed waters to blood, and did so many signs before him, his magicians did the like; upon which the king might thus reason with himself, that Moses had no other power but what his magicians had, though he might think him a more skilful magician; and therefore there was no reason to believe his message as being from God, seeing his miracles might be no other than the effect of his art to countenance a pretended command from heaven.

Applic. This insolency of Satan may inform us, First, *Of the great patience of God*, that sees these outrageous mockings, and yet doth not by a strong hand put a stop to them. Secondly, *Of the great power and pride of Satan*, that he both can—though not without permission from God—and dare attempt things of this nature. Thirdly, *The great power of delusion*, that can so blind men, that they not only are drawn to act a part in such designs, but believe confidently a divine impulse and heavenly warrant for their so doing. Fourthly, *The miserable slavery of such vassals of Satan* that are thus led by him, who are therefore sadly to be pitied and lamented, as being under such strong chains of captivity.

Obs. 3. Thirdly, *We cannot pass by the art which the devil here useth to set off the temptation, and to make it plausible.* He sets before him the world in all its glory. Here observe, *That Satan, in his temptations to worldly pleasures, doth usually paint the object with all its utmost beauty.*

When I have sometime observed a mountebank upon a stage, giving excessive commendations of a trivial medicine, asserting it good almost for every disease, and with a great many lies and boastings enforcing it upon the credulous multitude, it hath put me in mind of this spiritual mountebankery of the devil. How doth he gull and delude the foolish by laying out the pleasures of sin! and no otherwise doth he keep them at a gazing admiration of worldly pomp, delights, and satisfaction, which he promiseth them from iniquity, than the serpent Scytale doth with passengers, whom she stays, by amazing them with her beautiful colours, till she have stung them.447 The art of Satan in this matter lies in four things:—

[1.] First, *If there be anything that can be called a delight, or may any way conduce to a satisfaction in any sin, he will be sure to speak of it in its highest praises.* He not only stretcheth his rhetoric to the height in giving commendations to the most noted pleasures that men propound to themselves, but he seeks out the hidden things of delight, and raiseth in men an itch of desire after the improvement of delight, by the contrivances of wit or art. Thus he tells them of jollity, ravishing mirth, high satisfaction, and, if they will believe him, of unspeakable delight to be had by giving themselves up to the world and the course of it. Nay, he hides nothing that will bear any praise; the least advantage, the smallest gratification that any sin can afford to human desire, he will be sure to speak of it.

[2.] Secondly, *He carries on this design by lying.* He promiseth more than ever sin can give, and he sends his proselytes out after sin under the highest expectations, and when they come to enjoy it, they often find the pleasure falls short of his boast. He whispers honours, preferments, and riches, in the ear of their hearts, and often pays them with poverty and disgraces, and gives them *pro thesauro carbones*, stones for bread, a serpent for a fish. Witches give frequent accounts of Satan's lying promises; he tells them of feasts, of gold, of riches, but they find themselves deluded; he sends them oft hungry away from those banquets, so that they have no more than when a man dreams he eats. He gives that which seems gold in appearance, but at last they find it to be slates or shells. We find in this temptation he is liberal and large in his offers to Christ, and what he requires he will have in present payment, but the reward for the service is future. It is his business to engage men in sin by his promise of advantage, but being once engaged, he takes not himself concerned in honour or ingenuity for performance. Hence doth the Scripture fitly call the pleasures of sin 'lying vanities,' a 'vain show,' a 'dream;' thereby warning men from a forward belief of Satan's promises, in that they find by experience they shall be at last but lies and disappointments.

[3.] Thirdly, To make his bait more taking, *he conceals all the inconveniences that may attend these worldly delights.* He offers here the kingdoms of the world to Christ, as if all were made up of pleasure. Those cares, troubles, and vexations that attend greatness and rule, he mentions not; their burden, hazard, and disquiet, he passeth over. Thus in common temptations he is careful to hide from men the miseries that follow these empty pleasures. So that often men do not consider the mischief, till 'a dart strike through their liver,' Prov. vii. 23, and till a dear-bought experience doth inform them of their mistakes.

[4.] Fourthly, His power and work upon the fancies of men, is none of the least of his ways whereby he advanceth the pleasures of sin. That he hath such a power, hath been discoursed before, and that a fancy raised to a great expectation makes things appear otherwise than what they are, is evident from common experience. The value of most things depends rather upon fancy than the internal worth of them, and men are more engaged to a pursuit of things by the estimation which fancy hath begat in their minds, than by certain principles of knowledge. Children by fancy have a value of their toys, and are so powerfully swayed by it, that things of far greater price cannot stay their designs, nor divert their course. Satan knows that the best of men are sometimes childish, apt to be led about by their conceits, and apt in their conceits to apprehend things far otherwise than what they are in truth. Hence is it, as one observes,448 that of thousands of men that return from Jerusalem, or from Mount Sion, or from the river Jordan, scarce can we find one which brings back the admiration which he had conceived before he had seen them. Fancy doth pre-occupate the mind with a high opinion of things; and these exorbitant imaginations pass to such an excess, that men think to find a satisfaction beyond the nature of these pleasures they aim at, which hath these two inconveniences: the one, that this affects and draws as powerfully as if they were all as real and high as they are conceited to be; the other, that sight and fruition takes away the estimation, and by a disappointment doth deaden and dull the affections to what may be really found there. Thus Satan by one deceit makes men believe that sin hath pleasure, which indeed it hath not, and by that belief leads them on powerfully to endeavour an embracement of them, and at last urgeth them with a delusion.

Applic. In opposition to this deceit of the devil, we must learn to esteem worldly delights as low as he would value them high. And to this purpose the Scripture speaks of them in undervaluing language, calling worldly pomp an opinion, a fantasy, a fashion or figure, an imagination rather than a reality; and further enjoins us not to admire these things in others, not to envy them that enjoyment of them, nor to fret at our want of them, much less to be transported with any angry passion about them, nor to concern ourselves in any earnest pursuit of them.449

Obs. 4. Fourthly, *Satan in this temptation did not bravely speak of these things, nor only make an offer in discourse, but he thought it most conducible to his design to present them to his sight.* He knew full well that the heart is more affected by sensible discoveries than by rational discourses.

Note here, *That Satan in temptations of worldly pleasure, endeavours to engage the affections by the senses.*

That it is Satan's great business to work upon the affections, I have shewed at large. Here he endeavoured to prepare the affections of Christ, that so the motion, when it came, might not die, as a spark falling upon wet tinder, but that the affections being stirred up might cherish the offer, and that the offer by a mutual warmth might more inflame the affections that were heated before.

To this end he works by the senses, and would have Christ's eye to raise his affections of love, desire, hope, and whatever else might wing his soul to activity. There is a great connexion betwixt the senses and the affections. The senses bring intelligence unavoidably, and are apt to stir up our powers to action. As the jackal is said to hunt the prey for the lion, so do the senses for the affections, and both for Satan.

It is also remarkable that Satan, endeavouring to make the eyes of Christ traitors to his affections, and that he thinking it necessary to give him a view of what he proffered him, should not give him time to take a full survey of these kingdoms, but should huddle it up in such a haste, that all, as Luke tells us, was done in 'a moment of time.' Was Satan in haste? or was he unwilling to part with what he so liberally proffered? Surely no, but this transient view was his subtlety, to entice him the more, and to inflame his heart with greater desires.

Obs. 5. Observe then, *That where Satan is most liberal in his proffers, he there manageth his overtures of advantage with a seeming shyness.* And this he doth, *First,* To heighten the worth of them in our estimation, as if they were jewels not to be gazed at, or curious pieces not fit to be exposed to common view. *Secondly,* By this art he makes men more eager in the pursuit. Our natural curiosity presseth us with great earnestness after things of difficult access, and we have also strange desires kindled in us from a prohibition, so that what we list not to choose if we have a liberty of enjoyment, when we are forbidden, we are troubled with impatient longings for it, and cannot be at quiet till we do enjoy it: *nitimur in vetitum.*

When Satan makes nice with men, offering the pleasures of the world, and yet hedging up the way with difficulties, they should make no other construction of it, but that Satan doth, so far as he is concerned, more strongly entice them. He plays at peep with them, that he may make them more earnest to follow him, and to bid high for the possession of these delights.

Malo me Galatea petit, ...
Et fugit ad salices, et se cupit ante videri.

CHAPTER XIX

These observations, which the preparation to the temptation hath afforded us, being despatched, the temptation itself follows, which is this, 'fall down and worship me.'

This motion, from such a one as Satan, to such a one as Christ, who was holy and undefiled, God and man, seems to be an incredible piece of arrogancy, pride, and malice; for to propound himself as the object of divine worship, was certainly a desperate assault. It includes, [1.] the highest blasphemy; [2.] the grossest idolatry imaginable. Both these are frequently noted as the design of this temptation.450 But [3.] the comprehension of this motion takes in the whole withdrawing of the mind from God and religion, or the care of the soul and eternal life; in which sense Satan doth frequently practise this temptation upon men by the motive of worldly pleasures. I shall consider the temptation first, as blasphemous, and so it will give us this observation:—

Obs. 6. That the best of God's children may be troubled with most vile and hideous blasphemous injections.

Blasphemy, in the largest sense, is anything spoken or done, by which the honour and fame of God may be wounded or prejudiced; but the formality of blasphemy lies in the purpose or intendment of reproaching God. Such was the blasphemy of the Israelitish woman's son, recorded in Lev. xxiv. 11, where blaspheming is explained by the addition of the word cursing, which in the original— ללק —comes from a word that signifies to 'set light by one.'451 So that hence, and from the circumstances of the story, we may safely conjecture that this man having an Egyptian to his father, which probably might in scorn be objected to him by his contending adversary, he more readily might be drawn out to vilify the true God; but, be it what it will, it was certainly more than that blasphemy which the Rabbins fancy to be in the repetition of naming the word Jehovah, which in reverence they either leave out, as when they say, 'the arm of the Almighty,' or change it into some other, as Adonai, or the like; and accordingly we may observe, that reproaching God and blaspheming God are joined together, as Ps. xliv. 16; Isa. xxxvii. 23.

In blasphemy, as the matter, there must be thoughts, words, or actions that may aptly express a contempt or reproach of God; so also, as to the form of it, there must be an intendment of reproaching. Now though this be a sin which the heart of a servant of God would most abhor, yet Satan doth sometimes trouble the best with it. We have an instance in Job. His design was to bring him to curse God, for so he professeth in express terms; chap. i. 11, ii. 5, 'Lay thine hand upon him, and he will curse thee to thy face.' And in prosecution of this his boast, he breaks the matter plainly to him by his wife, chap. ii. 9, 'Curse God and die.' Whatever may be spoken of the word as signifying blessing, though some affirm the word ברך, in the proper idiom of that language, and not by an antiphrasis or euphemismus, as some think,452 signifies as properly to 'curse' as to 'bless,' and is determinable to its signification either way by the circumstances of the place, or whatever men endeavour to excuse his wife, it is plain, not only by Job's answer, that it was evil counsel, but also by Satan's avowed design, that it was directly for cursing God. Besides this instance, if we consider the expression of 'fiery darts,' Eph. vi. 16, we shall find that this temptation is more common to all sorts of Christians than we would imagine. It is plain that these words allude to the poisoned arrows which Scythians and others used. These not only wounded but poisoned, and the venom inflamed with a fiery heat the part or member pierced. By this similitude, it must be granted that not common temptations are hereby understood, but such as were more than ordinarily hurtful, vexing, and dangerous. It may be persecutions are one of these darts, but all reckon temptations of spiritual terrors, and blasphemy, to be undoubtedly pointed at.453

The ways of Satan in this temptation are three:—

(1.) First, He endeavours to bring men to blaspheme, by secret and subtle ways of ensnaring them; and this is most-what practised in consequential and covert blasphemies, when, though men do not directly intend an open outrage against God, yet Satan brings them to that which might be so interpreted. This seems to have been the case of Job's sons, according to his jealousy of them; 'It may be my sons have sinned, and cursed God in their heart,' Job i. 5; not that they were open blasphemers, for they were surely better educated, neither doth Job express such a fear of them; but that in their mirth their hearts might have been so loosened from the fear of God, that they might be tempted to undue thoughts of God, slighting his threatenings or goodness. To this purpose Broughton translates, 'They have little blessed God in their hearts.'454 The same thing we may observe in Job himself. When the devil could not prevail with him to 'charge God foolishly,' chap. i. 22, yet he pressed him so hard by his miseries, that he hoped at last to bring him to utter the anguish of his mind in impatient and reflecting expressions, and so far prevailed, that he bitterly 'Curseth the day wherein he was born,' chap. ii. 3, and wisheth that he had 'given up the ghost when he came out of the belly;' which though it came far short of what Satan had boasted of in his achievement against him, yet it had such an unwarrantable tendency that way, that when his friend Eliphaz took notice of his expressions, as savouring of too much distrust, he is forced to make apology for himself, and to excuse it by the desperateness of his condition; chap. vi. 26, 'Do you imagine to reprove words and the speeches of one that is desperate?' In such cases, the devil provokes men beyond their intentions, to speak in their haste so inconsiderately, that they know not or mind not, the just consequence of their speeches. It was a degree of blasphemy in David to say, though in his haste, that 'all men were liars;' it was an unbelieving reflection on the promise given him by Samuel. In Mal. iii. 13, the people did not believe that they had 'spoken so much against God,' when yet their words had been 'stout against him.'

(2.) Secondly, Satan endeavours this *by violent injections of blasphemous thoughts that are directly such*. In this I shall note to you,

[1.] First, *That the vilest thoughts of God, of his ways and providences, of Scripture, and of Christ, are frequently suggested*. Things of greatest outrage against heaven, and contempt of the Almighty, as Bernard expresseth it, *Terribilia de fide, horribilia de divinitate*; as, there is no God, or that he is not just, or not faithful to his promises; or that Christ was but an impostor. He sticks at nothing in this kind, though never so contrary to the hope and persuasion of those whom he thus molests.

[2.] Secondly, These are frequently reiterated upon them, and their minds so troubled by them, that they cannot free themselves from such thoughts, but he follows on and clamours in their ears, as Gerson455 observes, Nega Deum, maledic Deo—Deny God, curse God.

[3.] Thirdly, And this with so great *a force and impetuosity, that they are compelled to form these thoughts in their minds, and to speak contrary to what they would*, as if their thoughts and tongues were not under their own government, the devil not satisfying himself to bear in these thoughts upon them, but he endeavours, as it were, to make them say after him, and to cast his suggestions into their own mould, that so they might seem properly to be their own; and this they are forced to whether they will or no, even then when their minds are filled with horror, their heart with grief, and their body with trembling. I have discoursed with some who have bitterly complained that their tongues and their thoughts seemed not to be their own, but that Satan ruled them at his pleasure; and that when in opposition to the temptation they would have formed their tongues to speak blessing of God, they have spoken cursing instead of blessing; and that when a blasphemous thought had been cast into their mind, they could not be at rest till they had thought it again.

[4.] Fourthly, These troublesome temptations are oft of long continuance. Joannes Climacus tells us456 of a monk that was troubled with blasphemous thoughts for twenty years together, and could not quit himself of them, though he had macerated his body with watchings and fastings. Some have them going away and returning again by fits, according as the prevalency and ferment of their melancholy gives Satan the advantage of dealing thus with them. For if we inquire why it is thus, especially with the children of God, we must partly resolve it into the 'unsearchable wisdom of God,' who for holy ends of teaching and disciplining his servants, permits Satan thus to molest them; and partly into those particular advantages which Satan hath against them according to the variety of their conditions, which usually are these: —

First, He takes advantage of such *bodily distempers as do deprive men of the use of their reason,* as fevers, frenzies, madness. In these he oft forms the tongues of men to horrid blasphemous speeches.

Secondly, A pressure of outward afflictions gives him his desired opportunity; and this he knows to be generally so successful, that he promised himself by this means a victory over Job. Ordinarily, straits and miseries do produce blaspheming. Isa. viii. 21, the prophet notes that when the people should be 'hardly bestead and hungry,' they should 'fret themselves, and curse their king and their God, and look upward,' as avouching what they had done.

Thirdly, Worldly plenty, fulness, and pleasure lay often foundations of this temptation. When their cups are full, and their hearts high, Satan can easily make them 'set their mouth against heaven.' A proud heart will readily say, 'Our tongue is our own, or, Who is the Lord?' [Ps. xii. 4.] This was the engine which the devil managed, if it were as Job suspected, against the sons and daughters of Job, to make them curse God in their hearts; and by this did he seek to prevail upon Christ in this blasphemous temptation.

Fourthly, A melancholy distemper doth usually invite Satan to give blasphemous suggestions. The disturbed and pliable fancies of such, are the advantages which he improves against them.

Fifthly, Inward terrors and distresses of conscience are also an occasion to Satan to move them, as by a desperate humour, to utter hard things of God and against themselves.

But there is yet a third way by which Satan tempts men to blaspheming, *by sudden glances of blasphemous imaginations,* which like lightnings do astonish the heart and then suddenly vanish. These are very common, and the best of men observe them frequently. Satan seems as it were rather to frolic and sport himself in these suggestions, than to intend a serious temptation. Their danger is not so much, yet are they not to be despised, lest these often visits, carelessly entertained, and not dismissed with just abhorrency, do secretly envenom the soul, and prepare it for stronger assaults.

I shall next inquire into the reasons of this trouble which Satan gives the children of God.

[1.] First, These temptations are very affrighting; though they prevail not, yet they are full of perplexing annoyance. Corrupt nature startles at them, and receives them not without dread and horror. It is sadly troublesome to hear others blaspheme God. 'The reproaches of those that reproached thee,' saith David, 'fell upon me.' It was as 'a sword in his bones' to hear the blasphemous scoffs of the wicked, when they said to him, 'Where is thy God?' And if it were confusion and shame to him to hear 'the enemy reproach and blaspheme,' as he professeth it was, Ps. xliv. 15, 16, how sadly afflicting would it be for any child of God to observe such things in his own imaginations! If there were no more in it than this, it is enough to put Satan upon that design, because it is a troublesome kind of martyrdom.457

[2.] Secondly, *This is also a spiteful revenge against God.* All he can do is to blaspheme and rage, and it is a kind of delight to put this force upon those that carry his own image. He would do all he can to make his own children to vilify and reproach their heavenly Father, and to render cursing for blessing.

[3.] Thirdly, This temptation, though it have not the consent or compliance of God's children, yet it opens a way to many other sins, as murmuring, distrust, despair, weariness of God's ways and services. When we find Satan thus to run upon us, it is apt to breed 'strange thoughts of God,' that thus permits Satan to take us by the throat, or to make us judge of ourselves as rejected of God, and given up to Satan's power; and if it do this, his labour is not in vain; we are, as one observes,458 more to fear his subtlety in bringing us by this into other snares, than the violence of the adversary in this suggestion.

[4.] Fourthly, This is a stratagem for laying the foundation of direful accusations. The devil in this doth as the Russians are459 reported to do. They, when they have a spite against any of their neighbours, hide secretly some of their goods in their houses, and then accuse them of theft. When blasphemous thoughts are injected, and men refuse to consent, then Satan raiseth an accusation against them, as Joseph's mistress did, as if they were guilty of all that blasphemy that he tempted them unto; and it is a difficult task to persuade them that these things should be in their minds, and that they should not be the proper issues of their own heart. And very often doth he from hence accuse them of sinning against the Holy Ghost, because of the hideous blasphemies which he had first suggested to them.

Applic. First, This will give us considerations of *consolation*, and that—(1.) *In regard of others.* We observe often our sick friends speak what we would not willingly hear, and it cannot choose but be sadly afflictive to hear their curses and blasphemous speeches; but when we consider the advantage that Satan takes of their distemper, if their lives heretofore have been pious and religious, we comfort ourselves in this, that it is more his malice than their own inclinations; neither should we suffer our hope or charity to be distressed on their behalf. (2.) It is the like ground of consolation for ourselves or others that are violently afflicted with blasphemous thoughts. For,

[1.] First, *If we call to mind that our Lord and Master suffered such things, we that are of his household need not think we receive a strange or unusual measure in that we are molested as he was.*

[2.] Secondly, If we consider that Christ was tempted *without sin on his part*, then may we fetch this conclusion from it, *that it is possible that such thoughts should be cast upon us, and yet that we may not be chargeable with them as our iniquities.*

Thirdly, We may hence see that such temptations are more frightful than hurtful. These, as one observes,460 seldom take, they carry with them so much horror, to those that believe and love the true God, that it keeps them from a participation with Satan in the sin itself, nay, it fills them with fear and striving against it; they rather, as bugbears, scare and disquiet them, than produce the real effects of compliance with them.

Applic. Secondly, The consideration of this kind of temptation may *fill the hearts and mouths of those of us as have not hitherto been troubled with it, with praise for so merciful a preservation.* If we have not been under this kind of exercise. it is not from any good will that Satan hath to us, but because our God withholds a commission from him. A poor weak Christian wonders that Satan hath not made him a mark for this arrow, that he hath not broken him with this tempest. To answer that wonder, he may know that the same tenderness in God, that will not put 'new wine into old crazy bottles,' nor a 'new stiff piece of cloth into an old tender garment,' nor that will oppress the weak and infirm with strong exercise or burdens; that same tenderness of a compassionate Father doth keep off such trials, because he will not suffer them 'to be tempted above what they are able.'

Applic. Thirdly, This temptation calls for *advice to those that are under it*, to whom I shall direct a few things.

[1.] First, When any are troubled with blasphemous thoughts, let it be considered *in what state and temper their body is*. If it be distempered with melancholy, as is most usual, then the prescription of an able physician is necessary in the first place, without which he that would spiritually advise or counsel shall but beat the air, and his words be so far from the fastness of nails that they shall be as wind. I have known many under great complaints and fears by reason hereof, that have been cured by physic alone; for when, in this case, the fuel is withdrawn, the fire goes out. Correct the melancholy temper that gives the devil this advantage, and the trouble will cease.

[2.] Secondly, It is of great consequence to understand *the nature of these temptations*. If the tempted could see these to be their sufferings rather than their sins, they would with greater ease bear it as an affliction. And to those that complain, abhor, resist, and pray against them, they are not sins, no more than when a harlot layeth her child at an honest woman's door, that child is to be reckoned as the fruit of her wickedness. A giant may dash the son against his father, but so far will the father be from imputing it as rebellious insolence in his child, that he will pity him the more, as suffering by a double injury; for it is not only against his natural affection and reverence to his parent, but it is a bodily hurt beside. Thus will God much more pity his children under these sufferings.

[3.] Thirdly, We must not suffer such thoughts *to lodge in us*, but before they settle, if possible, we must repel them; as Abraham drove away the fowls that came down upon his sacrifice. I know the tempted will say this advice is not practicable; they find these thoughts swarm about them as bees, and when one is driven back another straight comes in its place. But to them I answer, that blasphemous thoughts are repelled two ways. (1.) By stout and resolute resistance. This, though it do not extinguish them, nor free us of the trouble, yet it keeps them from settling upon us, and us from the guilt of them. (2.) By diversion, which the work of a lawful employment, or good society, and other discourses may do. This may give some ease from the molestation, and the other preserves us innocent.

[4.] Fourthly, In temptations to blasphemy confident refusals do better than disputings.461 Here we are to resist with courage and a holy contempt of Satan. If we be too timorous and fearful, he insults the more upon us; as dogs when they are observed follow the passenger with greater eagerness and noise. Abhorrences and positive discharges, like that of Christ in the same case, 'Get thee hence, Satan,' do more for us than to debate the matter with him.

CHAPTER XX

Thus have I considered the temptation as blasphemous. I proceed next to consider it as idolatrous. The words ἐὰν πεσὼν προσκυνήσῃς, if thou wilt fall down and worship, do give us the true notion of idolatry. The word which we call worship comes from κύω, which signifies to kiss, or from κυὼν, which signifies a dog, both being to the same purpose, and signifying any action of reverence by which we signify the respect of our minds. To kiss the hand, or to fawn as a dog, are gestures which express the honour we would give, and being applied to divine worship before, or with respect unto, an undue object, is idolatry; and as such doth Christ reject it in his answer, 'Thou shalt worship the Lord thy God, and him only shalt thou serve.' We worship God, when in ways and actions commanded or prescribed, we testify our belief and resentment of his incommunicable attributes. It is idolatry when either we use the same actions of prescribed worship to that which is not God, or when we testify our respects to the true God in an undue way of our own devising. Here might I take occasion to shew the vanity of the popish subterfuges; their distinction of latria and dulia is, as Dr [Henry] More observes, hereby overthrown.462 Satan doth not here set himself up as the omnipotent God, for he acknowledgeth one superior to himself, in that he confesseth that the power he had of the kingdoms of the world was given to him, Luke iv. 6, and therefore not the latria but the dulia is required of him; and yet this, Christ denies him as being idolatry, in that no religious worship—for that must needs be the sense of his answer—is due to any but God alone. Their other distinction of worshipping an idol, saint, angel, cross, &c., and before such a creature, is also hereby crushed, as is commonly observed:463 for what the evangelist Matthew expresseth by προσκυνήσῃς μοι, Luke calls ἐνώπιόν μου, before me; so that the Scripture makes no difference betwixt these two, shewing it to be idolatry to use religious worship to that which is not God, or before it. But these things I shall not prosecute; keeping therefore to my design, I shall observe,

Obs. 7. *That it is one of Satan's great designs to corrupt the worship of God.* That this is so will appear,

(1.) First, *If we consider what varieties of worship hath been in the world.* God gave a fixed and stable law, and yet this so little prevailed, that men were upon new inventions presently. I shall not need to reckon up the almost numberless varieties of this kind among the heathen. The instance is plain enough in those that professed the name of the true God; they were still changing for new fashions in religion, borrowing patterns from their neighbours, so that if there were but a new altar at Damascus, or a new idol in any strange city, they must presently have the like, till, as the prophet tells them, 'according to their cities so were their gods,' [Jer. ii. 28.] He that will call to mind that the husbandman did first 'sow good seed in his field,' and that there is such variety of tares and false worship, notwithstanding the plain and positive command of God, fixing and determining his worship, must needs conclude that an enemy, Satan, hath done it.

(2.) Secondly, *If we call to mind how in all ages there hath been a constancy in this inconstant variety.* We hear of it among the heathens. We read enough of it among the Jews, and when they were out of the humour of more shameful idolatries, they yet corrupted the worship of God by their traditions; and of these they were so fond, that they caused the law of God itself to give place to them, and made it void by them. The times of the gospel were not free. Though Christ came to seek such worshippers as should 'worship him in spirit and in truth,' yet before the apostles' deaths, while yet they were persuading to the contrary, there arose up some that corrupted the worship, by leading the people back again to the Jewish ceremonies, and others laboured to bring in 'worshipping of angels,' and at last to 'eat things offered to idols,' with greater defilements. Since the apostles' days the same design hath been carried on in the churches. Rome hath patched together a great deal of Jewish and heathenish ceremonies; and when the man of sin shall be revealed, yet a higher flood of such abominations is to be expected. Who hath wrought all this, but Satan? This is still the same design, and though the work be not in all parts like itself, yet the whole of it evidenceth the working of the same spirit in all.

(3.) Thirdly, Let us observe how early this began. We cannot say but that in the days of Adam, who doubtless had received particular commands from God, in which he would not fail to instruct his children, they were seeking to themselves 'many inventions,' Gen. iv. 26. At the birth of Enos, as some conjecture, there were such defilements brought into use in worship, that Seth had respect to it when he called his son Enos, Sorrowful, as lamenting that profanation which was then begun in 'calling upon the name of the Lord,' for so do many interpret that passage, which in our English we read thus, 'Then began men to call upon the name of the Lord.' The word in the original is לחזה, which signifieth both to profane and to begin, and may be as properly translated, then 'profaned they in calling upon the name of the Lord.' And there are several reasons that move learned men464 to fix upon this translation. As (1.) That it is not probable that men began then to call upon God, or publicly to do so, as some would interpret, and not before, as the present English would imply. (2.) That age was noted as corrupt, and therefore it is noted as a rarity that Enoch walked with God. (3.) The Rabbins generally translate ללח to profane; but if we should grant the present English, 'Then began men to call upon the name of the Lord,' it would imply that the worship practised by Adam and Abel had been corrupted, and now it was restored again and reformed; which will make the corruption of worship to be yet more early. And after that we read of corruption crept into the family of Seth, as well as now in the family of Cain, Gen. vi. 2; so that the worship of God stood not long in its honour, though Adam and Seth were alive to instruct them; which shews that it was a rebellious departure from the way, fomented and brought on by the malignant spirit Satan.

(4.) Fourthly, But to make all sure, *the Scripture lays all these kinds of corruption of worship at Satan's door.* The defilements of worship taught in Thyatira, by Jezebel, are called 'the depth of Satan,' Rev. ii. 24; the corruptions introduced by antichrist, are from 'the workings of Satan,' 2 Thes. ii. 9. What was promoted by false apostles to that purpose, they had it from their great teacher Satan, who 'transforms himself for such ends into an angel of light,' 2 Cor. xi. 13, 14; so that nothing can be more plain than that this is an old and constant design of Satan.

The particular ways by which Satan effects this design I shall not now touch, but shall in lieu of that give you the reasons of his endeavours this way.

[1.] First, *He knows that this is a sin of a high provocation.* Worship is the proper tribute that is due to God, and it is peculiarly his prerogative to prescribe the way and manner of it. Neither of these honours will he give to any other, but will express his jealousy when any invasion is made upon these his sole prerogatives. Now his worship cannot be corrupted, but one of these at least will in some degree or other be touched. If we set up another object of worship, we deny him to be God; if we worship him in a way of our own invention, we deny his wisdom, and set up ourselves above him, as if we could order his worship better than he hath done in his word.

[2.] Secondly, *If the worship be corrupted, all the exercise of the affections of the heart, and all the service itself is lost, and become unacceptable.* He knows that such worshippers shall meet with this answer, 'Who hath required this at your hands?' [Isa. i. 12.]

[3.] Thirdly, *Corruption in worship*, Satan by long experience knows to have been the ground of those hatreds, quarrels, persecutions, and troubles under which the church hath groaned in all ages, every difference imposing their way and persuasion upon all dissenters, to the disturbance of peace, breach and decay of love, hindrance of the growth of piety, to the biting and devouring of one another.

[4.] Fourthly, Besides God is provoked by this to *leave his sanctuary*, to remove his glory and his candlestick, to make his vineyard a desolation, and his churches as Shiloh.

[5.] Fifthly, Satan is the more industrious in this, because *his ways are capable of many advantages to further his design, and many specious pretences to cover it*. In Col. ii. 8, he made use of philosophy to corrupt religion, and by unsound principles of some heathens famous for that learning, introduced 'worshipping of angels.' What that could not effect he laboured to perform by 'the traditions of men,' and where that came short, 'the rudiments of the world'—the Mosaical ceremonies were so called here, and in the Epistle to the Hebrews—were his engine by which he battered the plain worship of the New Testament. And as to pretences, the apostle doth there and elsewhere note that decency and order, humility, wisdom, and self-denial, are things very taking, and yet usually pretended for such bold innovations as may corrupt the pure streams of the sanctuary.

Applic. Hence may I leave with you a few memorials.

[1.] First, *This may make us jealous of any alterations in the way of Gods worship*. We have reason under the most plausible pretexts to suspect the hand of Satan, because it is one of his main businesses to corrupt the worship.

[2.] Secondly, *This may justify those that out of a conscientious fear of complying with Satan's design, dare not admit of a pin in the tabernacle beside what God hath prescribed, nor leave behind a shoe-latchet of what he hath enjoined.*

[3.] Thirdly, *This will tell us that that worship is best and safest that hath least of mixture of human invention*. We cannot offend in keeping close to the rule, though the worship thereby become more plain, and not so gorgeous in outward appearance. We may soon overdo it by the least addition, and cannot be so certain of God's acceptation, as we are of pleasing the senses of men, by such introducements.

This motion of Satan, 'Fall down and worship me,' is now in the last place to be considered as a particular instance of Satan's general design *of drawing the hearts of men from God his service and ways, to the pleasures of sin*; as if he should say to him, follow my advice, give up thyself to my service, and thou shalt be gratified with all the delights that the world can give thee. To this doth the bait here offered most fitly agree. Hence observe,

Obs. 8. *That it is Satan's general design to withdraw the hearts of men from God, that they may be enslaved to him in the service of sin.*

That the devil doth level all his endeavours to this, cannot be doubted; for,

(1.) First, *He hath a kingdom in this world*, from which he is denominated 'the prince of this world.' And this is not only a rule of exterior force, such as conquerors have over their captivated slaves, who are compelled to subject their bodies, while yet their minds are full of hatred against him who hath thus forced them to subjection; but it is a rule over the hearts and affections of men, working in 'the children of disobedience' a love and liking of these ways, and begetting in them the image of Satan; so that what work he imposeth they are pleased withal, and 'love to have it so.' Therefore he is not only called their prince, but their god and their father: 'Ye are of your father the devil,' in that with a kind of inward devotion they will and endeavour to perform the lusts which he propounds to them.

(2.) Secondly, *This kingdom is contrary to Gods spiritual kingdom*, that being of darkness, this of light; and it is managed by Satan with an envious competition and co-rivalship to that of God; so that as God invites men to the happiness of his kingdom, and sends his Spirit in his word and ordinances to persuade them, Satan doth the like. He sends out his spirit, which the apostle calls 'the spirit of the world,' 1 Cor. ii. 12, and employs all his agents to engage men for him. He requires the heart as God doth, he promiseth his rewards of pleasure, honour, riches, if they will fall down and worship him. Now it is so natural to prosecute an interest thus espoused in a way of opposition, especially to any other that set up for themselves in a contradictory competitorship, that the very natural laws of Satan's kingdom will engage him to stand up for it, and to enlarge it all he can.

Those upon whom he prevails are of two sorts—

(1.) First, Some are visibly in his service. These answer the character which was given of Ahab, 1 Kings xxi. 20, 'who sold himself to work wickedness in the sight of the Lord.' The first expression shews that such are wholly in Satan's power and disposal—as things sold are in the possession and power of the buyer—they are at Satan's will. If he say to them, 'Go, they go,' and if he say, 'Come, they come.' Their bodies and spirits are Satan's, they are not their own; and they are his for the ends of sin, for that employment only, so that they are 'wholly corrupt and abominable.' The latter expression, that he did so 'in the sight of the Lord,' manifests their shameless impudency in sin, that they 'declare their sin as Sodom, and hide it not,' that they do not blush, but openly wear the devil's livery and avouch his service. As the works of the flesh are manifest, so these in their practice of such works are manifestly Satan's subjects. These kind of men are frequently in the Old Testament styled 'sons of Belial,'465 a name very significant, shewing either their devoting of themselves to the devil's service, in that they reject the yoke of God's law, in that they 'break his bonds, and cast his cords from them,' or their pride that they will have none above them, not considering that there is a God, or that the Most High rules, or their averseness to what is good, being 'wholly unprofitable, and to every good work reprobate.' [Titus i. 16.]

(2.) Secondly, *Some are secretly his servants*. They come to the devil, as Nicodemus did to Christ, by night. They will not openly profess him, but yet their hearts are wholly his. Such are called by the name of hypocrites. The pharisees and scribes seemed to declare for God, called themselves Abraham's seed, fasted, gave alms, made long prayers, and yet were a 'generation of vipers,' and 'of their father the devil.' The secrecy of this underhand engagement to hell is such, that many who are in a league with the devil, and at an agreement with death, do neither know nor believe it concerning themselves. For,

[1.] First, *This private covenant may be where there are the greatest seeming defilements of Satan and high professions of service to God*. The pharisees, as have been said, were the devil's servants, under all the fair show they made of religion and zeal for the law, and yet when Christ plainly told them that they were not Abraham's seed but the devil's seed, they with high indignation and scorn throw back the accusation to Christ, 'Thou art a Samaritan, and hast a devil; we are Abraham's children,' [John viii. 48,] so little believed they the truth when it was told them.

[2.] Secondly, *This may consist with some designment and intention to give God glory*. The Jews, though they submitted not to the righteousness of God, yet, by the testimony of Paul, they had a zeal to God. The very heathens that sacrifice to devils had not formal intentions so to do, as appears by their inscription on the altar at Athens, Acts xvii. 23, 'To the unknown God.' The true God, though unknown, they propounded as the object of their worship; yet falling into those ways of devotion which the devil had prescribed, these intentions could not hinder but that they became his servants.

[3.] Thirdly, *Men may be servants to Satan under great assurances and confidences of their interest in God*. Many go to hell that have lived with Lord, Lord in their mouths. Those mentioned in Isa. xlviii. 2, that had no interest in truth and righteousness when they solemnly sware by the name of the Lord, 'yet they called themselves of the holy city, and stayed themselves upon the God of Israel,' [Isa. xlviii. 2.]

Obj. If it seem strange to any that these professions, intentions, and confidences are not enough to secure men from this charge, but that they may be secretly slaves to hell, I answer,

Ans. 1. First, *That those do not necessarily conclude that the heart of such men is right with God.* Formality, natural conscience, and the power of education may do much of this; for though we grant that such are not conscious to themselves of any real design of serving Satan, yet they may either so far miss it in the way of their service, offering that as well-pleasing to God, which indeed he hates, and that through wilful and affected ignorance, as those of whom Christ speaks, John xvi. 2, that should think the killing of God's children a piece of acceptable service; or they may be so mistaken as to the sincerity of their hearts that they may think they have a design to please God in doing of what he requires in order thereunto, when indeed it may not be singly for God but for themselves that they work, in a self-gratification of their natural zeal for their way; or their esteem, credit, and advantage may privately influence them, rather than a spirit of life and power.

Ans. 2. Secondly, *The work which they do, and the ends they serve, will be evidence against professions and intentions.* It is a sure rule, that the work shews to whom men are related as servants, and it is laid down as a certain standard to measure the hearts of men by, when pretences and persuasions seem to carry all before them: Rom. vi. 16, 'His servants ye are to whom ye obey;' 1 John iii. 8, 10, 'He that committeth sin is of the devil: in this the children of God are manifest, and the children of the devil'—that is, when it becomes a question to whom a man belongs, whose child and servant he is, it must be determined by the works he doth. If he engage in the ways of sin, he is of the devil, let him profess what he will to the contrary. This same balance Christ useth to try the truth of the Jews' pretences to God: John viii. 34, 'Whosoever committeth sin, is the servant of sin;' they boasted high, but he shews them that seeing their designs and works were hatred, envy, murder, &c., which are apparently from Satan, it was evident they had learned these of him; and he concludes by this proof, ver. 44, 'that they were of their father the devil.' Thus may we say of those that pretend they honour God, they deify the devil, they intend well, if yet they give themselves up to the pleasing of the flesh, if worldly-minded, if they live in pride, strife, envy, maliciousness, &c.,—which are works of the devil,—it is not all their pretences that will entitle them to God, but they are, for all this, the devil's servants, as doing his works.

Applic. This may put men upon inquiries, *Who are ye for? whose servants are ye?* There are but two that can lay claim to you, and these two divide the whole world betwixt them. There is no state of neutrality: you are either

God's servants or the devil's. Ye cannot serve them both; 'now if the Lord be God, serve him.' Satan's service is base, dishonourable, slavish; the service of God, freedom, honour, life, and peace; there is indeed no comparison betwixt them. Happy, then, is that man that can say the Lord is his lot and portion; that can come into God's presence, and there in his integrity avouch the Lord for his God—that can stand upon it. 'My soul hath said unto the Lord, Thou art my God, and I have none besides thee; other lords have had dominion over us, but we will make mention of thy name only,' [Isa. xxvi. 13.]

This temptation, though it were in itself horrid, and as a brood of vipers knotted together, which at once could send out several stings, and make many wounds,—as hath been noted,—yet in the way of propounding, Satan seems to insinuate the largeness of his proffer, and the smallness and inconsiderableness of the service required, as if he should say, 'See how free I am in my kindness; I will not stick to give thee the kingdoms of the world, and the glory of them, and all this for so small a matter as bowing before me, or doing me a little reverence.' This gives us to observe,

Obs. 9. *That when Satan doth design no less than to enslave men to his service, yet he will propound sin as a small thing, or but one act of sin, as a thing not valuable, to engage them to him.* Not but that he desires to run men to excess in wickedness, and delights to see them with both hands earnestly work iniquity with greediness; yet where he sees the consciences of men squeamish, and that they cannot bear temptations to open and common profaneness without danger of revolt from him, there he seems modest, and requires but some small thing, at least at first, till the ways of sin become more familiar to them, and then when they can better bear it, he doubles the tale of bricks, and with greater confidence can urge them to things of greater shame and enormity. That this is his way appears,

[1.] First, *From the common argument which he useth at first to those whom he would draw off from a more careful conversation,* which is this: Do such a thing, it is but for once, and but little; others do the like, and demur not, or the best do as great matters as this comes to. It is but a small thing, considering the strait, or the advantage that may accrue. This is his usual note to candidate iniquity, as experience of all doth testify.

[2.] Secondly, That this is so is also evident from a consideration of *the several ways and courses of sinners.* Some are tempted and overcome by one kind of sin, and not at all urged to others. Some go to hell in a way of covetousness; others are pretty unblameable in most of their carriages, but are overcome by a proud humour; others are given to drink, and yet will not steal nor deal falsely; others take a more cleanly way to hell, rely upon their own righteousness, or are engaged in error, and their life otherwise smooth and fair. The Jews in Christ's time were only engaged against Christ, and for their traditions, but not molested with temptations to open idolatry as formerly. Those who are ignorant are not troubled with temptations to despair, or inward terrors. The reasons of his dealing thus are these: —

[1.] First, *He sees that one sin heartily prosecuted is enough to signify homage to him, and to give him possession.* As we take possession of land by a turf or a twig, so by one sin admitted with full purpose of mind, Satan is let into the heart. As a penny will be sufficient earnest for a bargain of a thousand pounds, so may one sin be a pledge or earnest for the whole soul in a league with hell.

[2.] Secondly, *He knows that one sin persisted in may be enough to destroy the soul;* as one wound may kill, one leak may sink a ship.

[3.] Thirdly, *He knows that one sin breaks the covenant of God,* and turns the heart from him, if men give up themselves to it.

[4.] Fourthly, *One sin wilfully pursued makes a man guilty of the breach of the whole law.* It destroys love and respect to God, undervalues his authority, contemns his threatenings and promises.

[5.] Fifthly, *One sin is enough to make way for more.* Where Satan would have more, yet at first he is pleased with it as a hopeful beginning. It makes room enough for the serpent's head, and then he will afterwards easily wind in his whole body.

Applic. This may warn us not to be emboldened to any sin by the plea *of diminution;* not to venture because it may seem little, or be but for once. A true Christian should be a perfect universalist; he should be universally against all sin, and universally for all duty.

CHAPTER XXI

I come now to the argument which Satan used for all this, 'All these things will I give thee.' He casts a golden apple before him, and seeks to entangle him by worldly greatness and delight. I shall not examine how true or false Satan spake when he called all these things his, and that he could give them to whom he would. It is enough for our purpose to take notice of his pretence, so far as might make his offer probable; and then observe,

Obs. 10. *That the great engine which Satan useth to draw away the heart from God to his service is worldly pleasures and delights.*

I shall first shew that this is Satan's great engine, and then explain what is in it that fits it so much for his purpose. The first of these is evidenced by these particulars:—

1. First, The Scripture doth particularly note to us a deceit or guile to be in worldly pleasures. Christ, in Mat. xiii. 22, speaks of 'the deceitfulness of riches;' and that deceit is expressed by such a word as signifies 'a drawing out of the way,' a misleading;466 so that he means not the uncertainty of these delights, in which sense it is said 'that riches take themselves wings and fly away,' [Prov. xxiii. 5,] which often disappoint and deceive the expectations of those that do most hug them. Nor can this be understood of riches in an active sense, as we attribute deceit to men, who as rational agents can contrive and devise snares; but it only means that these are so objective as things that are abused by Satan to delude and betray the sons of men: and these are so frequently made use of by him for such purposes, and with such advantages of power and provocation, that Christ elsewhere, Mat. xix. 23, speaks of it as a thing almost impossible, to have riches and not to be ensnared by them: 'A rich man shall hardly enter into the kingdom of heaven,' [Mat. xix. 23,] which Mark and Luke express by an affectionate amazement, 'Oh, how hardly can a rich man be saved!' [Mark x. 23-25, and Luke xviii. 24, 25.]

2. Secondly, *These are Satan's great net which encloseth multitudes*; a general bait, by which most are hooked into the service of sin. Most temptations come from this ocean as springs from the sea. 'The lust of the flesh, the lust of the eyes, the pride of life,' have their original from the world, 1 John ii. 16. Christ speaks of this 'mammon of unrighteousness' as the only thing

that stands up in competition for the hearts of men against God, Mat. vi. 24; and the apostle, 2 Tim. iii. 4, reckoning up the various ways of particular lusts, as covetousness, boasting, pride, blaspheming, &c., concludes them all under this, that they 'are lovers of pleasures more than lovers of God;' shewing us thereby, that though the lusts of men might run out diverse ways, and be exercised upon diverse particular objects, yet they all borrow their original from worldly pleasures, and their design is nothing but that in the general. Hence it is that some make the world the great traitor to God; for though they reckon up three great enemies to God and man, 'the world, the flesh, and the devil,' yet 'these three agree in one;' the pleasing of the flesh is the great end and desire of natural men; the world is the storehouse, from which men draw out several pleasures, according to the several ways they take in gratifying their lusts and humours, and the devil is only officious to help all this forward, by enticing and persuading them to 'make these provisions for the flesh.' And who can think other, but that this must be Satan's great engine, when, as hath been said, *first*, the world, and the pleasures of it, is the sum of all iniquity, containing in it virtually or actually the transgression of the whole law. The root it is of all evil, 1 Tim. vi. 10; all profaneness against God, all neglect of duty, all outrage, wrong, or injustice to man, may, and usually doth, spring from hence, insomuch that some have particularly traced it through every command of the decalogue, and found it guilty, either as principal or accessary, of every iniquity. *Second*, Our thoughts may be the more confirmed in this when we see all men entangled by it; for albeit that some temptations seem directly to carry men from a love or care of the world, as despair, terrors of mind, voluntary humility, neglecting of the body, and others of the same kind; yet if the matter be considered, the truth in hand cannot be prejudiced by such an objection. For, [1.] Those who seem in distress of conscience most to loathe the world were yet first entangled by it, and the consideration of that guilt, whether at present justly or unjustly charged upon them, is the usual occasion of these troubles. And, [2.] Those who seem to undervalue money, riches, plenty, &c., are, it may be, no less slaves to other worldly lusts; for pleasures of the world comprehend whatsoever may arise from anything that is in the world to the delight of life. Honour, pride, ambition, prodigality, are 'worldly lusts,' as well as covetousness and desire of power or rule. And those that seem to deny themselves of 'faring deliciously,' or 'wearing soft raiment,' may be as much distressed with an inward desire of applause and honour, as those that would gratify their senses are by sensual lusts.

3. Thirdly, How much the world stands Satan in stead may be observed from *the force of that temptation upon those that have very much engaged in their*

profession of the ways of God. It hath often fetched off those that seemed to have given up themselves to God. Demas was once commended by Paul as his fellow-labourer, Philem. 24; yet at last it so prevailed upon him that he complained, 2 Tim. iv. 10, that 'Demas had forsaken him,' and turned his back upon his profession, and so far, if Dorotheus do him right, that he became an idol-priest in Thessalonica, the cause of which horrid apostasy was his 'love to the present world.' Balaam seemed resolute not to act anything against Israel, yet 'the ways of unrighteousness' so far blinded him, that he taught Balak 'to cast a stumbling-block before the children of Israel.' The highest of nominal professors, noted by the 'thorny ground' in Mat. xiii. 22,—who seemed to differ from the good ground only in this, that their fruit was green and not ripe, as Luke expresseth it, 'They brought not fruit to perfection,'—they were choked in these fair beginnings and offers for holiness by the 'cares and pleasures of the world.' All ages abound with instances of this kind. Æneas Sylvius preached against the pope, set up the council above him, commended the Germans for opposing him; but preferment made him alter his note, and at last he became pope himself. Bonner, the persecutor, seemed at first a good man, a favourer of Luther's doctrine, but advancement changed him to a bloody wolf, a cruel tiger. Spalato forsook popery, but, missing those dignities which he aimed at in England, was, upon hopes of greater preferment, induced to lick up his vomit, and to own popery again. How many examples have we of those who, the higher they grew in the world, became more careless of religion; as Sixtus Quintus, who went as fast back in religion as he went forward in promotion; so that he that at first entering into orders, had a good hope of his salvation, by that time he came to be pope, he became so wicked that he despaired of happiness.

4. Fourthly, This temptation is one of Satan's last refuges, and often prevails where persecution cannot. The thorny-ground hearers were above those of the stony ground in this, that they stood out the storm, and bore the scorching heat of persecution, but then the world choked them. Sad experience tells us that churches that did thrive and grow as the palm-tree under their pressures, were spoiled by ease and plenty, which so cherished the seeds of pride, vanity, and contention, that they grew up amain, and did more to their desolation than the cruelty of all their fiercest enemies. Julian, who, by the greatest art and policy, studied to overthrow the Christian's name, so observed this, that he made it his rule rather to corrupt men by honours than to compel them by torments.467 We have also found that though the Roman synagogue join force to subtlety in the advancement of their dagon, yet they have still looked upon this temptation of the world as most likely to gain the hearts of their rational opposers. Cruelty could

overawe the senseless multitude, and could take out of the way those of whose opposition they were afraid, but it seldom with success wrought upon persons guided by light and conscience, to a compliance that would hold long; for though at first some good men were overawed to make subscription and to recant, as it did with Bilney, Bainham, Cranmer, and several others,468 yet upon the working of conscience, after the stound and dazzle of the temptation was over, they recoiled so resolutely upon them, that they lost more than they gained that way. But those that were willing to nibble at preferments became theirs wholly. Thus they set upon Luther, Galeaceus, Carracciolus, Dr Taylor, and a great many more, though to no purpose, for they were ready to bid their money 'perish with them,' and to bid defiance to their favour as well as to their frowns. Notwithstanding they have made many real conquests by this weapon, and accordingly this is reckoned among the temptations of greatest force: Heb. xi. 37, 'They were stoned, they were sawn asunder, they were tempted,' that is, by the pleasures and preferments of the world. It seems the Holy Ghost would point at this, how fair and plausible soever it be, as one of the devil's most powerful engines.

Next, I promised to discover what it is in the world which makes it so fit for Satan's designs.

(1.) First, *The world brings or affords fit matter to be made the fuel of lust.* For this reason the apostle in the place afore-cited, 1 John ii. 16, forbids us so earnestly to love the world, or the things of the world, because there is nothing in it which is not improveable, as an occasion or provocation to lust. Whatsoever is in the world is lust of flesh, or eyes, or heart; and there is no lust but it may be furnished with a proper object from hence. The appetite, senses, or affections fetch all their delights from hence.

(2.) Secondly, Besides the common materials of sin that are digged out of this mine, the world hath something *of an aptitude in it to tempt.* Not that it hath properly and formally, *insidiationis animum,* an active subtlety to lay snares for men, but yet it is not so purely passive as to make it altogether innocent. There is something of a curse upon it ever since, by the fall of man. It was loosened from its proper, primitive ends; and as the devil spake by the serpent, so doth he urge, speak, tempt, and insinuate by the world, so that it is still an occasion of danger to us, and hath a special advantage over our affections, upon several accounts. As, [1.] In that it is in itself lawful to be used. [2.] In that it is suitable to our desires and tempers. [3.] In some respects it might be necessary and advantageous for the comfort of life, for the support of families, and to enable us to be helpful to others. [4.] It is near to us, under our eye; we have familiar converse with it, it is still with us. [5.] We have a natural propensity to be in love with it; the flesh would fain be pleased, and nothing is more answerable to it than the pleasures of the world. We need not wonder then, when we see it so highly captivating the affections of men, and leading them bound in chains and fetters. Some make it their god; gain is all their godliness and religion; they seek their 'portion in this life,' Ps. xvii. 14; this is their treasure, and here is their heart; and it would be no less wonder if Satan should be guilty of so much oversight, as to neglect the use of an instrument which is every way so fitted for his purpose.

(3.) Thirdly, Besides this fair prospect which it gives to sin, it hath an enmity to God and his ways, which is no less advantageous to the devil. This is positively affirmed, James iv. 4, 'The friendship of this world is enmity with God;' not only is this true in a lower sense, as a hindrance, being backward and averse to it, but it is a direct opposition and contrariety to God and his service. Its drawing back and hindering is charge enough against it: for it [1.] withdraws those thoughts, affections, time, care, and endeavours, which should be laid out upon better things, so that holiness must needs be obstructed, dwindle, and decay by it. [2.] It hinders the influence of heaven; it shuts out the light casually, quencheth and resisteth the Spirit, and, meritoriously also, it provokes God to withdraw, to remove his glory, and to give over his striving with them; but the contrariety that it hath to all the parts of holiness is yet more: Christ notes it, Mat. vi. 24. These two masters, God and the world, are contrary in their designs, in their commands, in their natures, so that it is impossible for any man to serve them both. They both require the heart, and they both require it to contrary and incompatible services and ends. These, then, are such masters as would be domini in solidum, masters of the whole.469 Now there cannot be two masters of one thing in that sense; neither, if there were, could the hearts of men serve these different commands, but their work would necessarily engage their affections to one only; they would either 'love the one and hate the other, or hold to the one and despise the other.' This very consideration, if there were no more, doth render the world a desirable instrument for Satan.

(4.) Fourthly, In all this the world hath so many *cunning disguises, and plausible shifts, that it becomes thereby wonderfully serviceable to Satan.* It is the perfection of wicked policy to manage wicked designs under plausible pretences. These the world hath in readiness when it is accused of rebellion and treachery against God. The pleas of necessity, of prosecution of a lawful calling, of providing for a family, of not neglecting the benefits of God, of cheering the heart, and taking the comforts of the labours of their hands, and a great many more, are ready excuses to ward off the force of the convincing word. These the devil drives home, and fastens them into such strong persuasions, that the deluded sinner cannot see the danger that is before him, nor the spiritual adultery or idolatry of his soul, in his excessive love to worldly pleasures.

(5.) Fifthly, The world hath also *a spiritual fascination and witchcraft*, by which, where it hath once prevailed, men are enchanted to an utter forgetfulness of themselves and God, and being drunk with pleasures, they are easily engaged to a madness and height of folly. Some, like foolish children, are made to keep a great stir in the world for very trifles, for a vain show; they think themselves great, honourable, excellent, and for this make a great bustle, when the world hath not added 'one cubit to their stature' of real worth. Others are by this Circe transformed into savage creatures, and act the part of lions and tigers. Others, like swine, wallow in the lusts of uncleanness. Others are unmanned, putting off all natural affections, care not who they ride over, so they may rule or be made great. Others are taken with ridiculous frenzies, so that a man that stands in the cool shade of a sedate composure would judge them out of their wits. It would make a man admire to read of the frisks of Caius Caligula, Xerxes, Alexander, and many others, who because they were above many men, thought themselves above human nature. They forgot they were born, and must die, and did such things as would have made them, but that their greatness overawed it, a laughing-stock and common scorn to children. Neither must we think that these were but some few or rare instances of worldly intoxication, when the Scripture notes it as a general distemper of all that bow down to worship this idol. They live 'without God in the world,' saith the apostle, [Eph. ii. 12,] that is, they so carry it as if there were no God to take notice of them, to check them for their madness. 'God is not in all his thoughts,' saith David, Ps. x. 4, 5. 'The judgments of God are far above out of their sight;' he puffs at his enemies, and saith in his heart, 'he shall never be moved,' &c. The whole psalm describes the worldling as a man that hath lost all understanding, and were acting the part of a frantic bedlam. What then can be a more fit engine for the devil to work with than the pleasures of the world?

Applic. I shall briefly apply this to two sorts of men, those that are straitened with want and necessities, and those whose 'cups run over,' having all 'that their heart can wish.'

(1.) First, To those that think their measure of outward comforts little, I would from the doctrine now explained tell them that *they have not so much cause to vex and disquiet themselves for their poverty or troubles as they apprehend.* The world is not so desirable a thing as many dream. Did but men consider how great a snare it is, and what dangers attend the fulness of it, they would not so earnestly covet it, nor so passionately lament when it flies from them. If thou hast so much godliness as can quiet thy heart in a contented enjoyment of thy little, that little which thou hast is better than great riches of the wicked. Thou little knowest from what pride, insolency, contempt of God and men, and many other temptations and lusts, God doth preserve thee, by denying thee earthly things. Thou art now, it may be, often looking up to God, striving to believe his word, often examining thy heart, labouring to live upon God and his all-sufficiency, looking after the bread that endures to eternal life; when if thou hadst the temptations of plenty, it may be feared thou wouldst be another man, and be carried away to forget God, to be careless of holy walking, and so make way for bitterness and sorrow at last.

(2.) Secondly, I would also caution poor men not *to enlarge their desires too much after the world, but to fear the temptations of the world.* It is not only a snare to those that enjoy it, but to those that want it: for while they admire it, and engage their affections for it, it ensnares them in sinful undertakings; they are tempted to lie, cheat, dissemble, to use unlawful shifts, to rob, steal, overreach in bargaining, and to neglect the care of the soul in all. Let such call to mind, [1.] That often the providence of God doth of purpose thwart and cross the designs of such, so that though they toil and sweat, running from market to market, 'rising early and sitting up late,' yet he blows upon their gettings, and they wither to nothing, 'while it is yet in their hand;' or if they seem to keep them longer, yet all the end they make with them is but to put them into a 'bag with holes,' [Haggai i. 6,] they 'perish by evil travail,' Eccles. v. 14. [2.] They often are at a great deal of labour in pursuit, and then when the desired object is within their reach, they are overwhelmed with their disappointment, as if providence designed to mock them for their folly. This is excellently set forth, in the emblem of a man climbing up a rock, with great labour, to reach a crown that hung upon the precipice, who when he had stretched himself to grasp it, falls down and breaks his neck. [3.] And when they do by great toil rake together a heap of riches, they are starved frequently in their plenty, and so cursed that they have no more than 'the beholding of their goods with their eyes,' in that God denies them a 'heart to use them,' Eccles. v. 11. [4.] Their gettings allay not their thirst for more, 'He that loveth silver, shall not be satisfied with silver,' Eccles. v. 10. [5.] Often they are given as a scourge and plague; as the quails given to the Israelites 'came out of their nostrils.' The wise man notes it, Eccles. v. 13, 'Riches are kept for the owners thereof to their hurt.'

(3.) Thirdly, To those that have the delights of the world, plentiful estates, full tables, beautiful houses, rich tradings, honours, and dignities, I would desire to give the greatest caution, that they take heed to themselves, because they walk in the midst of snares. They should consider, [1.] That the great God hath laid most serious charges upon them, 'not to love the world,' but to withdraw their affections from it, nay, to be crucified to it, as to any captivating delight, and to use it with such an indifference of mind, that they should be in their deportments towards it as 'if they used it not.' [2.] They should have their danger in their eye. How careful is he of his steps that knows he walks in the midst of serpents which are ready to sting him; the thoughts of this should blunt the edge of our delights. If you were at a feast where you knew there were poisoned dishes, you would be afraid to eat anything. Do you think that Captain Smith470 when he was taken by the savages of America, and had plenty of meat set before him, which he knew was given to fatten him that he might be better meat when he was killed, had any stomach to eat or to drink? Was that feast pleasing to him that sat under a sharp sword hung over his head in a horse hair, when he expected every moment it should fall upon him and kill him?471 Such are great men, rich men. With what fear and care should they use these things, when they know there is hazard of mischief from them upon every occasion! How much doth Christ speak in that one sentence, 'It is easier for a camel to go through the eye of a needle, than for a rich man to enter into the kingdom of heaven'! [Mat. xix. 24.] He means not that it is absolutely impossible, but extremely difficult, and the difficulty lies in the hindrances which their riches casts before them. [3.] They should carefully consider for what ends God gives these, and to what use they are to be put. Rich men are but God's pursers; they do but 'carry the bag,' and what is put therein, for public uses. If accordingly, as faithful stewards, they lay it out upon those that have need, they shall 'make friends of the unrighteous mammon,' and it will turn to a spiritual account: but if they think that all is for themselves, and so shut their bowels and purses from others, then they carry the bag no otherwise than as Judas did, and will be easily persuaded to sell Christ and heaven for a little more of earth.

CHAPTER XXII

These answers of Christ to the several temptations, which are now to be explained, are different as to their matter, yet the general purport of them being the same, I shall therefore handle them together. They may be considered two ways:—

1. First, *As they are fit and pertinent answers to particular temptations, of distrust, of presumption, of debauching the heart by worldly delights to the service of Satan*; and thus may they be useful in their consideration, to those who are directly moved by Satan to such sins. And when at any time we are tempted in straits to cast away our reliance upon the careful providence of God, we may look upon Christ's answer, that man's life doth not so depend upon the usual means, but that any other thing blessed by divine appointment may be useful to that end. When we are enticed to presume of extraordinary supports, then by Christ's example the temptation may be resisted, by considering, that however God be to be trusted, yet he is at no time to be tempted by unnecessary expectations in the neglect of the ordinary means. If our hearts be wooed by worldly delights to cast off our care of God and religion, we may then call to mind that this is abominable idolatry, and so may we turn off our hearts from sinful compliance by charging our souls with the opposite duties, upon a true discovery of the vileness and inconvenience of the transgressions urged upon us.

2. But, secondly, They may be considered as they give *instruction for the management of our spiritual armour against all Satan's wiles in the general*; and in this sense I shall endeavour to open them, laying down first these two conclusions:—

(1.) First, *That the whole business of these temptations, as permitted to Satan, and submitted unto by Christ, was certainly upon design.* The same wisdom that contrived the wonderful method of the salvation of men by a Redeemer, did also order these temptations; for else Christ could have prevented them, or by a divine authority commanded silence to the tempter, and by his power might have chased him away. As Christ told Pilate, 'Thou couldst have no power at all against me, except it were given thee from above,' [John xix. 11;] thereby manifesting that his suffering was from a higher design than he was aware of; so might he have said to the devil, 'Except this had been designed by an eternal counsel, thou couldst not have made this attempt.' So that we must look further for the spring and rise of this, than to any supposed occasional outbreaking of satanical malice upon him.

(2.) Secondly, That this design, however it touched upon the person and offices of Christ, as mediator and second Adam, for thus it became him to overcome the enemy at the same weapon by which he overcame our first parents, and by this personal experience, to be fitted with feeling compassions to the tempted, yet was it *wholly for our sakes*, as may appear by two things:—

[1.] First, In that Christ, if his answers had only concerned himself, might have given other fit replies to the first temptation, of turning stones to bread He could have retorted the argument upon Satan, as Jerome and others observe.472 If I am not the Son of God, it is in vain to require a miracle of me. If I am, it is in vain to tempt me. Or he might have answered, 'That as the Father hath life in himself, so hath he given to the Son to have life in himself, and that by this divine power he could sustain himself without bread.'473 To the second it might have been a sufficient answer to have excepted against his unfaithfulness in citing that testimony out of Ps. xci., where, by discovering his wilful omission of the clause, 'in all thy ways;' 'He shall keep thee in all thy ways;' his temptation might have fallen to the ground, as no way encouraged from that promise. To the third might have been returned such answers as these: that Satan's offer was a lie; that it was not in his power to dispose of the kingdoms of the world—that these were Christ's already; that these were vain arguments to draw him from the glory of a heavenly kingdom; and finally, that of all creatures Satan, being God's sworn enemy, had least reason to expect divine honour.

[2.] Secondly, In that all Christ's answers were from Scripture, which is properly a 'light to the steps of men,' and all these scriptures cited shew man's duty. He saith not, 'the Son of God shall not live by bread alone,' but 'man lives not by bread alone;' he saith not, Christ must not tempt, but thou, man, shalt not tempt the Lord thy God, &c. By all which we may discern that Christ answered not by arguments peculiarly agreeable to his person and nature, but by such as suit the general state of God's children. And this certainly was for our advantage. He conquered with such weapons, not for any necessity that he had to take that course, but for the need that we had of such instruction; for hereby we see that Satan is conquerable, and also how we must use our weapons.474 In this also he left us 'an example, that we should follow his steps;' as Gideon said to his soldiers, 'As you see me do, so do you likewise,' [Judges vii. 17.] Thus, as it were, doth our Lord speak to us: For your sakes suffered I these temptations, that I might teach your hands to war, and your fingers to fight; for your sakes I used these weapons of yours, rather than my own, that I might shew you the use of your sword and shield, and how your adversary may be overcome by them; dealing herein with us as a master at arms, — it is Musculus's comparison, — who, for the better instructing and animating of his tyro, takes rather his disciple's sword than his own, to beat his adversary withal, minding not only the conquest of an enemy, but also the encouragement of a young soldier.475

If any carry a suspicion in their mind that Christ had not our instruction so much in his eye as hath been said, because he gives not such particular instructions for our spiritual welfare476 as the apostle in Eph. vi., expecting that our Saviour should have been more punctual in making particular applications from every part of his carriage to our use, and drawing out from thence some positive conclusions or draughts of the way and manner of resistance, they may know that there is no other difference betwixt Eph. vi. and Mat. iv. than there is betwixt precept and example. What the apostle there prescribed in the theory, here Christ teacheth in the practice; here we have in their use the girdle of truth, the shield of faith, the sword of the Spirit, the helmet of salvation, and all the other parts of that armour; and withal we may know that this is a far more advantageous way of teaching young beginners, to let them see things in a plain example, than only to give general precepts. But besides, we are to consider that Christ did many things, the meaning whereof the disciples then present with him did not know as yet, neither was it expected from them that they should; like to what he said to Peter, John xiii. 7, 'What I do thou knowest not now, but thou shalt know hereafter;' but were intended to be laid up in store to be more fully made use of, as after-directions should come in to give them information. He therefore that had purposed to give further light in this matter by his apostle and servant, was now doing that which his design led him to in his personal actings, with a secret respect also to those instructions which he intended after to communicate. We have then no reason to be jealous that these temptations were not intended for our use, but the more to assure ourselves that it was even so, because we find that those very weapons which here Christ in his own person wielded against Satan, are afterwards recommended to us.

Having thus laid the foundation, we must then, if we will imitate our captain, carefully observe his deportment from point to point, that we may draw out those instructions which he intended for us.

And the first thing that I shall take notice of, shall be the courage and magnanimity of our leader. He had endured temptations forty days and nights before, and yet he keeps the field without any appearance of shrinking or running away. Satan no sooner tempts than he is repelled. From this consideration we have this instruction: —

Direct. 1. *That he that would successfully resist temptations, must not fly, but with a courageous resolve set himself to oppose.*

Christians are apt to fear, when Satan comes up against them, and ready to turn their backs: as the Israelites were dismayed at the appearance of Goliath, and fled before him. But if we would conquer, we must, as David, go out against him in 'the name of the Lord.' To this we are called, 1 Cor. xvi. 13, 'Stand fast in the faith, quit yourselves like men, be strong;' and Eph. vi. 14, 'Stand, having your loins girt with truth,' &c. This courage recommended is not a contempt and negligent slighting of danger, nor is it a bold adventurousness upon occasions of sin; it is a holy, humble courage, and doth admit of a threefold fear.

(1.) First, *Of a fear of sin*, that is, a hatred of it. We must fear sin as the greatest evil. This is no cowardice, but tends to the strongest resolution and highest endeavours against it. From this principle is it that men oppose sin as their mortal enemy, and excite their utmost courage to fight against it. As the Philistines being afraid of Israel, and yet hating to serve the Hebrews, mutually encouraged one another, 'Be strong, and quit yourselves like men, O ye Philistines.' A fear of hatred begets boldness.

(2.) Secondly, Courage admits *of a preventing fear and a provident avoidance*. Occasions of sin are to be fled. We are not with greater earnestness called upon to stand, than we are warned in this case 'to fly.' So the apostle often, 'fly fornication,' 'fly idolatry,' 'fly youthful lusts.' Occasions are best opposed by flying, where calling and duty doth not engage: Prov. iv. 14, 'Enter not into the path of the wicked, and go not in the way of evil men.' He fights best that flies most, where necessity doth not bid him stay, 1 Cor. vi. 18, x. 14, and 2 Tim. ii. 22.

(3.) Thirdly, It also admits of the fear *of a holy jealousy*; such a distrust of ourselves, as puts us to seek to 'the rock which is higher than we' for shelter. God calls us to 'turn into our stronghold,' Nahum i. 7, and to 'lay hold upon his strength,' [Isa. xxvii. 5.] It is rashness or desperateness, and not true courage, to adventure ourselves without our guard or shield. But however we must fear sin, suspect our strength, and fly occasions, yet Satan we must not fly. Here we are bid to stand, for these reasons:—

[1.] First, *It is impossible to fly from him*. He can follow us wherever we go. If we go to holy assemblies, he can come thither. If we shut up ourselves in our closets, he can meet us there. If we betake ourselves to a wilderness or to a crowd, to be sure he will find us out.

[2.] Secondly, *We are expressly charged to make resistance*: James iv. 7, 'Resist the devil;' 1 Peter v. 9, 'whom resist.' This plainly speaks positive endeavours and opposition on our part.

[3.] Thirdly, *A fainting fear is an unbelieving distrust of Gods power*, as if he were not 'able to save to the uttermost,' [Heb. vii. 25,] and of Christ's compassionate tenderness, as if he would not 'succour those that are tempted,' [Heb. ii. 18.]

[4.] Fourthly, *Our fainting makes Satan insult.* He triumphs when we turn our backs, and besides hath the greater advantage to wound us or to tread us down at pleasure. It is observed that God provides armour for head and breast, and all the fore parts, by a shield in case of resistance; but if we fly, so little encouragement is there for cowardice, there is no armour for the back.

[5.] Fifthly, *It is most suitable to Christian courage to die in the place, and to put it to the utmost hazard rather than to yield.* According to Vespasian's motto, *Oportet imperatorem stantem mori.* Every Christian should say, 'Shall such a one as I fly?' [Neh. vi. 11;] one that hath given up my name to God; one that hath professed holiness afore men; one that hath so many advantages for resistance, and such sweet encouragements from a victorious general!

Quest. But the great question is, What is this fear that is forbidden, and the courage which is enjoined?

Ans. The fear forbidden is an unbelieving weakness and pusillanimity, through which, as hopeless of success, men throw down their weapons and yield themselves up to Satan, when the hearts of men fail them to the giving up of the victory.

Spiritual courage, on the contrary, is a serious resolve of fighting it out in the strength of the Lord, and it consists of these two parts:—

First, A sincere resolution to be on Christ's side against all iniquity, a deliberate unfeigned determination to stand for God and his holy ways, against Satan and sin. [1.] The ground of this determination is a conviction of the evil of sin, even to a hatred of it. He that hath not thoroughly weighed the misery of living in sin, and fully purposed within himself to forsake it, can have no true Christian courage when it comes to a pinch. [2.] From this ground he lays himself under solemn engagements to Christ his general, as soldiers list themselves under their captains, that he will follow him and observe his commands; he gives up himself to God by covenant. So that now he is no longer his own, but Christ's servant, bound for his work. [3.] And this with such or so much belief of his promises for aid and victory, that he hath some hopes or expectations at least, that God may at last so assist him that he may attain to some real degree of the mortification of the 'flesh, with the affections and lusts thereof,' [Gal. v. 24.]

Secondly, The second part of this courage consists in a suitable management of this undertaking. Courage is not only seen in the first onset, but in the prosecution of the warfare; and this lies in two things. [1.] When there are real endeavours against sin, answerable to this undertaking, in all ways of striving to oppose it. When men do not engage against sin with big words only; or as the children of Ephraim—who, arming themselves and carrying bows, seemed to have stout resolves, but then 'turned back in the day of battle;' but with real and conscientious wrestlings, setting themselves with all their might and care against every temptation, and studying to pursue the victory, where in any degree it is obtained, to a greater height. [2.] When these endeavours are sincerely persisted in, without being quite wearied out or utter fainting, so that it never comes to this, though they may be sometime under Satan's feet, that they relinquish their first solemn engagement, or repent of their undertaking, and then turn their backs upon God, listing themselves under Satan's colours. Such a fainting as this would bereave men of their crown; 'Ye shall reap in due time if ye faint not,' Gal. vi. 9. Upon this hazard are the children of God cautioned, Heb. xii. 3, 'Lest ye be wearied and faint in your mind.' [3.] There is also a particular kind of courage expressed in a holy and humble contempt of Satan's suggestions, when after all means used they cease not to be troublesome. This is not to slight sin but to slight Satan, who, though he is resisted, ceaseth not to molest.477

Applic. I shall particularly apply this first direction, [1.] To those that propound ease to themselves in their race or warfare, which is a thing impossible to one that doth the work of a soldier, not considering that work and courageous endeavours do abide them. [2.] To those that pretend themselves Christ's soldiers, courage and Christian magnanimity is your cognizance. By this must you be known. How do ye stand? what are your resolutions and undertakings? Those Christians that have 'joy and peace in believing' can more easily satisfy themselves in this; but those that fight in tears and grief, in disquiets and troubled thoughts, are apt to conclude themselves unbelieving, because they are fearful; or to think that they look not up to Jesus, the 'author and finisher of their faith,' because they apprehend themselves weary and 'faint in their minds.' For the ease and help of such, I shall shew in a few things that there is as real a Christian courage in such mourners as in some that sing songs of triumph.

[1.] First, It is a real courage and undertaking against sin for any to resolve his utmost, *out of detestation of it, before he can satisfy himself that God will accept of it.* To oppose sin under such a discouragement, or at such a venture, is a courageous hatred; and yet so do these mourners.

[2.] Secondly, *To be under continual grievings because of miscarriages, so that other things of outward enjoyment cease to be pleasing,* is a courageous hatred; but this is their case.

[3.] Thirdly, *To wrestle against sin under high discouragements*, when afflicted and tossed, when Satan runs upon them and shakes them by the neck, and yet they continue their wrestling and withstanding as they are able; this is faithful resistance, 'a resistance unto blood, striving against sin,' Heb. xii. 4; that is, if that expression be proverbial, like that, *ad sanguinem usque*, they resist sin faithfully, under great hazards and inconveniencies, even to wounds and blood, till they have broken heads and broken faces; and can say to God, though we have been 'broken in the place of dragons,' and have these wounds to shew, yet 'have we not departed from thee,' [Ps. xliv. 19,] nor quitted our desires after thee and holiness, for all these buffetings of Satan; but this is the character of these dejected ones.

[4.] Fourthly, It is a courageous hatred that cannot *suffer a sinful motion to fall upon the soul, but it puts all into a combustion within, and raiseth disquiet;* for it is an argument that there is a contrariety betwixt the heart and sin; but this is their case also.

[5.] Fifthly, It is courage and constancy *to hold on in gracious endeavours and strivings;* so that when they fall, as soon as they can re-collect their strength they set on where they left, and renew the battle, never changing their first resolve for holiness against sin. This is implied in the apostle's phrase of 'standing,'—Eph. vi., 'That ye may withstand, and when ye have done all, to stand.' He is accounted to stand that runs not out of the field, but stands to his holy resolve to the last, though the battle go sore against him by fits; but such are these mourners.

There is true courage under mourning and disquiet of heart, so that we may say to such, 'O thou afflicted and tossed,' fear not, 'the glory of the Lord shall shine upon thee,' [Isa. lx. 1.] They that are weak in this sense shall be strong as David.

CHAPTER XXIII

The next thing observable in Christ's carriage to Satan is this, that Christ, though he rejected every temptation by giving a reason of his refusal from the command of God, did not suffer Satan to dispute his temptations further than the first proposal, and in his answers he takes no notice of the reasons or motives by which he laboured to make his temptations prevailing. In the two first temptations he gives no reply to what Satan insinuated by his supposition, 'If thou be the Son of God,' neither by affirming that he was so, nor discovering to him his knowledge of the secret subtlety which he had wrapped up under these plausible pretences. In the third he answers not a word to the vanity and falsehood of his deceitful offer of 'the kingdoms of the world,' though, as hath been observed, he might have opposed strong reasons against them all; and besides, when Satan became insolent and impudent in tempting Christ 'to fall down and worship him,' he chaseth him away with a severe abomination, 'Get thee hence, Satan;' from which we have a second direction, which is this:—

Direct. 2. That temptations to sin are to be opposed by peremptory denials rather than by disputings.

This is a note which most commentators have on this place; but it stands in need of a distinct application, because it is not a rule so general but that the practice of God's children have made exception against it. For the clearer explanation of it, I shall,

1. First, *Give you the several kinds of disputings, by which we may see that all are not alike*; for,

(1.) First, *The serious working of the thoughts in a quick denial of a temptation with a reason implied or expressed, though it admit not Satan to any further dispute or argument, may in some sense be called a disputing*; for the Scripture useth διαλογισμὸς for any inward, serious thought. Such a kind of disputing as this is necessary. It cannot be wanting to any that refuse a sinful motion, this being, as we shall see afterward, one of those directions which Christ intended us by his example, and the very thing which Christ practised in every temptation; for he contented not himself to give a naked denial, but still adds a reason of such refusal. Those who in general terms urge that temptations are not to be disputed, do not reckon this as any disputing;

and others that do, taking disputing for the refusal of a thing with a reason assigned, think that his procedure in the two first temptations is not imitable by us, but only that of the third, wherein he chased away the devil with angry denial; but the mistake is obvious.

(2.) Secondly, *There is a disputing of unnecessary curiosity and conference.* This is when a sinful motion injected into our hearts is not directly consented to, but then instead of a full denial men begin to raise questions and make objections of lesser moment, or some impertinent queries which strike not at the root; as one observed of himself, that instead of denying a sinful motion, he began to dispute whether it came from Satan or his own inclination; and so, instead of quenching the fire, he busied himself to inquire whence it came. Men deal with temptations in this case as they who being asked whether they will buy such a commodity, hastily answer no, but yet call back the party again and ask whence it came, or what it must cost, and by such entanglements of curiosity engage themselves at last to buy it. Eve failed by such an inconsiderate conference with Satan, for the abrupt beginning of the serpent's speech, 'Yea, hath God said ye shall not eat,' &c., and the summing up of the arguments which prevailed with her to eat, 'When the woman saw that the tree was good for food, and pleasant to the eyes,' &c., [Gen. iii. 6,] do clearly evidence that there was more discourse than is there expressed, and that also tending to ascertain the goodness, pleasantness, and profit of the fruit. This kind of disputing is always unlawful and dangerous, for it is but a wanton dalliance with a temptation, a playing upon the hole of the asp, and commonly ends in a sinful compliance.

(3.) Thirdly, *There is a disputing of a deliberating and parleying indifferency.* This is when the devil puts a thought of sin into their minds, and, while they seem not to be forward to embrace it, leaves it to further consideration, and then they float betwixt resolved and unresolved, betwixt *pro* and *con*, being at a great dispute within themselves what is best to be done, whether the conveniences on the one hand will weigh down the inconveniences on the other. This, in cases of apparent sin, is a wicked halting betwixt two, always unlawful.

(4.) Fourthly, *There are also treacherous partial arguings, wherein the heart takes part with Satan.* These are those debates that are to be found in natural men, about the doing or not doing of sinful things. This looks so like the combat betwixt the flesh and the Spirit, that it hath occasioned an inquiry how they may be distinguished each from other. It is generally concluded that in that strife of the natural man, the light of the understanding and conscience gives opposition to the bent of the affections, and the same faculties, though sanctified in part in the regenerate, are the parties that give opposition each to other; but with this principal difference, that in this strife of the flesh and Spirit the man takes part with God, whereas in the other the affections take the devil's part, and in a malignant averseness to the light, strive to put it out and to get over the conviction of conscience, so that the man strives to sin, and to stop the mouth of such objections as come in to the contrary: this kind of disputing is always sinful.

(5.) Fifthly, *There is yet a disputing in a strict sense, which is a full and solemn debating of a satanical injection, by giving it the full hearing, and admitting Satan to be a respondent to our objections.* Of this it is queried how far it may be convenient and how far inconvenient, because we see Christ in this place did not thus dispute with Satan, and yet we find instances in Scripture of some holy men that have been unavoidably engaged to dispute a temptation to the utmost.

To answer this query, I shall, secondly, shew in what cases it may be necessary or convenient to enter the lists with Satan in a holy arguing, and in what cases it is inconvenient and dangerous. There are four cases in which we may dispute a temptation:—

[1.] First, When the motion is of things *doubtful and disputable, whether they be lawful or not.* Here it cannot be avoided; for albeit, as the apostle adviseth, Rom. xiv. 1, 'doubtful disputations' are not to be imposed upon others, so as to tie them up to our persuasions, yet in these things every man, before he can act clearly, is to endeavour his own satisfaction in the lawfulness or unlawfulness of the thing, that so he may be 'fully persuaded in his own mind,' ver. 5. And he gives two strong reasons of this, ver. 22, 23: (1.) From the rack and trouble which otherwise the man may be put upon, while his conscience, unsatisfied, 'condemneth him in that which,' by a contrary practice, 'he alloweth.' (2.) In that this condemnation of conscience, while he doth that, the lawfulness whereof he believeth not, is an evidence of his sin, as well as an occasion of his trouble.

[2.] Secondly, Disputings have place, when *a temptation hath taken hold upon the thoughts, and so far possessed itself that our corruption riseth up in the defence of the suggestion.* Satan will not quit that hold, though he be an intruder without our leave, till he be beat out of his quarters. The apostle, Eph. vi. 16, implies so much by that expression, of 'quenching the fiery darts' of Satan. It is not proper to understand it of a refusal of the first motion of sin—though interpreters do usually make it comprehensive both of the keeping out of the dart and the plucking it out—because this evidently supposeth that the dart hath pierced the soul, and now begins to burn and inflame, which will require more labour for the quenching of it, than a refusal of the first motion would put us to. As when fire hath taken hold upon our houses, we shall be forced to bring water for the extinguishing of the flame, which before it had broke out upon the building, an ordinary care might have prevented. And this we [are] further taught by a distinction which the same apostle useth in the same place, of στῆναι and ἀντιστῆναι, standing and withstanding. We must keep off the temptation, that it enter not, by standing against the assault in a peremptory refusal; but if it do enter, then we must be put to it, by a force of holy arguing, to pull out the arrow, and to withstand it.

[3.] Thirdly, Much more need have we of disputing, when the present temptation is *a motion of such a sin which we are habituated unto, and have long practised*; for these kind of sinful motions are not cast out easily. In this case, David adviseth his enemies, Ps. iv. 2-4, who had for a long time, 'loved vanity, and sought after leasing,' that by 'communing with their own heart,' and by disputing against their sinful practices, they should bring themselves under a holy awe, and by that means stop the course of their sinning, ver. 4. This, indeed, is the great thing that sinners are called to by God, to ponder their estate, to consider their ways, to study the evil and danger of sin, to examine themselves, and to reason together with God about the wickedness and ingratitude of their actions, and about the contrary loveliness, blessedness, and happiness of the ways of God, that so they may be brought to repentance; all which are done only by a serious arguing of their case and hazard.

[4.] Fourthly, It is convenient, and in some cases necessary, to dispute a temptation which Satan offers to us, *by the mouths of men, who entice us to share with them in their wickedness*; for here, by arguing, we may not only discourage their further solicitation, and so free ourselves from the like temptation for the future, but we also, by the exercise of a holy charity, endeavour to 'pull them out of the fire,' Jude 23. When Joseph's mistress tempted him, he considered that he had to deal both with the devil and his mistress, Gen. xxxix. 7, 8, and therefore that he might 'resist the devil,' he peremptorily refused the temptation; but that he might take off his mistress from her unlawful prosecution, he argues with her about the ingratitude, danger, and unlawfulness of such an act, 'My master wotteth not what is with me in the house, and he hath committed all that he hath to my hand: there is none greater in this house than I, neither hath he kept anything back from me but thee, because thou art his wife: how then can I do this great wickedness, and sin against God?' When sinners do entice us to cast in our lot amongst them, pity to them, and care of ourselves, will engage us to argue the folly and danger of their ways with them, except they behave themselves as dogs and swine; their carriage giving us just ground to conclude, that they are so set on wickedness, that it may endanger us, rather than profit them, to debate with them. And so was it likely—and the text seems to hint so much—that when Joseph perceived his mistress was resolved upon the pursuit, and that his reasonings were not minded, he persisted in his denial, but forbore his arguings.

But however it may be convenient to dispute, in the last mentioned sense, in these four cases—and others may probably be added—yet there are cases in which it will be inconvenient and hazardous to dispute or argue, and of this order I shall reckon four.

[1.] First, It is not safe to dispute the matter in vile, infectious temptations, such as are either suitable to our inclinations, or may receive a favourable aspect and countenance from the posture of our affairs and condition. These temptations, even in our debating against them, are like the opening of a sepulchre, which sends forth a poisonous stream478 which may infect those that loathe and resist it. It is dangerous to admit fire into the same room where there is gunpowder, though there be no intention to kindle it. It hath been an old observation, that the very confession of infectious sins, though designed to beget shame, and resolution against them for the future, have kindled a new flame, by the unnecessary declaration of the manner and circumstances, so that they have returned from the confessor more infected than when they went; and those very persons whose care it should have been to have put the highest disgrace upon sins so confessed, to the begetting of loathing and abhorrency in the parties and themselves, have by too curious an inquiry received such poison at the ear, that the heart hath been forthwith infected. The like hazard remains to those that are willing to debate such sins with Satan; for though they begin upon the score of resistance, yet the very dwelling on such a subject, when admitted to lay itself open, doth convey such amorous looks unto the treacherous affections, that the heart is in danger of a secret poison. There is no better way in such cases than to command all such thoughts and considerations out of our coasts, and, as we do when the city or town we live in is infected, to withdraw ourselves from the air of such a temptation. We may observe the like care in Joseph, though he thought himself concerned at first, as hath been said, to oppose the unlawful suit of his mistress, yet seeing her desperately set upon her folly, he declined all communication with her, and would not be with her, Gen. xxxix. 10; and at last, when she caught him by his garment, 'he left it in her hand and fled,' ver. 12. He might easily have rescued his garment from her, had he not been aware that his contesting against her might have been an occasion of ensnarement to himself. Christ himself, when he was tempted by Peter to spare himself, [Mat. xvi. 22,]—which was a temptation very taking to human nature, especially when suffering and death is in view,—is more short and sparing in his reasoning against it, than he was when the devil tempted him. He gives no positive reasons against it, as he did when he was tempted to 'fall down and worship the devil,' but dischargeth himself from any further consideration of the matter by a declared abhorrency of the thing, 'Get thee behind me, Satan, for thou savourest not the things that be of God, but the things which be of men.' Which is as if he had plainly said, This is so apparently from the devil, and so much abhorred by me, because so suitable to my condition, that I will not so much as discourse of it or consider it.

[2.] Secondly, Generally in all temptations, though they have not the advantage of our present special estate or inclination, as hath been noted, of an apparent withdrawment from obedience, or of things unquestionably sinful, it is not convenient to dispute them, but to dismiss them by a denial, except some of the forementioned considerations do alter the case. In known cases we need not parley, but stoutly deny. Our resolutions for duty, and against sin, should not be to seek. We are certain that sin is to be avoided, and duty to be practised; here we should be peremptory. Abraham being certain of duty, when God called him to 'a place which he should afterward receive for an inheritance,' he disputed not the uncertainty, the danger or inconvenience that possibly might attend his removal, but went out, 'not knowing whither he went,' Heb. xi. 8. Paul being called by God to preach among the heathen, though 'flesh and blood' were ready with arguments against it, yet he would not so much as confer with them, but immediately obeyed, Gal. i. 16. Like instances I might fetch from other holy men. Cyprian, when the president gave it to his own choice whether he would obey or be put to death, commanding him to take it into consideration, he readily replied, In re tam sancta non est deliberandum, that it was not to deliberate in so plain a case. Mrs Ann Askew, when at the stake ready to be burnt, a pardon was offered by the Lord Chancellor; she would not so much as look on it, but returned this answer, that she came not thither 'to deny her Lord and Master.' Bishop Hooker,479 in the same condition, had a box laid before him with a pardon in it, which when he understood—he was so afraid of tampering with a temptation—he cried out, 'If ye love my soul, away with it; if ye love my soul, away with it.' And many others there were in all ages, so far from accepting such 'unlawful deliverances,' that they would not take into consideration the unrighteous terms upon which they might have escaped.

[3.] Thirdly, When a temptation, after all means used, continues to be troublesome, and is rather an annoyance than an infection, then must we not dispute it, but by a holy contempt despise it. Temptations to blasphemy are oft of this nature, as hath been noted in its place, and there are other things by which Satan creates to God's children great disquiet, while they in the meantime abhor the sin, and cry out of the trial. Here when the 'messenger of Satan' will not depart, it is an advice that hath the general approbation of holy experienced men,480 that we should despise the temptation, as an approved way to our quiet and ease; for while we think to repel such assaults by struggling with arguments, we do but increase the force of them; as he that thinks to shelter himself against the wind, by holding up his cloak before him, doth but derive upon himself a stronger blast.

[4.] Fourthly, *In temptations of inward trouble and terror, it is not convenient to dispute the matter with Satan.* David in Ps. xlii. 11, seems to correct himself for his mistake; his soul was 'cast down within him,' and for the cure of that temptation, he had prepared himself by arguments for a dispute; but perceiving himself in a wrong course, he calls off his soul from, disquiet to an immediate application to God and the promises, 'Trust still in God, for I shall yet praise him;' but in Ps. xi. 1, he is more aforehand with his work, for while his enemies were acted by Satan to discourage him, he rejects the temptation at first, before it settled upon his thoughts, and chaseth it away as a thing that he would not give ear to: 'In thee, Lord, do I put my trust; how say ye then to my soul, Flee as a bird to your mountain?' And there are weighty reasons that should dissuade us from entering the lists with Satan in temptations of inward trouble. As,

[1.] First, The determination of the sincerity of the soul and its converted state is a question of no small difficulty—a knotty controversy, more intricate and abstruse than those controversies that in the schools are of greatest name for difficulty; for this is liable to more weighty objections, and stands in need of nicer distinction. As Dr Goodwin observes,481 'They that converse with dejected spirits, find so much quickness and nimbleness of reasoning, turning every way to ward off the force of an argument brought for their consolation, that even wise and able heads are oft put to a stand, and know not what to answer.' Would it then be fit to give Satan this advantage? or to admit him so far into our reasoning? He that will invite Satan to such a contest, shall be sure to have his hands full.

[2.] Secondly, This kind of temptation doth usually *disable men for arguing*; it oftentimes confounds the brain, stupifies the understanding, and weakens the memory. Heman complains of himself as 'distracted by terrors,' [Ps. lxxxviii. 15.] Job calls himself desperate, [chap. vi. 26.] Such persons are not surely in a fit case to manage a temptation with so cunning a sophister as Satan.

[3.] Thirdly, If they descend into the battle, he is not only *too strong for them, but commonly after a while they take Satan's part against themselves, and comply with him, concluding against their own peace.*

[4.] Fourthly, *There is also a better way at hand than to enter into a dispute;* and that is, by going to God by a present faith, love or repentance, when the truth of any of these is questioned. It is a difficult task to prove sometime that former acts of faith, love, or other graces were sincere. This may admit of such objections from a wounded spirit, that it will be hard to answer them; but in this case it is a nearer way to see if there be not in all these complainings some present acts of these graces; whether such complainants are not willing to embrace Christ upon any terms, whether they do not hate sin, whether they would not unfeignedly be reconciled to God, &c. It oft falls out that this doth stay the trouble when examinations of former acts do nothing for them. Some men are at more pains, as one saith, to repair and fit an old building, than would serve to rear a new one. Yet must it be remembered that though it were the best course to resist temptations of this nature at first, by avoiding unnecessary disputings, notwithstanding when this—as I noted before of other temptations—hath seized upon the heart and taken possession, then shall we be forced to 'fill our mouths with arguments,' and whether we will or no, must we undergo a contest. As we see in David, who when his troubles had prevailed upon him, was forced to plead with God, with himself, with the temptation, and to have recourse to former experience, 'the days of old, and the years of the right hand of the Most High,' [Ps. lxxvii. 10,] and all little enough.

All that I shall further say concerning the inconveniences of disputing with Satan, shall be to give you *the reasons manifesting these unnecessary communings with him to be every way hazardous and unsuitable.* As,

(1.) First, *It is an honour to Satan, and a disgrace to ourselves.* Men are loath to be seen contesting with persons of a far inferior rank, especially in such things which have procured to such a noted infamy. It is a usual piece of generosity in men of spirit that they scorn to strive with a scold, or contend with a beggar, or be found in company of those that are under an evil name deservedly; and in matters that are vile and base, it is highly disgraceful to admit them to a debate. Such things will either get more credit than they deserve, while they seem to be countenanced by a dispute, or else shall communicate their discredit to those that shall shew such familiarity with them.

(2.) Secondly, *By refusing to dispute temptations, we raise up in our hearts an active abhorrency of them, and by that abhorrency we are cautioned and strengthened against them.* It must needs awaken our hatred into a present activity against that sin, which our consideration at first view presents to us so abominable, that it deserves no other answer but to be whipped out of our sight. And when our heart is thus alarmed, it cannot but stand upon its guard. It is a course that holy men have taken to keep men at a greater distance from sin, to present it as a thing of greatest abhorrency; and that is the intendment of that expression, Rom. vi. 1, 'Shall we sin, that grace may abound? God forbid,' The vileness of that abuse of gospel grace he shews by setting it below the merit of any serious thought; he sharpens their apprehensions against it by an outcry of detestation. The like he doth, Eph. v. 3, where he endeavours to set their hearts against uncleanness and coveteousness, by telling them that it was unbecoming saintship that such things should be 'so much as once named by them.'

(3.) Thirdly, *Disputing is a secret invitation to the devil to urge the temptation further.* We do but toy with him, and give him occasion to follow us. Eve found the truth of this by sad experience; she so managed herself, that she plainly intimated she had a mind to hear what the devil could say for the eating of the forbidden fruit; and so urged the prohibition of God, and the threatening, that she sought from Satan a confirmation of her secret unbelief rather than faithfully endeavoured a repulse of the temptation, and mentioned the threatening under such terms of uncertainty and peradventure, as an objection which she desired might be removed, rather than from a firm belief of that death spoken of, fortifying herself in her duty; by all which Satan was so encouraged to proceed, that he presently confirmed her in her distrust.

(4.) Fourthly, *These disputings usually return nothing of advantage to our account, but to Satan's.* We unnecessarily enter the lists with him, and that upon very unequal terms, he being, as Saul said of Goliath and David, a 'man of war from his youth,' and we but weak, unskilful striplings. We go out of our trenches and leave our weapons behind us. We expose our naked breasts to all his darts, and by discoursing with him he gains time wherein the poison may more powerfully work upon our affections. If he was too hard for our first parents at this weapon, we, whose hearts are not so faithful to God as theirs in innocency, but corrupted by Satan, who hath also a party in us, are not likely to come off with triumph.

(5.) Fifthly, *These presage, consequently, an overthrow.* A parleying city holds not long out. It implies in itself an inclination to yield, when armies are willing to treat. Daily examples and experience of those that give up themselves to sin after communication with Satan sadly witness this truth.

The sum of this direction is this, that when a motion of sin is put into our heart, instead of disputing where it may be avoided, we should peremptorily deny it and send it away with an angry rebuke or severe abomination: I may not do it; How can I do this wickedness? Get thee hence; or, 'The Lord rebuke thee, Satan.'

CHAPTER XXIV

The magnanimity of Christ, and the peremptoriness of his denial, we have noted. We must further observe the immediateness of his answer; he suffered not any of these motions to stay long with him; here was not a *Cras tibi respondebo*, Come again to-morrow and I will answer. He would not take time with the devil, but had his answer ready. No sooner was he tempted, but the temptation was repelled; for these expressions—'But he answered and said;' 'Jesus said unto him;' 'Then saith Jesus unto him,'—shew the quickness and speediness of these returns, that he answered presently, forthwith. Hence we have a third direction in our resisting of Satan, which is this:—

Direct. 3. *Temptations are best answered when they are presently denied and forthwith repelled.* The direction is of great importance; it is not for us to pass by a temptation with silence, or to defer an answer. For these reasons:—

(1.) First, The nature of temptations, as dangerous or infectious, doth sufficiently enforce a necessity of their speedy removal. Things of danger require a sudden stop. If poison be taken into the body, we speedily labour to cast it up, or to overcome it by antidotes. We labour to stay the spreading of a gangrene presently. Who thinks it fit to delay when fire hath taken hold upon a house? The very opportunity of help is in the speediness of the endeavour. It is too late to bring water when the house is consumed, too late to apply a remedy when the disease hath conquered. They that consider what a temptation is, will see no reason to move slowly in opposing.482

(2.) Secondly, *Silence encourageth Satan.* It is not with him as it is with men; it is the policy of some to overlook their petitioners, and by silence to scare them from any further address; but Satan hath more impudence than to be put out of countenance by delay, and more active malice than to be discouraged by silence; nay, it doth on the contrary embolden him. Modest requests are disheartened by silence, but such motions which, by their nature, imply a disgrace, and carry no reason for their acceptance but what they expect to find in the consent of those to whom they are made, if they be not presently refused, they give encouragement to hope for entertainment. An immodest request to a chaste matron, if not forthwith expressly abominated, encourageth to further attempts. Sin being so great an affront to a holy heart, the motion of it cannot be entertained with silence, but Satan is emboldened to expect consent in time, and follows his advantage accordingly. He usually flies at a valiant peremptory resistance; but if the pulse of the soul beat slowly upon the motion, he grounds his hope upon that, and is animated to a further procedure.

(3.) Thirdly, *Our wills are apt to be inclined by delay*. Though grace have made straight our crooked natures, yet we still carry such a sway to our former dispositions, that a small thing, having the advantage of our natural bias and inclination, makes us, like a deceitful bow, turn to our old stand. For the understanding and will of the regenerate are but imperfectly good, the faculties that should obey are unruly. In such a case how dangerous may delays prove! Who will suffer a seditious incendiary in an army, formerly inclined to mutiny? Who will permit leaven to remain in that mass, which he desires may not be leavened, and not quickly remove it? Who will neglect a spark upon dry tinder, that would not have it consumed, and not instantly put it out? If it was so great a mischief to Eve in innocency, as hath been said, to delay her peremptory denial, of how much greater hazard is it to us! Delays are dangerous to a very proverb, and silence may end in consent.

(4.) Fourthly, Silence is also some degree of consent. It is strange to find a man delaying an answer to temptation, and yet no way guilty of consenting. In things that are to be opposed with care and hatred, no man can withhold his hand without blame. He that is not against Satan, who is to be perpetually resisted, is so far for him as he is not against him. He that delays justice which is due, denies it. The judge in the parable was called unjust, not because he had devoured the widow's house, but because he deferred to do her right.483 He that hinders not evil when and as soon as he can, doth command and approve it. These are received axioms amongst men, and have the same truth in them if applied to resistance of temptations. And this may further appear by considering, [1.] The weakness of the will in the regenerate. When our wills are really set upon good and against evil, yet we cannot say they are perfectly for the one and against the other, but that there is still some degree of averseness to good, and of inclination to evil in our wills, or else we should not meet with complainings of imperfections under sincere resistances; as in the apostle, 'The evil that I would not, that do I,' [Rom. vii. 19.] [2.] The acts of the will in consenting may be so sudden, short, and quick, that they may be almost insensible, and as forward and ready as the motion. [3.] The will may be interpretatively voluntary and consenting, when yet it forms not in itself any positive approbation. It may be guilty, in that it doth not more strongly and speedily dissent: for the suspension or negation of the will's act, where it ought to act, cannot avoid the charge of coming short of duty.

(5.) Fifthly, Not to answer presently, is to lose the best opportunity of answering. It is less dangerous, more easy, more comfortable to be speedy in denial. The sooner fire is put out, or the disease is stayed, the less hurt is done; and it is far less labour to quench a spark than a flame; to pluck up a young plant than an old standard; to kill the cockatrice in the egg. A temptation opposed speedily, is with greater ease overcome, than after it hath settled though but a little: for it presently makes a party within us; our affections are soon engaged, our understanding soon bribed, and then we have not only Satan but ourselves to oppose; and this self so divided, that when we come to fight, our wills are against our wills, our affections against our affections, our wishes and prayers clash and contradict each other. As Austin confesseth of himself: 'I prayed,' said he, 'and then feared lest thou shouldst hear me too soon; I desired to satisfy, rather than to extinguish lust.'484 At the first assault the soul is oft in a better posture, more unanimous and consistent with itself; then is the golden opportunity of resistance. For, as one saith,485 it is better to do it while reason is on our side, than when both reason and affection conspire against us. And, lastly, it would be more honour and satisfaction to us, rather not to have admitted such a guest, than after such admittance into our thoughts to be forced to cast him out.486 In the review of our actions we shall have more comfort to have been resolute against any sin than to hold our peace.

The necessity of a quick and speedy rejection of a sinful motion is then beyond dispute, and there needs no more to be said for the explanation of this direction, but an account of what is implied in a speedy denial. It contains these four things:—

[1.] First, *That it must issue from a fixed determination against sin.* Some refuse a temptation with the same mind that carried Lot's wife out of Sodom, and are forced beyond their own inclination, but these go not far till they 'look back;' and no wonder: for if he that is sincerely peremptory against sin at the first motion, may by the solicitation of the flesh be inclined afterward, there is little expectation that he whom the first motion finds indifferent and but coldly denying, should hold out long. But that refusal that must give any encouragement to hopes of success, must be an answer of holy indignation against the offer of temptation, and that confirmed into a serious resolve of heart not to yield.

[2.] Secondly, *This positive denial must be also wisely jealous of Satan, in motions that are unlikely, or that may seem light, little, and not directly intended.* Though it may be but a transient glance, or a thing that is out of our road, yet must nothing be contemned or undervalued. Jealousy will take notice of small actions or circumstances, and no less suspicious must we be of every proffer made to us, lest Satan by any means get an advantage against us.

[3.] Thirdly, *The refusal must be so quick, that it may be ready to take the temptation by the throat.* At the first motion or rising of it in our mind, we must endeavour to stifle it in the birth, that it may be as the 'untimely fruit of a woman that never sees the sun,' [Job iii. 16;] we must not give it time to grow up to a rod of wickedness, but must nip it in the earliest buddings of it. It is the nature of grace, if we do but faithfully pursue the inclinations of it, to be quick in its opposition. So doth the apostle's phrase teach us, Gal. v. 17, 'The flesh lusteth against the spirit, and the spirit against the flesh:' the spirit is as ready to repel, as the flesh to suggest. No sooner doth the one stir, but the other is ready with an opposition, and the reason of it is from the active contrariety that is betwixt them; for so the word, ἀντίκειται, there used, would express it; they are sworn enemies, animated by principles of constant opposition, as water and fire are, which cannot meet in peace together, but a present noise and combat is raised from this conjunction.

[4.] Fourthly, When this is done, *we must endeavour to maintain and stick to our first disallowance.* A child of God, I know, in sinful yieldings of infirmity, may say as the apostle, 'What I do, I allow not,'—that is, [1.] What he then consents to, he did not allow at the first, till importunity prevailed. [2.] Though his affections incline to sin, yet his constant settled judgment is against it; and though he do it, he cannot say he approves it. Neither of these are the things I aim at; but this, that as the first motions of sins are disallowed, we should endeavour to keep at that, to stand our ground, to withhold the least after-delight or approbation. Not but that we must be forced sadly to acknowledge the real truth of what the apostle speaks in the place last cited, that these different principles, which of them soever carry the victory, do so impede one another, that when grace carries it, yet it cannot do the utmost it would or aims at; so that in the stoutest oppositions, there may be some secret degrees of allowance unavoidably; notwithstanding we must so manage our denial, that, if it were possible, we should not afford the smallest inclination toward it; the least, the better and nobler conquest.

CHAPTER XXV

The next particular in Christ's answers to be observed by us is his citations of Scripture as an invincible reason against all the devil's temptations; he beats them all back with this weapon, 'It is written.' That this was written for our learning, and that, otherwise than for our instruction, he lay not under any necessity of using this method, hath been evidenced before, and it is a thing which all commentators487 do take notice of. From this we have another direction for the right way and order of resisting temptations, which is,

Direct. 4. *That temptations are best repelled by arguments drawn from the word of God.*

For the explanation of this, it may be considered what is first *presupposed in this direction*; for when it is affirmed that we must answer by reasons from Scripture, this implies —

(1.) First, *That temptations are not to be opposed by groundless refusals.* It is no way safe to say we will not, because we will not, nor to insist upon our own bare resolve; for this would be wilfulness, rather than an obediential refusal, and unwarrantable self-confidence, rather than a humble wrestling. There are some, of whom it may be said, as the prophet once charged the Jews, Isa. xxii. 11, that when Satan comes up against them, they look in that day 'to the armour of the house of the forest,' they 'repair the wall,' and 'cast ditches for fortification;' they prepare themselves to the battle 'in their own strength, but they look not unto the maker thereof,' to him who by his mighty power must fashion our hearts to resistance. The vanity of such undertakings is enough manifested in the event, for commonly such men go on in a bravado of resolution, but are so altered at the first appearance of the enemy, that they yield without a stroke. Who could be more confident than Peter that he would not deny his Master, whatever others did? and yet how soon did his heart fail him. We may warrantably deny a sinful motion, without being explicit in our reason against it, especially in usual temptations, and when they thrust themselves into our minds at such times when our thoughts are charged with an attendance upon other duties, in which nevertheless the heart hath a secret and implicit regard to the command of God; but in no case must we go down to the battle in the strength of a wilfulness, lest it go against us. And thus do they who, when they are reproved for some miscarriage, as of drinking, will presently with great confidence make engagements not to drink wine or strong drink, not to go into a tavern or alehouse without any humble respect to duty, or the power of God for the conquest of the sin; and accordingly we see that usually such promises and obligations do not hold; either they wilfully break them, or they become sinfully witty to make evasions for the practice of sin, without the breach of the oath or promise.

(2.) Secondly, The direction supposeth that *we must deny the sin with the arguments of greatest strength and authority*. There were occasions and hints of other answers to these temptations that offered themselves in Christ's way, and yet he waives them all, fixing only upon Scripture reasons as the best and strongest. It is no Christian wisdom to urge those inferior considerations of shame, loss, inconvenience, &c. Some have no other reason betwixt them and sin, but *What will men say?* or *What will become of me?* But besides that, these would only be a train to bring on disputings, and that it is no way safe to venture our souls upon such defences, when better may be had; for who will venture his life upon a staff when he may have a sword? It is easy for Satan to break these bows, and to cut these spears in sunder. He can balance such reasons with equal reasons, and presently make us believe that we have as good reason to commit the sin as those urged by us for the not committing of it.

(3.) Thirdly, This direction of using Scripture reason doth clearly imply that the force and power of Scripture is not in the words or characters, but in the mind and reason of it; not that Scripture used as a charm or spell, as if the devil were afraid of the sound and words of it, can beat back the devil, but it is the authority of its command which works upon the mind the highest impressions of fear and care, and as a strong argument prevails with us to forbear. Notwithstanding the plainness and undeniableness of this inference, not only do ignorant men bless themselves against the devil by repeating some phrases or sentences of Scripture impertinently, and such as have no direct signification of the matter in hand betwixt Satan and them, as if the devil could not endure to hear the paternoster, or durst not come within the sound of the name Jehovah, but also papists—and of them such as might be supposed more considerate than to be carried by such conceits—have placed a virtue in the words and sounds of Scripture, and therefore do they command, though under some limitations and restrictions, the hanging of sentences of Scripture about the neck in scrolls, for the driving away of evil spirits, though in a clear contradiction to the reason which they give in the general against this course, which is this, that the 'power of Scripture is not in the figures and characters, but in the mind and understanding of it;' and therefore profits as 'pondered in the heart,' not as 'hung about the neck;' and upon as slender grounds do they place a more than ordinary virtue, in the angelical salutation, in the seven words upon the cross, in the triumphal title, 'Jesus of Nazareth, King of the Jews,' &c.488 Such kind of oppositions are but a mock to Satan. We cannot think to 'bore the jaw of this leviathan with a thorn,' or to come to him with 'this bridle,' or to 'play with him as with a bird,' [Job xli. 2;] he durst allege scripture himself to Christ, and therefore it is not the phrase or sound that affrights him.

(4.) Fourthly, The direction doth imply *an argumentative, proper, and fit use of Scripture commands or promises.* We see Christ urged not any scripture indifferently, but he used fit words, and chose to himself select smooth stones out of this brook to sling against this spiritual Goliath. Every temptation had an answer that doth most fully and properly confront it. He regarded the main of the temptation, and suffered not himself to be diverted from that prosecution, by engaging himself in that which might have been perplexed and controversial, though he had a fit opportunity to reprove Satan for a dishonest craft of representing scripture in a sense of his own making, and so might have rejected the temptation of casting himself down, as leaning upon a false foundation, in that God did not promise in Ps. xci. to preserve any that should presumptuously expect a protection while they run out of God's ways; yet he waived this answer, and opposed the assault by a plain scripture which chargeth the contrary duty.

Secondly, Having seen what this direction doth imply in these things that are to be removed from the sense and intendment of it, I shall next, for ascertaining of the reality and importance of it, shew that temptations are to be resisted by Scripture arguments, by these two evidences:—

(1.) First, *God's recommending of the commands of Scripture for such a purpose*: Deut. vi. 6, 'These words which I command thee this day, shall be in thine heart: and thou shalt bind them for a sign upon thine hand, and they shall be as frontlets between thine eyes,' &c. Whether the latter part of the command is to be understood literally, as the Jews apprehended and practised, though some think otherwise, is not necessary to be asserted, seeing it is granted by all that they were to have the commands of the law so ready in their minds and memories, as if they had been written on their hands and upon their foreheads. That God designed this precept for the resistance of sin and temptation cannot be doubted, and that the advantage which might hence arise to them was not only the information of their minds, in point of sin and duty, is as unavoidable; for that and more is intended by that part of the injunction, 'These words which I command thee, shall be in thine heart;' but when? Besides this information, which the knowledge of the law would afford them, and their humble compliance with it, as just and good, which would enable them to say, 'Thy law, O Lord, is within my heart;' he further enjoins them the quick and ready remembrances of these laws, as if they were 'frontlets between their eyes, and signs on their hands.' It can signify no less than this, that in so doing they would be able to resist those motions by which Satan would seek to engage them to the violation of these commands. Neither need we to doubt hereof, when Christ himself hath so fully taught us, by his own example, in resisting temptations, the particular use of the remembrance of the law. In the New Testament the apostle is most express in this matter: Eph. vi. 17, 'Take the sword of the Spirit, which is the word of God,' where not only the use of Scripture commands and promises against Satan's suggestions is taught, but also the high avail and potency of this weapon in reference to its end. It is called a sword, and in that comparison it shews the active resistance which may be made by it; and it is called, not a sword of flesh, for 'the weapons of our warfare are not carnal,' but 'of the Spirit,' to shew how mighty it is in repelling Satan.

(2.) Secondly, Another evidence of its usefulness is from the success which the children of God have had in the right management of this weapon. It is observable that while Christ answered by Scripture, Satan was silenced, and had not what to reply to the answer, but was forced to betake himself to a new temptation. David in many places highly magnifies the power of the command, in the success he had by it; Ps. xvii. 4, he shews how available it was to preserve him in his common converse from the sinful snares laid before him, 'Concerning the works of men, by the word of thy lips I have kept me from the paths of the destroyer.' In Ps. xviii. 22, 23, he tells us that he was shielded from the sins of his inclination and love, which are hardest to prevent, by the opposition that he gave to the motions of them, in setting up the statutes of God against them; 'All his judgments were before me, and I did not put away his statutes from me; I was also upright before him, and I kept myself from mine iniquity.' In Ps. cxix. 11, he puts his probatum est upon the head of this receipt, and speaks of it as his constant refuge, 'Thy word have I hid in my heart, that I might not sin against thee.' In Ps. xxxvii. 31, he speaks of it as a tried case of common experience to all the children of God, 'The law of God is in his heart, none of his steps shall slide.' I shall add to this the experience of Luther, when, saith he, in Epistle to the Galatians, 'the motions of the flesh do rage, the only remedy is, to take the sword of the Spirit, that is, the word of salvation, and to fight against them; of this I myself have good experience; I have suffered many great passions and vehement, but so soon as I laid hold of any place of Scripture, and stayed myself upon it, as upon an anchor, straightway my temptations did vanish away, which without the word had been impossible for me to endure, though but a little space, much less to overcome.'489

(3.) Thirdly, The excellency of this remedy will further appear from these following reasons:—

[1.] First, In that it is *a universal remedy*. There can be no temptation, either of seducement or of affrightment, but the Scripture will afford a suitable promise or command to repel it. So that it, like the flaming sword in the cherubim's hand at paradise, turns every way to guard the soul. I need not give instances of its power against sinful motions, having done that already, and of such temptations which war against the peace of the soul. I need but say this in the general, that as the nature of such temptations is to disguise God, and to render him dreadful to us, in the appearances of wrath and incompassionate implacableness—and this Luther sets down as a certain rule—so have we in Scripture such declarations of the mind and tender inclinations of God, and such full and clear promises to assure us of this, and those so adapted to every case, to every kind of hard thought which we might take up against him, that we may find enough in them to break all those malicious misrepresentations of Satan, and to keep up in our mind 'right thoughts of God;' which if we will adhere to, not suffering such promises to be wrested out of our hands, nor our hearts to give way to malignant impressions of cruelty, revenge, or unmercifulness in God, though we be cast into darkness, into the deeps, we may find some bottom on which to fix such beginnings of hope, as may at last grow up to a spirit of rejoicing in God our Saviour; and in this case, when our heart and Satan dictate to us that God is our enemy, we ought, as it were, to shut our eyes, to refuse to hearken to our own sense and feeling, and to follow the word; but if we once give up the word of promise, it is impossible the wound of conscience should be healed with any other consideration.

[2.] Secondly, *This remedy is comprehensive of most other remedies against Satan's temptations.* In Eph. vi., there are several other pieces of spiritual armour recommended, and yet there is such a manifest mutual respect betwixt this and those, that any may conclude that however they be distinguished in their names, yet they are conjoined in their operation. The girdle, so far as it relates to truth of judgment and opinion, depends on the word of Scripture for information; the shoes, which are defensive resolves to walk with a steady foot in the ways of religion, notwithstanding the hardships that attend holiness, are prepared to us, by the comfortable and peace-bringing promises of the gospel; the righteousness which is our breastplate, is only set forth and wrought out to us by the Scripture and its ordinances; faith which is our shield, and hope which is our helmet, they neither of them act without the warrant and encouragement of it; and whereas other parts of the armour are defensive, this of the Scripture is compared to the sword, which not only defends, but also offends and beats back the enemy. If the matter be seriously considered, all these parts of armour are but these two, the graces of the Spirit—faith, hope, patience in their sincere exercise, and the word of Scripture as the instrument by and in which they shew their operations; so that all this armour being put to use, in every particular temptation, it amounts to no more than this we are speaking of, viz., that sinful motions are to be rejected by a believing, sincerely resolute opposing of them, with arguments from the word of God.

[3.] Thirdly, Scripture, as it is the word and command of the great King of heaven, hath a daunting and commanding authority over the consciences of men. 'Where the word of a king is, there is power,' Eccles. viii. 4, and such is the majesty of a divine law, that it hath power over the consciences of those that are yet in their sins, and can wound, affright, constrain, and bind even the rebellious; so that so long as they retain any of their natural impressions of a divine power, they have some awe for his commands, which may be seen and argued, where it would be least expected, from the enragement of the hearts of sinners, when 'sin by the commandment,' accidentally, 'becomes exceeding sinful,' Rom. vii. 13, 14. For as that outrageous fierceness doth arise from the contrariety that is betwixt a carnal heart and a spiritual law; so that contrariety would never work if the authority of that law, having a power to restrain, and give check to the corruption of the heart, were not some way owned by the conscience; for where no countermanding law is owned, there can be no irritating, provoking restraint. This it can do to the vilest of men; but of how much more power may we imagine the word to be with good men, whose hearts tremble at the word, when they 'bind the law upon their heart,' and charge their consciences with it? It is surely 'quick and powerful, sharper than a two-edged sword,' [Heb. iv. 12;] nor doth it only, by unlovely affrightments, terrify them from sin, but by commanding duty make the heart in love with it, so that it becomes a delightful satisfaction to be preserved from the snare.490

[4.] Fourthly, There is no argument that can be used against temptations that can be more afflictively discouraging to Satan. Satan, as bad as he is, cannot but believe those truths which he knows, and he knows that there are many truths in Scripture which respect him, as threatenings of punishment and divine vengeance; he believes these things and trembles, James ii. 19. His unavoidable knowledge or remembrance of these things begets horror in him, he cannot but be under a dread of these truths. What can be supposed so to wound him as the bringing these things to memory, by urging the command of God against him? Dr Arrowsmith491 gives two instances of this kind, the one of Christopher Haas in Sweedland—from the epistle dedicatory to the five tomes of Brentius's works—the other of Daniel

Cramer, rector of a school at Stettin in Germany; on both which the devil made a bold attempt in a personal appearance; from the first, demanding a catalogue of his sins in writing; from the other, demanding a paper in which one of the students had obliged himself to Satan's service; they both referred him to that text of Gen. iii. 15, 'The seed of the woman shall bruise the head of the serpent.' And this was retorted upon him with such a strong exercise of faith, that he presently desisted the suit and vanished.

[5.] Fifthly, *This weapon cannot easily he wrested out of our hands*. When we urge a divine prohibition against a temptation, what can he say in answer? he cannot deny it to be the word of God, or to be true, or that we are not obliged to it. He made none of these returns to Christ, but, by his silence, owned that it was God's holy command obliging us to duty. Neither dares he stand upon these exceptions to us, except he find our faith inclined to waver, or our minds weak and wounded by inward troubles of spirit; and when he puts on a boldness to deny Scripture to be the word of God, or that it signifies God's real intendments in his threatening—for by begetting unbelief of the truth of Scripture, and by suggesting hopes of escape and pardon, notwithstanding the violation of the commands of it, he wrests, when he doth prevail, this weapon out of our hands—yet he is forced to fetch a compass, and by many previous insinuations to make his way to these atheistical assertions. Thus he did with Eve, first, finding her a little inclinable, he dropped in privily something that might argue the improbability of the threatened penalty, and then at last positively denied it. But now if we hold to this, that 'the command is true and holy, and just and good,' he cannot wrest our plea from us.

[6.] Sixthly, *Nothing doth more undermine temptations, by rendering the reasons and motives thereof vain and empty, than doth the contrary commands of Scripture*. Temptation hath always some enticement of pleasure or profit, and these only seem to be taking or reasonable, while we consider not the word of God, as rotten wood or fish shine only in the dark; but when we are urged with sinful pleasures, how mean, base, dangerous, and unlovely be they, when the command to the contrary gives information that they are snares and lead to death, or the provocation of the Almighty.

[7.] Seventhly, *While we resist with Scripture arguments, we engage God, whose command we would stand by, to go down to the battle with us*. We 'lay hold upon his strength,' and put obligations upon him to take us out of the snare, and to deliver us from him who is 'too strong' for us.

(4.) Fourthly, It remains that, in a word, I shew *how the commands or arguments of Scripture are to be used in resisting Satan*, which is thus, When you have any sinful thought cast into your mind, presently reject the offer, by charging your heart with duty, from some opposite command; as if you be urged to acts of uncleanness, presently refuse, thus; No, I must not, God hath commanded the contrary, he hath said, 'Thou shalt not commit adultery.' If a covetous thought arise, reject it with this, God hath said, 'Thou shalt not covet.' If you be tempted to please the flesh, and follow vain delights, answer it with this, 'If ye live after the flesh, ye shall die;' and the like must be done in other temptations.

Obj. Some may perhaps think that this is easy work and quickly done, and that it seems to attribute a virtue and power to the words of Scripture, as if Satan were charmed by the language or phrase.

Ans. However at the first view this may seem easy, yet he that shall consider how much exercise of grace goes necessarily to the right use of Scripture opposition, shall not see cause to slight it as common, nor yet to think that any virtue is attributed to the words. For,

[1.] First, The Scripture here is only recommended *as a fit instrument, and no further or higher praise is given.* Though therefore we may attribute the whole of the conquest to the instrument alone, yet this hinders not, but that as an instrument peculiarly fitted for these ends, we may commend it above all other instruments, as we may justly commend bread for nourishing above a stone, and expect more from it than from a chip; so have we reason to expect more by the use of Scripture against Satan, than from other means of defence which God hath not set up for that service.

[2.] Secondly, *It is a concomitancy of divine power and aid that conquers for us.* The instrument is Scripture, but the power by which it works is from God.

[3.] Thirdly, *Neither is it any careless formal use of Scripture expressions that will give encouragement for expectation of a divine concurrence;* but the use of Scripture in this business implies an exercise of all graces, for it is an urging of Scripture under a fourfold consideration.

First, As being certainly persuaded of their truth, and fully keeping to that belief.

Secondly, As being thankfully apprehensive of the holiness, goodness, and profitableness of the commands, and cheerfully adhering to them as the only way and means to bring us to union with Christ, and to preserve us in it.

Thirdly, As being highly and indispensably obliged by them to perform the duty commanded therein, and to avoid the sins forbidden.

Fourthly, All this in a humble expectation of a divine help, according to the promise of God. Now he that can plead the command or promise against a temptation in this manner, doth not do an ordinary work, neither will he ascribe the success to the words and phrase of Scripture.

Some may, peradventure, wonder why Christ, by his example, had not recommended prayer, seeing it is of such unquestionable use in our undertakings against Satan. But that inquiry may be fully satisfied, if it be considered that Christ did peculiarly prepare himself to this encounter by 'solemn fasting,' ver. 2, which doth include praying; for such complicated duties are often denominated by that part which is extraordinary, and usually in Scripture a fast is only mentioned where prayer is chiefly intended. That this fast of Christ related to the temptation, and that also as a means of preservation, hath been spoken of in its place; it remains only that from hence I add a fifth direction.

CHAPTER XXVI

Direct. 5. That in all our endeavours of resistance, frequent and earnest prayers are not to be neglected.

This is so frequently recommended, and so fully handled by most authors, that I shall refer you to such authors as particularly treat of it; noting only that the apostle, in Eph. vi. 18, when he recommends it to us in these words, 'Praying always with all prayer and supplication in the Spirit, and watching thereunto with all perseverance, and supplication for all saints,' he doth mind us that he that expects the advantage of that duty must be peculiarly fitted, and seriously diligent in that work. For,

(1.) First, *He must have a praying frame of heart*; he must 'pray always,' or, as the apostle elsewhere, he must 'pray continually.' Not as if this duty must swallow up all the rest, and that a Christian had no other services to attend than prayer, but that he must be on a design to wrestle with God by prayer; and this must be constantly carried on, though the acts of prayer be intermitted; and besides that, in such cases, he may keep his usual stated times for that duty, he must have his heart so much upon his design, that every occasion or offer of temptation will presently put him upon the duty; nay, he must, in respect of the frequent intercourse of his heart with God in frequent ejaculations and breathings of soul, be as a man wholly resolved into that duty, as Paul was at his first conversion, who, as that expression 'behold he prays' [Acts ix. 11] doth intimate, seems to have been all prayer, and wholly taken up with that duty.

(2.) Secondly, *He must pray in the spirit*, his soul must be truly in the duty. A more than ordinary earnestness is necessary at solemn times, he must put out all his strength, he must cry mightily, and with his whole heart.

(3.) Thirdly, When his spirit grows dull, *he must reinforce it*, watch his heart he must; and if it be needful to quicken it up, he must add fasting or meditation, or whatever other means may be helpful.

(4.) Fourthly, In this course *he must continue without giving off the duty*. Though God behave himself as if he minded not his cry, or took no notice of his hazard, yet without weariness must our supplications follow him. It must be continued with 'all perseverance.'

(5.) Fifthly, *The heart that undertakes this must not be so narrow as to be centred upon his own concern only.* When he is melted into a spirit of meekness and compassion for others, and is not so solicitous for peace or ease, that he could hug himself in his private enjoyment without concerning himself to tender and help those that are in the same dangers, when his supplications are for 'all saints' as well as for himself, then may he expect to receive an olive branch of peace from heaven in the return of his prayer.

Obj. It is often objected by such, that they pray but are not heard; and that temptations continue, notwithstanding many cries and wrestlings.

Ans. [1.] First, *It is a great mistake to think that prayers are not heard or do not prevail, because the temptation is not quite removed.* Prayers may be acceptable to God, and recorded among his remembrances, where the temptation, for exercise and other holy ends, may be continued.

[2.] Secondly, *What God hath promised to such prayer, he fails not to make good.* He hath not promised to exempt us from temptation, but from the power and prevalency of it. If 'his grace be sufficient for us,' 2 Cor. xii. 9, in the meantime, it is an answer as good as Paul got when he was importunate; 'If together with the temptation he gives an issue, that we may be able to bear it,' 1 Cor. x. 13, there is his faithfulness in keeping promise. He nowhere promised that Satan should not tempt, but that he should not prevail. While we can hold up our hands in the mount to God, and our praying frame will ascertain us of this; 'for a man is never overcome by a temptation so long as he can pray against it;' for so long he delights not in it so long he consents not, and till he do consent Satan cannot prevail. Prayer will either make the temptation give way, or the temptation will make prayer give way; but so long as we hold out with earnestness, the temptation cannot prevail.

Obj. Some further object, that the more they pray they are the worse, and more infested by Satan than they were before they undertook that course.

Ans. 1. *It may be they may have more trouble from Satan.* David 'thought on God, and his trouble was increased,' [Ps. xxxix. 3,] and no wonder. Satan's spite and fury puts him upon giving greatest molestations to those of whom he despairs to subdue.

Ans. 2. Secondly, But though they may be more troubled, yet they may be furthest from conquest.492 These disquiets are like the trouble of the working of physic, which at first taking may make a man more sick, and yet bring him nearer to a state of health and strength; fear not then, faint not, resist faithfully, and to the utmost, and 'God shall bruise Satan under thy feet shortly,' [Rom. xvi. 20.]

INDEXES, &c.

II.—GENERAL MATTERS.

Satan tempts by,

Conclusions, direful,

Condition, Satan takes advantage of our, in temptation,

Confident, warning from temptations, to the over,

Confronting of Almighty by Satan,

Conscience, wounded,

in man,

scared,

molested,

scrupulosity of,

doubting,

evil,

denying,

how distinguish between terrors of, and melancholy,

total distress of,

terrors of,

Consent, by silence,

Consolation, for those troubled by blasphemy,

Contrary commands of Scripture to temptations,

Contrasts, between Christ and Satan,

Coveting,

Contempt,

of religion,

Satan seeks to bring Scripture under,

'Contemplative' heads,

Contentions and disputes,

Continuance, troubles of long,

temptations of long,

Contrivances,

curious,

'Conversation,' careful,

enlarge not,

Despagne,

Despair,

is presumptuous,

Devices,

Devil, though a 'spirit,' a proper subject of sin,

wickedness of, capable of increase,

has great occasions for malice, *ib.*;

fall of,

power of, as a,

meaning of, as a word,

denial of existence of,

Devils, large number of,

order among,

reality of existence of, argued,

believed in by the heathen,

'Devotional,' .

Diana,

Diascorides,

Dickson,

Differences, in God's children,

Dignity of God's children, a snare by Satan,

Diligence, of Satan,

instances of,seq.

Diodati,

Dionysius,

Directly and indirectly, Satan blinds,seq.

Disadvantage, fall of saints special,

Disappointment of Satan certain,

Discomposures of soul,

effects of,

Satan works on,

Fascination,

Fashion, sins out of,

Fast of Christ,seq.

why,seq.

Favour, special, a time of temptation,

Favourable, too, opinion of self,

Fears, suspicious,

impressions of,

come by fits,

return,

add to the weight of other troubles, *ib.*;

not always accompanying conversion,

an engine of temptation,

increase of,

prepare for Satan's most dismal suggestions,

make all seem the sword of an enemy, *ib.*;

no advice eases,

lead to conclusions of misery,

threefold,

what, forbidden,seq.

Februation,

Feigning departure,

Fenner,

'Finishing' of sin,seq.

First temptation, Christ's,seq.

Fixes, Satan, thoughts,

Follows, Satan, with a high hand,

Food of the soul, Satan robs of,

Foretell, Satan can,

'Formal' use of defences, Satan allows, and why,seq.

Guessing of Satan,

Haas,

Habits, vicious,

'Habituated' sin,

Hacket,

Han,

Hakluyt,

Happiness, impatient desire of,

Harvey,

Haste in sinning,

Hatred against Satan,

Hatred of Satan,

Hazard,

to life by some lusts,

and disadvantage by abuse of services,

of duties,

ways of religion said to be of intolerable,

ways of,

Heart, the stage of all action,

God and Satan meet in,

the 'deceits' of, point to Satan,

enticed,

sottish,

prepared for venomous impressions,

hard and impenitent,

Satan seeks to withdraw, from God and to enslave to sin, shewn,

prevails,

not right with God,

Heathen,

Heightening of duty,

of jealousies and fears against Satan,

Satan imitates God by pretence of teaching,

Impetuosity,

Impressions, dismal, of Satan,

Importunity,

impudent,

Impotent, mind rendered,

Impulses,

Incas,

Incessant, Satan in temptation,

things relating to such,

encouragement under,

Inclinations,

Indicia,

Indignation of Satan,

Indisposition of body,

of soul,

Indirect courses,

Infectious, temptations,

Infirmity,

'Ingenuousness,'

submissive,

feigned,

Injects, Satan's temptations,

impetuousness of,

injections of terror,

impetuous,

incessant, *ib.*;

odious,

abhorrency,

difference between atheistical injections and temptations,

of abominable sin,

Injury,

Insight, Satan has deep,

Insolency,

'Inspiration,' false,

Insult = triumph,

'Intercepting' of light by Satan,

Interest, Scripture contrary to,

'Interest' shaken by light,

'Internal' work,

Inventions, self-devised,

human, in divine worship,

Invisible, Satan in temptation usually,

Invitation, secret, to Satan by disputing,

Invocation of saints,

Inward temptations and outward distresses,

terrors and trouble,

reasons for not disputing with Satan in,seq.

Irenæus,

Jackson,

James,

Jenison,

Job and Satan,

Josephus,

Jostle,

Joy not received,

Jugglers' words,

Julian,

Junius,

Karsten,

Kert, maid of,

Kimchi,

Opinions, 'corrupt,'

Opportunity, suitable,

hindrances of,

best, for answering,

Origen,

Outbreakings against God,

Outcries, doleful,

Outward distress and inward temptations,

comforts those whose are little,

Outward not inward,

Ovid,

Owen,

Particular trust in God,

Passionateness,

Passions,

nature of,

discompose,

stirred up,

Satan sets on work,

Paterculus,

Peace, inward,

fruition of,

Satan's efforts against,

fruit of holiness,

gives inward strength, *ib.*;

to get, a duty,

a badge of kindness,

disturbed by Satan,

Performance, manner of, of duty,

Peripatetics,

Perkins,

Wilderness, scene of Christ's temptation,

why,

Will,

Willis,

Wills and shalls,

Witchcraft,

Wonders,

Working of thought,

Worldly pleasure, great engine of Satan,seq.

how so,

Worship, Satan sets himself up for,

'Wounded' spirits,

in regenerate and reprobate,

conscience by God and Satan, question on,

Wrath, Divine, sense of,

Wresting, import of Scripture, by Satan,

seen in results,

Scripture, a weapon not easily, out of our hands,

Xavier,

Young persons, troubled by Satan,

Zanchius,

Zeal, pretences of,

Zeilan,

Zembla, Nova,

FOOTNOTES:

362 Numb. iv. 3. Vide Lightfoot, 'Temple Service and Harmony.' Lev. viii. 6, 12.

363 Spanheim, Dub. Evan. in loc.

364 Non nobis expedit esse sine tentationibus; non rogamus ut non tentemur, sed ne inducat in tentationem.—Aug. in Ps. lxxiii.

365 Tentationem experiuntur ac sentiunt hi, qui ex animo pietati student.— Musculus, in loc.

366 Capel, 'Tempt.,' part 1, cap. 4, sec. 1.

367 Ibid., part 1, cap. 4.

368 Illæ plerumque suggerunt, quæ naturæ gratiora, idque placide et gradatim, ita ut mens sui compos maneat in ipso æstu, hæ autem impetu plusquam humano irruentes, fulguris instar, ocyus quam solent passiones dianoeticæ, &c.—Arrowsmith, Tactica [Sacra] I., lib. ii. cap. 7, sec. 6.

369 Horrore sui si implent animum, ut tantum non pectus ipsum expectorare videantur, dum ea perpetim dictitari sentit, et dolet, ad quoque præsentiam, natura vel depravatissima contremiscet.—Idem, Ibid.

370 Aliud est tentari, aliud tentationem recipere. Tentari et non in tentationem ferri non est malum.—Aug., De Bono Persever., lib. ii. cap. 6. Mordet Satan cum ad consensum trahit, latrat solum cum suggerit.— Bernard.

371 Musculus, in loc.

372 Vide Lightfoot, Harm. in loc.

373 Spanheim, Dub. Evan. in loc.

374 Spanheim, in loc.

375 Lightfoot, Harm. in loc.

376 Hobbes's Leviathan, cap. 45, p. 354.

377 Calvin, Scultetus.

378 Tenison Hobbes's 'Creed Exam.,' p. 65.

379 Spanheim, Dub. Evan. in loc.

380 Non mirum est Christum permisisse se circumduci a diabolo, qui permisit se a membris sui crucifigi.—Gregorius.

381 Aquinas, Sum. part 1, q. 114, art. 2. Homines instrumentaliter, mundus materialiter, Satanas efficienter.—Sclater on 1 Thes. iii. 5.

382 Piscat., in loc.

383 O Fratres adjuvate me, ne peream, nonne videtis Dæmonum agmina, qui me debellare, et ad Tartara ducere festinant, quid his astas cruenta bestia?—Cl. Senarclæus in Epist. ad M. Bucerum, &c., tells of a country man, at Tribury, ['Friburg'?—G.] in Germany, to whom the devil appeared in the shape of a tall man, claiming his soul, and offering to set down his sins in a scroll.

384 Putting into a 'dilemma.'—G.

385 Eccles. Hist., lib. iii. cap. 11.

386 Antiochus put Eleazer and the Maccabees in mind of this excuse, If it be a sin to do contrary to your law, compulsion doth excuse it.—Josephus on the lives of the Maccabees.

387 Timeo Danaos et dona ferentes.

388 Query: 'Thaumaturgia'?—G.

389 Spanheim, Dub. Evan. in loc., and Lightfoot, Harm. in loc.

390 Vide Lightfoot, Harmon. in Mat. iv. Pool Synopsis, in Deut. viii.

391 Query, 'Maintained'?—Ed.

392 Ps. cxvi. 11. Pool, Synopsis, in loc.

393 Alii damnatos se putant, et quod Deo curæ non sunt.—Platerus Tract. Melan., cap. 33.

394 Quis est ille Deus, ut serviam illi? quid proderit si oraverim? si præsens est, cur non succurrit? cur non me carcere, inedia, squalore confectum liberat? &c. Absit a me hujusmodi Deus.—Mercerus ad Gen. cap. xi fol. 230. [Misprinted in text and note 'Mercennus.' M.'s 'Commentary' on Genesis was a posthumous work, edited by Beza, 1598, folio.—G.]

395 Dr Reynolds, Serm, on Hosea xiv., ser. 4.

396 Query, 'Wearying'?—G.

397 Beza, Chemnitius.

398 Serm. de jejunio et tempt. Christi. Unitas naturarum excæcavit ℈.

399 See their relations in print. [Brooks, s.n.—G.]

400 Spanheim, Dub. Evan. in loc.

401 Bodin, p. 147.

402 Plurimum sunt præservativa locorum, hominum, et jumentorum, verba tituli triumphalis nostri salvatoris, dum scilicet per quatuor partes loci, in modum crucis inscribuntur, Jesus † Nazarenus † Rex † Judeorum †, ritibus ecclesiæ servatis et veneratis, ut per aquæ benedictæ aspersionem, salis consecrati sumptionem, et candelarum in die purificationis et frondium in die palmarum consecratorum, usum licitum vires dæmonis imminuunt, se muniunt.—Sprenger, Malleus Maleficarum, part 2, quest. 1. Licitum est aqua benedicta, quæcunque honesta loca, hominum et jumentorum, in salvationem hominum et jumentorum aspergere.—Id. ibid.

403 Query, 'warfare'?—Ed.

404 Sozomen, Eccles. Hist., lib. v. cap. 18.

405 Mal. Malefic., part 2, quest. 11, cap. 1, 3.

406 In Delic. Evang.

407 Spanheim, Dub. Evan. in loc.

408 Lightfoot, Harm. in loc.

409 Dr Kimchi, in loc.

410 Reynolds on Passions, chap. 23, p. 238.

411 Non ideo peccatur, quia nimis sperat in Deum; sed quia nimis leviter ac temere, sine ullo fundamento.—Ames, Medul., lib. ii. cap. 6, sec. 33.

412 Dickson, in loc.; Capel, Tempt., part 2, cap. 9.

413 Capel, Tempt., part 9, cap. 9, citing Augustine for it.

414 Capel, Tempt., ibid.

415 Seneca, De Providen. cap. 2. Liquet mihi cum magno spectasse gaudio deos—dum gladium sacro pectore infigit. Non fuit diis immortalibus satis spectare Catonem semel.

416 Aug., De Civit. Dei, P. 1, cap. 22. Major animus merito dicendus est, qui vitam ærumnosam magis potest ferre quam fugere. Et humanum judicium præ conscientiæ luce ac puritate contemnere.

417 As in the kingdoms of Biznagar—Purchas, Pilgr. lib. v. cap. 11—and in the Philippian islands.—Ibid., cap. 16.

418 Perire membratim et toties per stillicidia amittere animam.—Sen., epist. 101.

419 Cicero, 1 Tus. quest. Nihil urgebat aut calamitatis aut criminis—sed ad capessendam mortem—Sola affuit animi magnitudo.—De Civ. Dei, lib. i. cap. 22.

420 De Civit. Dei, lib. i. cap. 27.

421 Vide Boyle's Reflections, sec. 2, med. 10.

422 Query, 'Stukeley'?—G.

423 See the Narrative of Jo. Gilpin, called 'The Quakers Shaken.'

424 De Civit. Dei, lib. i. cap. 20. Non occides, non alterum, ergo nec te; neque enim qui se occidit, aliud quam hominem occidit.—Aug. De Civit. Dei, lib. i. cap. 22. Et Comment. Lod. Viv. Ibid.

425 Tempt., part 2, cap. 9.

426 Digito monstrari, et dicier, Hic est.—[Horace.—G.]

427 Quis vero tam bene modulo suo metiri se novit, ut eum assiduæ et immodicæ laudationes non moveant?—H. Stephens.

428 In Ps. xiv., In viis, nunquid in præcipitiis? Non est via hæc sed ruina, et si via, tua est, non illius.—Bernard.

429 Anthores se vitæ scelestæ immundæque testantur, perhibentur tamen in adytis suis secretisque penetralibus dare quædam bona præcepta de moribus, quibusdam velut electis sacratis suis; quod si ita est, hoc ipso callidior aduertenda est et convincenda malitia spirituum noxiorum.— Aug. Civit. Dei, lib. ii. cap. 26.

430 Mal. Malefic., part 2, Q. 1, cap. 9.

431 Jean D'Espagne, 'Popular Errors,' p. 76. [As before.—G.]

432 Holy War, lib. iii. cap. 24.

433 Wars of the Jews, lib. vii. cap. 13.

434 Funcius in his Chronol. tells the like of one in Crete, that called himself Moses, anno 434, who persuaded the Jews to follow him for the repossessing of Canaan. ['Funckius.'—G.]

435 Josephus, Anti. Jud., lib. xx. cap. 2.

436 Etsi semel videatur verax, millies est mendax, et semper fallax.

437 'Ingenuousness.'—G.

438 Though it was Scripture that Satan urged to Christ, yet he rejects his inference as false, because contrary to other plain scriptures prohibiting not to tempt the Lord.

439 Lightfoot, Harm. in loc.

440 Perkins, Com. in loc. Deut. xxxii. 49, and xxxiv. 1.

441 Hobbes's Leviath., cap. 45, p. 354.

442 Lightfoot, Harm. in loc.

443 So also Lucas Brugensis thinks in loc.

444 Varro, De Cultu Deorum.

445 De Civit. Dei, lib. vii. cap. 34, 35.

446 A long-exposed mistake, from a mis-reading of an inscription.—G.

447 Solinus, cap. xxvii. and xl.—G.

448 D'Espagne's Popular Errors, sec. 1, cap. 4. [As before.—G.]

449 Δόξα, φαντασία, σχῆμα, Ps. xxxvii. 1, and xlix. 16; Jer. xlv. 5.

450 Perkins, 'Combate,' in loc. Musculus, in loc.

451 Levis, nullius ponderis; leviter de aliquo sentire.—Jackson, in loc. Pool, Synopsis, Crit. in loc.

452 Selden and Leigh, 'Critica Sacra.' [As before.—G.]

453 Bayne, in loc. Arrowsmith, Tactica Sacra, lib. ii. cap. 8.

454 Caryl, in loc.

455 Tom. iv. col. 973.

456 Scala Paradisi, gradu 23.

457 Spiritus blasphemiæ, scaturigo est cogitationum adeo horribilium adeoque molestarum, ut ejus tentatio plerumque quasi martyrium est.—Guil. Paris, lib. de tenta. et resist.

458 Magis a dolo metuendum est quam a violentia adversarii, caveat æger ab impatientia, infidelitate, murmuratione aliisque peccatis quæ clam insinuantur.—Dickson, Therapeut. Sacra, lib. ii. cap. 29.

459 Heylin, 'Cosmogr.'

460 Capel 'Tempt.,' part 2, cap. 3.

461 Fæda tentatio magis vincitur fugiendo quam aggrediendo.—Gerson, tom. ix. col. 976.

462 Mystery of Iniquity, lib. i. cap. 9.

463 Musculus, in loc., and Perkins, in loc.

464 Drusius, Lightfoot, Tremellius, &c.

465 לעילב vel a ילב non et ליע jugem, absque jugo; vel a ילב non et לע supra, vel a ילב non, et לעי profuit, homo inutilis.

466 ἀπάτη, ab à priv. et πάτος, via.

467 Honoribus magis homines provocare quam tormentis cogere studuit. — Nazianzen.

468 Foxe, Acts and Mon. [Sub nominibus. — G.]

469 Grotius, in loc.

470 The famous Captain John Smith, the Founder of Virginia. — G.

471 Damocles. — G.

472 Si ad imperium ejus lapides possunt fieri panes, ergo frustra tentas; si autem non frustra, filium Dei suspicaris.

473 Musculus, in loc.

474 Vide arma quibus tibi non sibi vicit. — Ambrose.

475 Hæc armatura non tam Christo Filio Dei quam nobis illius tyrunculis convenit, uti tamen ille voluit, ut nos suo doceret exemplo, perinde atque si fortis quidam Gygas hostem non suis, sed tyrunculi sui armis feriat et prosternat. — Musculus.

476 Query, 'warfare' ? — Ed.

477 Capel, Tempt., part 2, cap. 9; Ames, Cas. Consc., lib. ii. cap. 18, sec. 14.

478 Query, 'steam' ? — Ed.

479 Hooper? — G.

480 Tentatus a Satana cum nullum evadendi modum sentis, simpliciter claude oculos, et nihil responde, et commenda causam Deo. — Luther, tom. iii. f. 396. Sicut tutissimum est canem latrantem contemnere, et præterire, ita una vincendi ratio est contemnere rationes Satanæ, neque cum iis disputare. Satan nihil minus ferre potest quam sui contemptum. — Id., f. 376; Ames, Cases of Consc., lib. i. cap. 6.

481 Child of Light, cap. 7, p. 41. [As before. — G.]

482   Sero medicina paratur,
          Cum mala per longas convaluere moras.

483 Differre justitiam est negare justitiam. Qui non prohibet cum potest, jubet.

484 Ego adolescens petieram a te castitatem, et dixeram; da mihi castitatem, sed noli modo; timebam enim ne me cito exaudires et cito sanares, malebam expleri quam extingui.—Confes., lib. viii. cap. 7.

485 Greenham on Ps. cxix. 101.

486 Turpius ejicitur quam non admittitur hospes.

487 Ideo Jesus omnes illas tentationes solis sacris Scripturis vicit, ut doceret nos sic pugnare et vincere.—Cajetan, in loc.; Jansenius, &c.

488 Malleus Mallefic, part 2, quæs. 11, cap. 6. Virtus evangelii est in intellectu et non in figuris, ergo melius in corde posita prosunt, quam circa collum suspensa.—Barthol., Sibilla Peregr., quæs. dec. 3, c. 9, q. 9.

489 Canon est, quod in omnibus tentationibus—alium fingimus Deum esse quàm sit, putamus enim Deum tunc non esse Deum sed horribile spectrum.—Tom. iv. f. 147. Reclamat (Sathan) in corde tuo, te non esse dignum ista promissione—est autem opus ardenti oratione, ne extorqueatur nobis promissio.—Luther in Gen., cap. 21, f. 188. Cor dictat Deum adversum verbum Dei, sequi debeo non sensum meum.—Idem, tom. iv. f. 156. Nulla alia re potest sanari hoc vulnus conscientiæ, quam verbo Divinæ promissionis.—Id. tom. iv. f. 400.

490 Quam suave mihi subitò factum est carere suavitatibus nugarum, et quas amittere metus fuerat, jam demittere gaudium erat.—Aug. Confes., lib. ix. cap. 1.

491 Tact. Sacr., lib. i. cap. 3, sec. 6.

492 That is, from being conquered.—G.